Over Here, Over There

The people and the places that made
the story of London and America

TERRY PHILPOT

Over Here, Over There

Terry Philpot

First published in Great Britain in 2019 by Step Beach Press Ltd, Brighton

Copyright © Terry Philpot 2019

A CIP catalogue record for this title is available from the British Library.

ISBN 978-1-908779-58-8

Picture credits: All illustrations are the author's, except where otherwise acknowledged.

Typeset in Brighton, UK by Step Beach Press Ltd

Printed and bound by L&S Printing, Worthing, West Sussex BN14 8NP

Step Beach Press Ltd, 28 Osborne Villas, Hove, East Sussex BN3 2RE

www.stepbeachpress.co.uk

For

John Pierson, who exemplifies the best values of his native country,
of which I have happy (and enlightening) memories of exploring with him.

and for

Robert Philpot, another fellow US traveller, for whom I may have
begun as the teacher but long ago became the pupil.

This book might not have been written without either of them
for which, many thanks, as always.

Author

Terry Philpot has written or edited 22 books, mainly on a wide range of social policy topics. More recently, his books have included *31 London Cemeteries to Visit Before You Die* (2012); *Beside the Seaside: Brighton's Places and Its People* (2015); *Secret Lewes* (2017); *Secret Rye* (2017); and *Secret Aldeburgh to Southwold* (2018). He has contributed 23 entries to the *Oxford Dictionary of National Biography* and writes and reviews regularly for *The Tablet*. He has written for a wide range of publications, including obituaries for *The Guardian*, *The Times* and *The Daily Telegraph*. A former editor, he has won several awards for journalism.

Contents

City of London

Croydon

Ealing

Greenwich

Hackney

Hounslow

Islington

Kensington and Chelsea

Acknowledgments

This book would not have been possible without the staff of the British Library, whom I have to thank once again.

There are a number of individuals who deserve thanks:

David Britten, parish manager of St Mary's Church, Battersea, gave great help in explaining the details of Benedict Arnold's burial in the church.

Rachel Bowen, account director of The Communications Store, informed me about the reconstruction of 1 (now 1–3) Grosvenor Square, the former US embassy.

Alexandra Edwards, visitor services manager at Two Temple Place, told me of William Waldorf Astor's London address, explaining, too, when he might have stayed at No 2. She also supplied photographs of No 2.

Marta Esteban supplied the photograph of Dennis Severs' House.

Deborah Gage, curator of Firle Place in Sussex, clarified General Thomas Gage's birthplace and the date of his birth.

Mark Hodgkin, verger of St Stephen's Church, Gloucester Road, gave information about the fate of the presbytery where TS Eliot lived.

William B McAllister, special projects division chief of Office of the Historian, US Department of State (a remarkable and lesser known US government agency, which I came upon by chance) helped with the problem of locating the site of the US legation when James Russell Lowell was minister. In this I was also assisted by Professor Patrick Salmon, chief historian of the British Foreign and Commonwealth Office, to whom Mr McAllister referred me. He cracked the problem. Mr McAllister also put me in touch with the US Army Center for Military History (for which, see overleaf).

James B Sinclair, chief executive of the Charles Ives Society, went out of his way to help me establish where Ives stayed on his visits to London.

Howard Spencer, senior historian of Blue Plaques at English Heritage, explained the identification complications arising from the Greater London Council's decision on the re-siting of the plaque on 2 Connaught Place, home of Lady Jennie and Lord Randolph Churchill.

1

Robert Trobridge, archivist of Harmonica UK, gave me Larry Adler's last address in London, while, helpful as ever, Alex May, senior editor of the *Oxford Dictionary of National Biography*, supplied me with two other Adler addresses.

The US Army Center for Military History and Kevin M Bailey, reference archivist of the Dwight D Eisenhower Library, Abilene, Kansas, helped me uncover the details of Dwight D Eisenhower's war-time use of 20 Grosvenor Square and Norfolk House, St James's Square in London.

Stephen Wickner, parish administrator of St George's, Hanover Square, made available the photograph of the church.

Simon Wartnaby, secretary of the Whistler Society, helped me with some of the dates and addresses of Whistler's homes in Chelsea.

Chris Parker, managing director and Karen Hobden, senior editor, respectively, of Step Beach Press, have supported me in this project. Lulah Ellender proved to be an essential 'eye' as copy editor.

Introduction

The traffic between what became the United States and Britain (London for the purposes of this book) is often assumed to be largely one way – east to west – until comparatively recently, coming long after the great push by colonists in the 17th century with the flow of immigrants into what by then had become the United States of America. However, from earliest times, the journeying was also west to east and this was not only settlers who came back to England or colonial officials who were required to return for short stays. According to Alden T Vaughan in his book *Transatlantic Encounters: American Indians in Britain, 1500–1776*, there were about 175 indigenous people and Inuits who came to the British Isles between 1500 and 1776. A few stayed, a few died coming or returning, but the majority completed a circular trip. Their homeland stretched from Baffin Island in north-east Canada to Brazil.

In the late 19th and early 20th century, the United States underwent great waves of European immigration and, among these, half a million people came from the UK each decade from 1860 to 1890. Many, of course, in seeking a new life found just that and lived well-settled, comparatively prosperous lives that were nevertheless ordinary to the point of being obscure. They live now only in family photographs and in the stories of family members. There were others, of course, who found fame and even notoriety. The same applied for the many who came – and continue to come – to settle in the UK.

Poor Lord North is remembered today only as the prime minister who 'lost' the colonies, but it is also worth remembering that at least two of his successors – Sir Winston Churchill and Harold Macmillan, later the Earl of Stockton – had American mothers. That inheritance had much to do with their personal attachment to the United States, which was expressed in their foreign policy and the so-called Special Relationship.

London attracts 2.3 million American visitors annually (2016) and 197,000 American citizens live in the UK. Despite the wrench of the Revolutionary War from 1775 to 1783 and the war of 1812 (in fact, 1812 to 1815) when

Britain did itself no favours by burning Washington DC (including the White House), the affection and ties between the two peoples remain strong. This has been forged both by the ancestral links, which many Americans have with Britain and Ireland, and also by two world wars in which the USA and the UK were the staunchest of allies.

This book concerns individual Americans who have come to London, some to settle, some for long stays; and Londoners who have made their name in the USA, most to settle, and have adopted US citizenship (the exception here is, of course, the early settlers who could be none other than British subjects). Their variety is all but infinite, far more so than I ever envisaged when beginning my research. They run from the first voyagers on the Mayflower and other ships to recent times – politicians to inventors, entrepreneurs to actors, and artists to soldiers – and even a spy. There are some Londoners who never visited the USA but who have marked its history. It hardly needs to be said that this book makes no claims to be comprehensive.

Whom to include, then, has been a formidable task. In order not to be overwhelmed and to give some shape to the entries, so far as people are concerned, for Londoners who made their names in the USA, I have listed only those who took US citizenship (like Elsa Lanchester and Charles Laughton or Bob Hope), and excluded those who never relinquished their British citizenship, including Charles Chaplin and Oliver Sacks (the latter remarking that he rather liked being labelled a 'resident alien'). Whether native-born Americans became British citizens or not has not been a factor.

I have also defined London within its present boundaries, last reorganised in 1965, so that some who left these shores or who came here in the past often did so not from or to what is now London but counties abutting it (none of the early colonists, for example, set sail from London as we know it).

A specific address (that is, a house number or name) has also been a qualification for inclusion, but that has led to me to exclude only one American in London: the film producer Carl Foreman, who lived in Hyde Park Gardens. I could not find his actual address despite much research and inquiry.

I have not included most US ambassadors (and no British ambassadors to the USA), whose number would demand a small book in itself. However, there are some whom I have included, with a number of their predecessors, then called ministers. I have also excluded those entertainers who came to make a film here or to perform on the stage, as they are too numerous. With the important exception of Madeleine Albright, the former US secretary of state, all those listed are dead. Ms Albright's was too extraordinary and inspiring a story to omit.

But this book is not only about people. I have also included several buildings and monuments in London either associated with Americans (for example, the American International Church) or, places like Westminster

Abbey and St Paul's Cathedral, where many Americans are memorialised, as well as the seven statues of US presidents.

This is obviously not a history of the relationship between the United States and London – nor between Americans and Londoners – but I hope that it does offer glimpses of the political, social, artistic, economic and military history that makes some kind of pattern.

For all the change in the demographics of the United States, London seems still to have a strong, even unique, pull for many Americans. The poet and diplomat James Russell Lowell felt himself back in 'the old home'. During his three-month stay in London, the novelist Nathaniel Hawthorne (then consul in Liverpool) noted 'the sight and actual presence of almost all the objects and renowned localities that I had read about, and which had made London the dream-city of my youth'. Sylvia Plath thought it conjured up the townscape of Dickens.

I hope that many of those who read this book and use it to walk the streets of the capital will recognise that feeling, which is not unknown even to native Londoners, like the present author.

Note on entries and addresses

All entries are listed under London boroughs and where there are areas within those boroughs (for example, Bloomsbury in Camden, Belgravia in Westminster, or Stoke Newington in Hackney), I have added these to the addresses, along with postcodes, to make buildings, places and monuments easier to locate.

Where there is more than one address for an entry, I have listed first the address that seemed the most significant by reason of, say, place of birth, length of stay, or some event that took place there. Otherwise, addresses are listed in order of residence. Many entries have more than one address and they may be in different boroughs. In which case, the entry appears under the borough of the first address.

Names in the text printed in **bold type** indicate a person or place with their own entry. Other addresses of lesser note but which may be of some interest I have *italicised* in the text.

I have done my best to ascertain if buildings are still standing and where they are not say so ('gone'). Where a plaque commemorates a person or event, this is indicated by **P**.

List of people and places by borough

BARNET

Acres, Birt (1854–1918), Photographer and film pioneer. Clovelly Cottage, 19 Park Road, Chipping Barnet EN5 5RY **P**

BROMLEY

Aldridge, Ira (c1807–1867), Actor. Luranah Villa, 5 Hamlet Road, Upper Norwood SE19 2AP **P**

CAMDEN

Acheson, Edward (1856–1931), Chemist and industrialist. Kings Court, 31 Prince Albert Road, Primrose Hill NW8 7LT (gone) **P**

Adler, Larry (1914–2001), Harmonica player and composer. 110 Eton Hall, Eton College Road, Hampstead NW3 2DN; and 4 Robert Close, Maida Vale, Westminster W9 1BY

Cartwright, John (1740–1824), Political reformer and first British advocate of American independence. 37 Cartwright Gardens (formerly 37 Burton Crescent) Bloomsbury WC1H 9EH

Doolittle, Hilda (HD) (1886–1961), Poet and novelist. 44 Mecklenburgh Square, Bloomsbury WC1N 2AB **P**

Eliot, TS (1888–1965), poet, critic, dramatist and publisher. 24 Russell Square, Bloomsbury WC1B 5EA **P**; 34 Russell Mansions, Bury Street, Bloomsbury WC1A 2JS; Flat 18, Crawford Mansions, Old Marylebone Road,

Westminster W1H 4JU **P**; St Stephen's Church, Gloucester Road, Kensington and Chelsea SW7 4RL; 19 Carlyle Mansions, Cheyne Walk, Chelsea SW3 5LS; and 3 Kensington Court Gardens, Kensington and Chelsea W8 5DL **P**

Emerson, Ralph Waldo (1803–1882), Philosopher, lecturer and essayist. 63 Russell Square, Bloomsbury WC1B 5BB (gone: now Imperial Hotel)

Fort, Charles (1874–1932), Writer and researcher into unexplained phenomena. 39 Marchmont Street, Bloomsbury WC1N 1AP **P**

Hutton, Barbara (1912–1979), Heiress, socialite and philanthropist. Residence of the American ambassador, Winfield House, Regent's Park NW1 4RT

Maxim, Sir Hiram (1840–1916), Inventor. 57d Hatton Garden, Holborn EC1N 8EG **P**; and Sandhurst Lodge, 382 Streatham High Road, Streatham, Lambeth SW16 6HP (gone: now Tesco)

Miller, Lee (1907–1977), Photographer. 21 Downshire Hill, Hampstead NW3 1NT **P**

Plath, Sylvia (1932–1963), Poet. 23 Fitzroy Road, Primrose Hill NW1 8TP; St George the Martyr, Queen Square, Bloomsbury WC1N 3AH; 18 Rugby Street, Bloomsbury WC1N 3QZ; and 3 Chalcot Square, Primrose Hill NW1 8YB **P**

Robeson, Paul (1898–1976), Singer, actor and political activist. The Chestnuts, Branch Hill, Hampstead NW3 7LT **P**; and 12 Glebe Place, Chelsea, Kensington and Chelsea SW3 5LB

Stewart, Donald Ogden (1894–1980), Screenwriter, novelist and humorist. 103 Frognal, Hampstead NW3 6XR

Vane, Sir Henry (1613–1662), Governor of Massachusetts Bay Colony, politician and author. Vane House, 65 Rosslyn Hill, Hampstead NW3 5UD (gone: now North Bridge Senior School) **P**

Wellcome, Sir Henry (1853–1936), Philanthropist and pharmacist. Wellcome Collection, 183 Euston Road, NW1 2BE; and 6 Gloucester Gate, Regent's Park NW1 4HG **P**

CITY OF LONDON

American Memorial Chapel, St Paul's Cathedral, St Paul's Churchyard EC4M 8AD

Billy Fiske Memorial, St Paul's Cathedral, St Paul's Churchyard EC4M 8AD

Penn, William (1644–1718), Founder of Pennsylvania. All Hallows by the Tower, Byward Street, Tower Hill EC3R 5BJ **P**

Williams, Roger (c 1606–1683), Founder of the Colony of Rhode Island and the Providence Plantations. St Sepulchre-without-Newgate, Holborn Viaduct, Holborn EC1A 2DQ

CROYDON

Chandler, Raymond (1888–1959), Novelist. 110 Auckland Road, Upper Norwood SE19 2BY **P**

EALING

Adams, John Quincy (1767–1848), US Minister to London and 6th president of the United States. Little Boston House, Windmill Lane, Ealing W5 4DL (gone: now Little Boston, 236 Windmill Road); and All Hallows by the Tower, Byward St, Tower Hill, City of London EC3R 5BJ

Merton, Thomas (1915–1968), Monk, mystic, writer, poet and political activist. 18 Carlton Road, Ealing W5 2AW

GREENWICH

Hawthorne, Nathaniel (1804–1864), Novelist. 4 (formerly 6) Pond Road, Blackheath SE3 9JL **P**

Hope, Bob (1903–2003), Comedian, actor and writer. 44 Craigton Road, Eltham SE9 1QG **P**

HACKNEY

Poe, Edgar Allan (1809–1849), Poet and short story writer. Manor House School, Stoke Newington Church Street, Stoke Newington N16 0JL (gone: now 172) **P**

HOUNSLOW

Pocahontas (c1596–1617), Algonquin princess. London Road, Brentford TW8 8AP (now the site of the Royal Mail Sorting Office, 50 London Road); Banqueting House, Whitehall, Westminster SW1A 2ER; and St Mary-le-Bow Church, Cheapside, Holborn, City of London EC2V 6AU

ISLINGTON

Paine, Thomas (1737–1809), Writer and revolutionary. Angel Square, The Angel EC1V 1NY (gone) **P**

KENSINGTON AND CHELSEA

Albright, Madeleine (1937–), US secretary of state. Princes House, 52 Kensington Park Road, Kensington W11 3BW

American Food Store, 2 Ladbroke Grove, Kensington W11 3BG

Bell, Alexander Graham (1847–1922), Inventor of the telephone. 57 West Cromwell Road, Kensington SW5 9QS; 115 Jermyn Street, Westminster SW1Yv4UH (gone); and Royal Society of Arts, 8 John Adam Street, Charing Cross, Wesstminster WC2N 6EZ

Benn, Caroline (1926–2000), Education reformer and writer. 12 Holland Park Avenue, Kensington W11 3QU **P**

Douglass, Frederick (c1817–1895), Abolitionist, author and diplomat. 5 Whitehead's Grove, Chelsea SW3 3HA (gone: now Nell Gwynne Court) **P**

Epstein, Sir Jacob (1880–1959), Sculptor. 18 Hyde Park Gate, Kensington SW7 5DH **P**; and 25 Queen's Gate, Kensington SW7 5JE

Gardner, Ava (1922–1990), Actress. Flat 3, 34 Ennismore Gardens, Knightsbridge SW7 1AE **P**

Gellhorn, Martha (1908–1998), War correspondent and writer. 72 Cadogan Square, Knightsbridge SW1X 0ED; 31 South Eaton Place, Belgravia, Westminster SW1W 9EL; and 20 Chester Square, Belgravia, Westminster SW1W 9HS

Harte, (Francis) Bret (1836–1902), Author. 74 (now 72–74) Lancaster Gate, Bayswater W2 3NH **P**

James, Henry (1843–1916), Novelist and short story writer. 13 De Vere Mansions, 34 De Vere Gardens, Kensington W8 5AQ **P**; 21 Carlyle Mansions, Cheyne Walk, Chelsea SW3 5LS; and 3 Bolton Street, Piccadilly, Westminster W1J 8BA (gone)

Kauffer, Edward McKnight (1890–1954) and **Dorn, Marion (1896–1964)**, Designers. 139 and 141 Swan Court, Chelsea Manor Street, Chelsea SW3 5RT **P**

Kennedy, John F (1917–1963), 35th president of the United States, and **Kennedy, Joseph (1888–1969)**, United States ambassador. 14 Princes Gate, Knightsbridge SW7 1PT **P**

Losey, Joseph (1909–1984), Film director. 29 Royal Avenue, Chelsea SW3 4QE **P**; and 60 Queen Anne Street, Marylebone, Westminster W1G 8HP

Morgan, Junius Spencer (1813–1890) and **Morgan Sr, John Pierpont (1837–1913)**, Financiers. 14 Princes Gate, Knightsbridge SW7 1PT **P**

Pound, Ezra (1885–1972), Poet. 10 Kensington Church Walk, Kensington W8 4NB **P**; 5 Holland Place Chambers, Kensington W8 4LS; and 48 Langham Street, Fitzrovia, Westminster W1W 7AR

Sargent, John Singer (1856–1925), Portrait and landscape painter and muralist. 31 and 33 Tite Street, Chelsea SW3 4JP **P**

Thompson, Sir Benjamin, Count Rumford (1753–1814), Soldier, physicist and inventor. 168 Brompton Road (formerly 45 Brompton Row), Knightsbridge SW3 1HW **P**

Twain, Mark (1835–1910), Writer and humourist. 23 Tedworth Square, Chelsea SW3 4DR **P**

Welch, Elisabeth (1904–2003), Singer, actress and cabaret artist. 1 Ovington Court, Ovington Gardens, off Brompton Road, Kensington SW5 1LB **P**

Whistler, James Abbott McNeill (1834–1903), Painter. 96 Cheyne Walk, Chelsea SW10 0DQ (formerly 2 Lindsey Row) **P**; 31 and 33 Tite Street, Chelsea SW3 4JP **P**; and 74 Cheyne Walk, Chelsea SW3 5TT (gone)

LEWISHAM

McMillan, Margaret (1860–1931), Pioneer of nursery education and socialist propagandist, and **McMillan, Rachel (1859–1917)**, Health visitor and educationalist. 51 Tweedy Road, Bromley BR1 3HN **P**

SOUTHWARK

Harvard, John (1607–1638), Benefactor of Harvard University. St Saviour's Church (now Southwark Cathedral), London Bridge SE1 9DA

Southwark Cathedral, Memorials. London Bridge SE1 9DA

Wanamaker, Sam (1919–1993), Actor, director, creator of the Globe Theatre. Globe Theatre, 21 New Globe Walk, Bankside SE1 9DT **P**; and 7 Bentinck Close, 76–82 Prince Albert Road, St John's Wood, Westminster NW8 7RY **P**

Weyonomon, Mahomet (c1700–1736), Mohegan tribal chief. Southwark Cathedral, London Bridge SE1 9DA

Yeardley, Sir George (1587–1627), Colonial governor of Virginia. St Saviour's Church (now Southwark Cathedral), London Bridge SE1 9DA

TOWER HAMLETS

Jefferson, Jane Randolph (1720–1776), Mother of Thomas Jefferson, 3rd president of the United States. St Paul's Church, 302 The Highway, Shadwell E1 3WD

Jones Jr, Christopher (c1570–1622), Captain of the *Mayflower*. Blackwall Stairs, Blackwall Way, Yabsley Street, Poplar E14; The Mayflower Pub, 117 Rotherhithe Street, Rotherhithe, Southwark SE16 4NF; and St Mary's Church, Rotherhithe, Southwark SE16 4JH **P**

Severs, Dennis (1948–1999), Museum creator. Dennis Severs House, 18 Folgate Street, Spitalfields E1 6BX

Virginia Quay Settlers Monument, Virginia Quay, Jamestown Way, Poplar E14 2DE

Whitechapel Bell Foundry (gone), First Liberty Bell struck here. 32–34 Whitechapel Road, Whitechapel E1 1DY

WALTHAM FOREST

Hitchcock, Alfred (1899–1980), Film director. 517 Leytonstone High Road, Leytonstone E11 4QH **P**; 175 Salmon Lane, Limehouse E14 7EU (gone); Gainsborough Studios, Poole Street, Hoxton, Hackney N1 7BG **P**; and 153 Cromwell Road, Kensington, Kensington and Chelsea SW5 0TQ

WANDSWORTH

Hartley, David (1732–1813), Signatory to the Treaty of Paris, MP, abolitionist and inventor. Tibbet's Corner, near Widcroft Road, Kingston Road, Putney Heath SW15 3EL (obelisk)

CITY OF WESTMINSTER

Adams, John (1735–1826), Minister to London and 2nd president of the United States. 9 Grosvenor Square, Mayfair W1K 5AE **P**

Adams, Henry (1838–1918), Writer and historian. 98 Portland Place (formerly 5 Upper Portland Place), Marylebone W1B 1LT 🅟

American Bar, Stafford Hotel, 16–18 St James's Place, St James's SW1A 1NJ

American International Church, 79a Tottenham Court Road, Fitzrovia W1T 4TB

Arnold, Benedict (1722–1801), Hero of the American Revolution and traitor to its cause. 62 Gloucester Place, Marylebone W1U 8HW 🅟; and St Mary's Church, Battersea Church Road, Battersea, Wandsworth SW11 3NA

Astor, William Waldorf, 1st Viscount Astor (1848–1919), Property owner and newspaper proprietor. 2 Temple Place, Victoria Embankment WC2P 3BD; and 18 Carlton House Terrace, St James's SW1Y 5AH

Astor, Nancy (1879–1964), First woman to take her seat in the House of Commons and **Astor, Waldorf, 2nd Viscount Astor (1879–1952)**, Politician, race horse owner–breeder and newspaper proprietor. 4 St James's Square, St James's SW1Y 4JU 🅟 (now the In & Out Club)

Burgoyne, John (1723–1792), General, politician, and playwright. 10 Hertford Street, Mayfair W1J 7RL 🅟

Channon, Sir Henry ('Chips') (1897–1958), Diarist and Conservative MP. 5 Belgrave Square, Belgravia SW1X 8PH

Churchill, Jennie (1854–1921), Society hostess and writer. 48 Charles Street, Mayfair W1J 5EN; 2 Connaught Place, Hyde Park W2 2ET; 35a Great Cumberland Place, Marble Arch (now the Rose Court Hotel) W1H 7DS; and 8 Westbourne Street, Hyde Park W2 2TZ

Cree (unknown–1734), Yamacraw leader. St John's Garden, Horseferry Road, Westminster SW1P 4DA

Cunard, Lady Emerald (1872–1948), Social hostess. 7 Grosvenor Square, Mayfair W1K 4AG (gone: now apartments, numbered 7); and Dorchester Hotel, 53 Park Lane, Mayfair W1K 1QA

Eisenhower, Dwight D (1890–1969), Supreme Allied Commander Europe and 34th president of the United States. Norfolk House, 13 St James's Square, St James's SW1 4JR 🅟; 20 Grosvenor Square, Mayfair W1K 6LE 🅟; and Telegraph Cottage, Warren Road, Kingston-upon-Thames KT2 7HU (gone)

Fairbanks Jnr, Douglas (1909–2000), Actor, businessman, socialite. 99 Park Lane, Hyde Park, Mayfair W1K 7TH; and 8 The Boltons, Brompton, Kensington & Chelsea SW10 9TB

Franklin, Benjamin (1706–1790), Pennsylvania agent to Britain, scientist, inventor, writer and statesman. 36 (formerly 7 and later 27) Craven Street, Strand, Charing Cross WC2 5NF 🅟

Gage, Thomas (1719/20–1787), Commander-in-chief of the British forces in North America and colonial governor. 41 (formerly 22, 29 and 54) Portland Place, Marylebone W1B 1QH 🅟

Harriman, Pamela Churchill (1920–1997), Diplomat and courtesan. 10 Downing Street, Westminster SW1A 2AA; and 49 Grosvenor Square, Mayfair W1K 2AH

Hendrix, Jimi (1942–1970), Rock musician and songwriter. 23 Brook Street, Mayfair W1K 4AH 🅟; and Samarkand Hotel, 22 Lansdowne Crescent, Notting Hill, Kensington and Chelsea W11 2NS

Ives, Charles (1874–1954), Composer. 18 Half Moon Street, Mayfair W1J 7BE (gone) 🅟

Kent, Tyler (1911–1988), Spy. 47 Gloucester Place, Marylebone W1U 8JE

Laughton, Charles (1890–1962), Actor, and **Lanchester, Elsa (1902–1986)**, Actor. 28 Dean Street, Soho W1D 3LL; 2nd Floor, 15 Percy Street, Fitzrovia W1T 1DS and 47 Farley Road, Hither Green, Lewisham SE6 2AA 🅟

Legation of the Republic of Texas, Pickering Place, 3 St James's Street, St James's SW1A 1EF 🅟

Lowell, James Russell (1819–1891), Poet, critic and American minister in London. 37 Lowndes Square, Belgravia SW1X 9HA

Melville, Herman (1819–1891), Novelist, short story writer and poet. 15 Craven Street, Strand, Charing Cross WC2N 5PB 🅟

Morse, Samuel (1791–1872), Painter and inventor of Morse code. 141 Cleveland Street (formerly 8 Buckingham Place), Fitzrovia W1T 4QG 🅟

Murrow, Edward R (1908–1965), Radio and television broadcaster. Flat 5, Weymouth House, 84–94 Hallam Street, Marylebone W1W 5HF 🅟

Page, Walter Hines (1855–1918), Journalist, publisher and American ambassador. 6 Grosvenor Square, Mayfair W1K 6LE (gone: now apartments, numbered 7) 🅟

Peabody, George (1795–1869), Merchant banker and philanthropist. 80 Eaton Square, Belgravia SW1 9AP 🅟

Radziwill, Lee (1933–2019), Socialite and sister of Jacqueline Kennedy. 4 Buckingham Place, Victoria SW1E 6HR

Roosevelt, Theodore (1858–1919), 26th president of the United States. St George's Church, Hanover Square, Mayfair W1S 1FX; and Brown's Hotel, 33 Albemarle Street, Mayfair W1S 4BP

Roosevelt, Franklin Delano (1882–1945), 32nd president of the United States and **Roosevelt, Eleanor (1884–1962)**, Politician, diplomat and activist. Brown's Hotel, 33 Albemarle Street, Mayfair W1S 4BP

Selfridge, Sir (Harry) Gordon (1858–1947), Department store owner. Selfridge's, 400 Oxford Street, Marylebone W1A 1AB; Lansdowne House (now the Lansdowne Club), 9 Fitzmaurice Place, Mayfair W1J 5JD **P**; and 2 Ross Court, Putney Hill, Putney Heath, Wandsworth SW15 3NY

Smithson, James (c 1765–1829), Founding donor of the Smithsonian Institution, mineralogist and chemist. 9 Bentinck Street, Marylebone W1U 2EH **P**

Statues of Presidents of the United States:

George Washington (1732–1799; served 1789–1797), Trafalgar Square, Westminster WC2N 5DX; *Abraham Lincoln (1809–1865; served 1861–1865)*, Parliament Square, Westminster SW1P 3PD; *Franklin Roosevelt (1882–1945; served 1933–1945)*; Grosvenor Square, Mayfair W1K 2HP; Franklin Roosevelt and Winston Churchill, New Bond Street, Mayfair W1S 3SU; *Dwight D Eisenhower (1890–1969; served 1953–1961)*, Grosvenor Square, Mayfair W1K 2HP; *John F Kennedy (1917–1963; served 1960–1963)*, Marylebone Road, Marylebone W1B 1PF; and *Ronald Reagan (1911–2004; served 1981–1989)*, Grosvenor Square, Mayfair W1K 2HP

St George's Church, Hanover Square, Mayfair W1S 1FX

Van Buren, Martin (1782–1862), Minister to Britain and 8th president of the United States. 7 Stratford Place, Marylebone W1C 1AY **P**; and 2 Chandos Street, Marylebone W1G 9DG; and **Irving, Washington (1783–1859)**, Writer, essayist, historian and diplomat. 8 Argyll Street, Soho W1F 7TF **P**

West, Benjamin (1738–1820), History painter. 14 Newman Street, Fitzrovia W1T 1PB (gone)

Westminster Abbey, Memorials. Dean's Yard, Westminster SW1P 3PA

Winant, John (1889–1947), US ambassador. 7 Aldford Street, Mayfair W1K 2AQ **P**

Windsor, Duchess of (Simpson, Bessie Wallis) (1896–1986), Socialite and royal consort. 5 Bryanston Court, Bryanston Square, Marylebone W1H 7HA

Entries

Acres, Birt (1854–1918)

Photographer and film pioneer

Clovelly Cottage, 19 Park Road, Chipping Barnet EN5 5RY P

Acres was born in Richmond, Virginia, to English parents, but was raised by an aunt after being orphaned during the American Civil War. When he came to England and was manager of a dry plate works in Barnet, he started experimenting with studies of clouds by use of chronophotographic time-lapse. While not a creative filmmaker, it is his work as an inventor and innovator which has been influential, even though today he is little recognised.

The first British 35mm moving picture camera and the first daylight loading home movie camera and projector were his inventions. Acres clocked up other notable 'firsts': as the first travelling newsreel reporter in international film history and the first European filmmaker to have his films screened in public in the USA.

In making cameras, projectors, film viewers, coating and slitting machines, and 35mm raw film stock he contributed much to the development of cinematography, as did his mobile newsreel reporting and the public projections of moving pictures.

Acres and his partner, the engineer and instrument maker Robert Paul, were the first people in the UK to construct a working 35mm camera. They developed a ciné camera and, in February 1895, made their first film experiment, showing their mutual friend Henry Short, wearing cricket whites, walking outside Clovelly Cottage. The film, sometimes called *Incident at Clovelly Cottage*, but not formally titled, also shows Acres' wife and infant son outside their home. Never shown commercially, this was the first real British film production.

However, Acres and Paul parted ways when the former patented the design of the 35mm camera in his own name. The last film they made together was of the Derby in 1895. Paul was to be far more successful with sales of his Theatrograph and Animatograph projectors, next to which Acres enjoyed only modest success with sales of his Kineoptikon projector.

In 1895 Acres went to Germany, sponsored by the German chocolate company Stollwerck, to film several scenes, including the opening of the Kiel Canal.

Acres gave the first public showing of moving pictures to a British audience when he displayed his film at the Lyonsdown Photographic Society at the Lytton Road Assembly Rooms in New Barnet on January 1896. That same month, the members of the society and their wives were treated to a demonstration of his Kineopticon system at the Queen's Hall, London.

While it was not his forte, he began to show films commercially with his Kineoptikon projector at Piccadilly Mansions, London. His early silent films included *The Oxford and Cambridge Boat Race*, as well as *The Arrest of a Pickpocket*, *The Comic Shoeblack*, *The Boxing Kangaroo* and *Performing Bears*.

In 1896 Acres attracted press criticism when, at the Cardiff exhibition, he filmed the Prince of Wales briefly scratching his head by tearing a hole in an exhibition wall (he claimed with permission). This seems not to have shocked the royal couple who invited him to their home, Marlborough House, to show the film.

Two years later, when a gantry collapsed at the launch of HMS Albion and many spectators were drowned, Acres and Paul both filmed the event. However, unlike Acres, Paul chose to show his film. Acres attacked his former partner in the press, accusing him of gross insensitivity. Paul's launch, though, saved a number of those in the water.

Acres' Northern Photographic Works began to produce celluloid film and in 1898 his Birtac, a miniature camera/projector, was launched for what was hoped to be a nascent home movie market. A fellow of the Royal Photographic Society, he pulled out of film production soon after 1900, but remained committed to film processing and celluloid manufacture. However, he was twice declared bankrupt.

He died in Whitechapel in 1918 and is buried in Walthamstow.

Aldridge, Ira (c1807–1867)

Actor

Luranah Villa, 5 Hamlet Road, Upper Norwood SE19 2AP

Aldridge was the first major African-American actor yet most of his performances were in Britain or on the continent. Despite what are very possibly fanciful claims about his origins – born in Senegal to royal blood – it is most likely that he was born in New York, the son of a

Portrait of Ira Aldridge in 1858 by Tara Shevchenko

free-born lay preacher (as the son was to be free born) and a mother who died when he was a youth.

Theatre was an interest to the child Ira and he went to his native city's Park Theatre. He was involved in the short-lived African Theatre, where he played in Sheridan's *Pizarro*.

He saw his best chance of success on the stage on the other side of the Atlantic and in 1824 he set sail for England. The next year he made his debut at London's Royal Coburg Theatre in *The Revolt of Surinam*, or, *A Slave's Revenge*. At the same theatre he also appeared in Thomas Morton's *The Slave* and JH Amherst's *The Death of Christophe*. In 1865 he married his first wife, Margaret Gill, who was seven years his senior. Their inter-racial marriage was criticised by the pro-slavery lobby. There were no children but she raised Ira Daniel, who was her husband's illegitimate child.

Aldridge's appearance attracted attention – he was tall and well-built and, says the *Oxford Dictionary of National Biography*, 'it was common for critics to note, with some surprise, that he was not as dark-skinned as actors in "blackface", but rather was "almost a light brown", with a "mulatto tint".' His voice was said to be 'rich and melodious', although some found it nasal or whiny. His accent was, it was said (unsurprisingly), 'strikingly un-English' in its pronunciation, while the novelist George Eliot found it intolerable.

He was known as the 'African Roscius' and specialised in tragic roles, but was also a notable comic player. In the earlier part of his career, he was known as 'Mr Keene' and toured the provincial circuit, taking in, among other places, Hull, Brighton, Manchester, Newcastle, Liverpool and Edinburgh, as well as London's East End.

In 1833 Aldridge made his West End debut as Othello at the Theatre Royal, Covent Garden where, up to his death only two weeks before, Edmund Kean had been playing the part. To defend the fact that he had succeeded Kean, Aldridge had to distribute hand bills.

The standards of the time and the uniqueness of having a black actor in a major role on the West End stage was reflected in some of the reviews: his performance was 'very *fair* for a black', the *Theatrical Observer* punningly recorded. It may have been the hostility of the press that caused the theatre to close for five days after two performances, and the rest of his run was cancelled. Yet other critics had remarked on his 'naturalness' and audiences were overwhelmingly supportive.

In 1852, after the provinces and Ireland, Aldridge embarked on a tour of the continent, where the theatre world warmed to him and he mixed with ease with aristocrats and artists in the Austro-Hungarian empire. His Othello was acclaimed in Switzerland and Germany, as well as popular performances in *The Padlock* and *Macbeth*.

A provincial tour and performances in East End theatres followed Aldridge's return to England in 1855. He was offered parts at the Lyceum when he burnished his reputation with a second tour on the continent and garnered a more approving coverage by the press. On visits to Russia in 1858 and 1862 he was said to have introduced a more naturalistic acting style and encouraged theatres to produce Shakespeare.

Margaret died in 1864 and the next year Aldridge married Amanda Pauline von Brandt. He had met her on a European tour in 1857 or 1858. They had four children: Irene (Luranah, 1860) and Ira Frederick (1862), who were born before their parents' marriage, Amanda, and then Rachel, who was born in 1868 after her father's death.

Aldridge acquired wealth, some of which he devoted to progressive black causes.

Continental audiences took far more to Aldridge than those in his adopted country, offering him greater artistic range and freedom. He died, apparently of a lung infection, in Łódz, Poland in August 1867 and rests in the city's evangelical cemetery.

Acheson, Edward (1856–1931)

Chemist and industrialist

Kings Court, 31 Prince Albert Road, Primrose Hill NW8 7LT (gone) P

Acheson enjoyed only three years of formal education growing up in the coal fields of south west Pennsylvania, leaving school at 16 on his father's death to work as a railway surveying assistant.

However, he must have had an inquiring and inventive mind as he spent his evenings largely carrying out

Edward Acheson in 1908 (*Popular Science Monthly*)

scientific experiments. He invented a battery which he sent to Thomas Edison in 1880, who, as a result, gave him a job. He worked for Edison for four years, during which he installed electric lighting in La Scala Opera in Milan and elsewhere in Europe.

When he left Edison, Acheson supervised a plant manufacturing electric lamps, where he invented silicon carbide, which he called carborundum and patented in 1893. He also built an electricity plant in 1891 in Port Huron. In 1894 he established the Carborundum Company. However, seven years later the Electrical Smelting and Aluminum Company was given 'priority broadly' 'for reducing ores and other substances by the incandescent method'. He appears to have established a company in London, EH Acheson Ltd, at 40 Wood Street, Westminster (gone) and lived in a house in Prince Albert Road from 1912 to 1915. Acheson took out 70 patents. He died in New York in 1931.

Adler, Larry (1914–2001)

Harmonica player and composer

110 Eton Hall, Eton College Road, Hampstead NW3 2DN
4 Robert Close, Maida Vale, Westminster W9 1BY

Not for Lawrence Cecil Adler of Baltimore, Maryland, was it ever the harmonica, but rather, the mouth organ, an instrument at which he not only excelled but which gave him a career that ranged across 20th century popular music from Ivor Novello to Elton John, and the Gershwin brothers to Sting. He performed at the BBC Proms and elsewhere played the work of

modern, as well as classical, composers. He created public and professional appreciation of the harmonica from what was considered a toy to an instrument of which he was a virtuoso.

The son of Jewish immigrants (his father was a plumber), Adler's talents got him out of his environment, where he had experienced anti-semitic abuse. His was a precocious gift – piano lessons at six; the youngest cantor in the Baltimore synagogue at ten. He studied music at Baltimore City College and the Peabody Conservatory of Music, from which he was expelled for playing *Yes, We Have No Bananas*, instead of Grieg's *Waltz in A Minor* at a recital.

Adler abandoned piano for the harmonica and won the state's harmonica championship in 1927 and then relocated to New York to find work as a professional musician. He rejected his parents' plea to return, preferring to try to join Borrah Minevitch's Harmonica Rascals, for which he was turned down when Minevitch did not recognise Adler's ability.

But Adler secured $100 a week to play in intervals in a tour of cinemas. Soon he was meeting people like Charles Chaplin, Greta Garbo, Noel Coward and even Al Capone.

He was not out of his teens yet had already worked with the comedian Eddie Cantor; auditioned for Florenz Ziegfeld's production of *Smiles*; appeared in a film, *Operator 13* (his first); and played at Grauman's Chinese Theatre in Los Angeles. Brought to London by the impresario Sir Charles Cochran, Adler enjoyed instant success in Cochran's revue, *Streamline,* and at 23 followed this with another Cochran vehicle, *Tune Inn*. A year later Adler was recording with Django Reinhardt and appeared in another film, *St Martin's Lane* with Vivien Leigh and **Charles Laughton**.

In 1939 Adler was a soloist with the Sydney Symphony Orchestra and played to troops in the Middle East and western Europe during the Second World War. He appeared for the first time at Carnegie Hall in 1943. There was a sweet irony for the Jewish harmonica player that at the war's end he performed *The Battle Hymn of the Republic* on the balcony of Hitler's Berlin Chancellery, and then the Jewish composer George Gershwin's *Rhapsody in Blue* at the Nuremberg stadium.

However, when Adler subscribed to the Committee for the First Amendment to support screenwriters and others being persecuted by McCarthyism, he came to the attention of the senator from Minnesota. He never came before the House Un-American Activities Committee but when labelled a communist (he had always been a fervent anti-fascist) by Senator McCarthy, he was blacklisted and unable to work.

This caused his migration to England where he became well established as a performer in both nightclubs and concert halls. At 24 Adler married a model named Eileen Walser and they lived at Stratford Court, Oxford Street (now the Radisson Blu Edwardian Berkshire Hotel). They went on to have a son and two daughters. Ralph Vaughan Williams composed *Romance for Harmonica and Orchestra* for him, which he performed at the Proms.

Adler's own foray into composing began with the music for the 1953 film *Genevieve*. He settled for 2.5 per cent of the royalties and netted more than £250,000 when the film was unexpectedly successful. However, in the USA, his name was deleted from the credits, and when the music was nominated for an Oscar, the composer was listed as Muir Mathieson, the conductor. (In 1993 the Academy sent Adler his nominee's certificate.)

More film compositions followed: *The Hellions*, *The Hook*, *King and Country*, *A High Wind in Jamaica*, and *The Great Chase*, as well as music for BBC television's *Midnight Madness*. At the Edinburgh Festival in 1963 he performed the first recitation of an unpublished quartet by Gershwin. Four years later, in 1967, he entertained Israeli troops during the Six Day War.

Adler divorced in 1961 and had a daughter with his second wife Sally Adler (she had changed her name by deed poll), with whom he lived in Maida Vale. The marriage lasted only eight years and they divorced in 1977. He never
remarried but had a ten-year relationship with the biographer Selina Hastings, his junior by 31 years.

Although he took up a second career as a writer – both of journalism and books – when the harmonica fell from fashion, Adler was always in demand. His work involved collaborations with Cher, Sting, Elton John, Elvis Costello, Meat Loaf and Peter Gabriel. He received enthusiastic reviews at the Edinburgh Festival in 1985.

For his 80th birthday he released an album, *The Glory of Gershwin*, which reached No 2 in the British pop charts. He was also often a guest and raconteur on TV chat shows, displaying his characteristic wit and charm.

Adler spent his final years in his Hampstead apartment and died of pneumonia, after suffering several strokes, at St Thomas's Hospital, London.

Cartwright, John (1740–1824)

Political reformer and first British advocate of American independence

37 Cartwright Gardens (formerly 37 Burton Crescent), Bloomsbury WC1H 9EH*

In July 1824, three months before Cartwright's death, Thomas Jefferson, former president of the United States, wrote to him congratulating him on his work. Touchingly, the great Virginian said that at their advanced ages they would soon be able to discuss good government for all eternity. Cartwright would not even wait for that because while plagued with ill health he published *A Problem*, one of his last books, in which he proposed the United States as an exemplary union for all nations.

Cartwright was born in Nottinghamshire to a well-to-do family, one of five brothers and five sisters. His early life was adventurous: he saw naval service and led exploratory expeditions, the latter injurious to his health. In 1780 he married Anne Dashwood, a woman from a similar family. It was a life-long and happy marriage, but childless.

Conscious of his poor education he took to reading voraciously, which developed his political outlook and led to his publishing 80 works between 1774 and 1824, becoming noted as the 'Father of Reform'.

In 1771 he published *American Independence: the Glory and Interest of Great Britain*, making him the first Englishman to support an independent United States, seeing a commonwealth of interest that would support a political union. And to advance his ideas of conciliation he published *A Letter to Edmund Burke, Esq*, in which he foresaw that transatlantic trade would transcend major political change.

His views would not allow him to serve in American waters under Lord Howe in 1775, and this refusal marked the end of his naval career. But he became Major Cartwright in the Nottinghamshire militia.

His study of the American War of Independence caused him to regard the British Parliament as corrupt and he published *Take Your Choice!*, his own programme for reform, whereby he became one of the first advocates of universal male suffrage. He later supported annual parliamentary elections, equal electoral districts, a secret ballot, the abolition of property qualifications for parliamentary candidates, and payment for members of parliament.

Cartwright saw politics as a pursuit for gentlemen and looked back to a time of Anglo-Saxon liberties, while propelling forward the English reform movement, deeply influencing the Chartists and the American Revolution. He not only wrote but was practical in working with diverse people, like Charles James Fox and others, often dissenters, and helped to found the Society for Constitutional Information. He twice (in 1806 and 1807) stood unsuccessfully for Parliament in Boston, Lincolnshire. The American colonies having become independent, the French Revolution further fomented his reformist zeal.

Reform and an interest in London politics led him to forsake Nottinghamshire, where he had amassed land, and move to the capital in 1819 and what was then Burton Crescent. His new colleagues included the radicals Francis Place and William Cobbett and he subsidised the radical *Black Dwarf* and founded the increasingly radical Hampden Club in London which spawned 150 clubs in the Midlands and the North. Cartwright addressed large outdoor meetings and, realising that Parliament would not reform itself, returned to his old theme

John Cartwright's statue in the gardens named after him (Terry Philpot)

of universal manhood suffrage. He escaped injury or death during the Peterloo Massacre in Manchester in 1819 and was found guilty of sedition in that same year at the age of 81, for which he paid a fine of £100.

Cartwright supported the Greek independence struggle in 1821, the same year that he published *The English Constitution Produced and Illustrated*, again praising political equality and the continued success of the American republican experiment.

He died at his home, and the crescent was later renamed in his honour. The bronze statue that stands by the gate of the crescent's park was erected in 1831, a year before the passing of the Great Reform Act.

---

* *No 37 is now numbered 36 and 37, with one door.*

Doolittle, Hilda (HD) (1886–1961)

Poet and novelist

44 Mecklenburgh Square, Bloomsbury WC1N 2AB 🅿

Hilda was HD to her friends and family in Pennsylvania long before she found literary fame using those initials. Her mother was a Moravian and she was brought up and educated in that faith. For a year she attended Bryn Mawr College, Philadelphia. It was there that she suffered an emotional breakdown brought on by the struggle between her mother's faith, her astronomer father's high academic expectations for her, and her need to find her place as the only girl among five brothers. She was only 15 when she developed a deep, life-long friendship with the young **Ezra Pound**, to whom she would be engaged.

It was about this time too that she began a long affair with an art student named Frances Gregg, and her understanding of her bisexuality was clarified when she underwent psychoanalysis with Sigmund Freud in Vienna in 1933. The conflict and confusion caused by her sexuality found expression in her autobiographical novels, which appeared after her death: *Her* (1981), *Asphodel* (1992) and *Paint it Today* (1992).

In 1911 Doolittle travelled to France and England with Gregg and Gregg's mother and when the two other women returned to the USA, Doolittle stayed in London. Here she fell in with the growing circle that Pound had gathered around him. The next year she met the writer and poet Richard Aldington, who was a member of Pound's Imagist group. When, after spending the summer in Paris, Aldington and Doolittle met Pound in a tea shop near the British Museum and showed him their translations from Greek poetry, Pound crossed out her name on her poems and substituted 'HD Imagiste', and she was known to the wider world from then on as HD.

Doolittle and Aldington married in London in 1913 and she gave birth to a still-born child in 1915. The next year *Sea Garden*, her first book of poems, appeared almost as Aldington left for the Western Front. Her work featured in various publications and from 1916 to 1917 she edited *The Egoist*. From 1917 to 1918 she lived at the Bloomsbury address.

Aldington began an extramarital affair in 1917 and Doolittle became lovers with Cecil Gray, musicologist and composer, a brief affair which, nevertheless, produced a daughter, Frances Perdita, in 1919. The last months of the marriage she relates in her novel *Bid Me Love*, published the year before her death. However, while they did not live together after his return from the war in 1919, Doolittle and Aldington did not divorce until 1938, so he could marry a lover who was pregnant with his child.

Aldington, to whom she continued to feel close, Pound and DH Lawrence, with whom she had an intimate friendship, featured in her poetry and prose, together with issues of gender, sexuality and artistic identity.

Doolittle had become friendly with Bryher (the novelist and journalist Annie Winifred Ellerman, a scion of the eponymous shipping family), who,

Hilda Doolittle's Mecklenburgh Square home

whilst being a manipulative person, did financially support and care for Doolittle and her child.

The outbreak of the Second World War, only 21 years after the end of the traumatic Great War, depressed Doolittle, and its conclusion disorientated her so much so that she sought treatment for a disabling breakdown in Zurich, Switzerland. She recovered but the rest of her life was spent in that country, either in hotels or clinics. Aldington visited twice but it became a friendship based on correspondence, as was her friendship with Bryher. Doolittle visited the USA several times in the 1950s to visit her daughter and grandchildren. It was in a Swiss clinic that she died of a brain haemorrhage in 1961, and her ashes are buried in the family plot in Bethlehem, Pennsylvania.

Unpublished novels, other prose and her book about Pound, *End to Torment*, appeared after her death.

Eliot, TS (1888–1965)

Poet, critic, dramatist and publisher

24 Russell Square, Bloomsbury WC1B 5EA 🅿
34 Russell Mansions, Bury Street, Bloomsbury WC1A 2JS*
Flat 18, Crawford Mansions, Old Marylebone Road, Westminster W1H 4JU 🅿
St Stephen's Church, Gloucester Road, Kensington, Kensington and Chelsea SW7 4RL
19 Carlyle Mansions, Cheyne Walk, Chelsea, Kensington and Chelsea SW3 5LS
3 Kensington Court Gardens, Kensington, Kensington and Chelsea W8 5DL 🅿

Thomas Stearns Eliot came from a patrician Unitarian family in St Louis, Missouri, where he was born, the last of his parents' six surviving children. His early interest in books intensified with the isolation from those of his own age caused by his congenital double hernia. As he attested: 'Missouri and the Mississippi have made a deeper impression on me than any other part of the world.'

He began to write poetry at 14 and enjoyed a classical education, going on to attend Harvard. It was in the college's union library in 1908 that he discovered Arthur Symons's *The Symbolist Movement in Literature*. Eliot said it was a communion with the dead. It opened him to his vocation as a poet and between 1911 and 1915 he wrote *The Love Song of J Alfred Prufrock*, *Portrait of a Lady*, *Preludes*, and *Rhapsody on a Windy Night*.

After a time as a philosophy assistant at the university he moved to Paris for a year's post-graduate study at the Sorbonne. Here Eliot made another discovery: Charles Maurras's conservative, monarchist Catholicism was to shape Eliot's later life and outlook. Then, after another three years at Harvard, Eliot gained a fellowship to Merton College, Oxford. It was not the happiest of experiences for, as he wrote to his friend the American poet Conrad Aiken, 'Oxford is very pretty, but I don't like to be dead'.

He spent much of his time in London where, in meeting **Ezra Pound**, he came into contact with one of the most significant people in his life. Pound thought the younger man 'worth watching' and he did much to promote Eliot. Eliot left Merton after a year and in 1915 was teaching English at the University of London's Birkbeck College in Bloomsbury.

That summer he and Vivienne (Vivien) Haigh-Wood married impulsively at Hampstead Registry Office. He was taken with her frankness, sophistication and charm. But there was more to it than that for him. He wrote later: 'I believe that I came to persuade myself that I was in love with her simply because I wanted to burn my boats and commit myself to staying in England'. He did: the philosopher Bertrand Russell lent them his flat in Bury Street as a home and they later lived at Crawford Mansions and Clarence Gate Gardens, Kensington. Eliot combined teaching, including in schools, with book reviewing to earn money. In 1917 a job in the foreign department of Lloyds Bank in London gave him financial stability and enabled him to write. That year he published *Prufrock and other Observations*.

While Russell brought Eliot into the Bloomsbury Group and the company of politicians like the former prime minister Herbert Asquith, Pound gave him an entrée into the international *avant-garde*. Such socialising had practical rewards: Lady Rothermere, wife of the newspaper magnate, offered him editorship of *The Criterion* that first appeared in 1922.

That year, too, *The Waste Land* appeared, which stemmed in part from his observations of London life but was also a work of great intensity and emotion. It came after a breakdown, occasioned by his father's death and the strain of his marriage, and rest cure.

In 1925 Eliot left Lloyds to become literary editor and a director of Faber and Gwyer (later Faber and Faber), a new publisher, at their Russell Square offices. He stayed with the firm up to his death with WH Auden, Stephen Spender and Ted Hughes numbered among the poets for whom he was responsible.

Two years later Eliot took two of the most important steps of his life when he converted to the Anglican faith in June and in November became a British citizen. For seven years from 1933 he lived at the Presbytery, 9 Grenville Place (gone: now 114a Cromwell Road) and served as warden of *St Stephen's Church, Gloucester Road, Kensington*. In a book of essays he referred to himself as a 'classicist in literature, royalist in politics, and anglo-catholic [*sic*] in religion'. Many years later he described his religious faith as one which combined the roots of his old and new countries: '… a Catholic cast of mind, a Calvinist

Plaque to TS Eliot at his last home, Kensington Court Gardens heritage, and a Puritanical temperament'. He took enthusiastically to the life of the Church, its debates and controversies, and he joined discussion groups and gave lectures.

The marriage became increasingly unhappy, partly due to Vivienne's physical and mental illness. In 1932 Eliot took a year's teaching at Harvard and they separated in 1933. He saw her only once between then and her death in 1947 in a psychiatric hospital, where he never visited her, and to which her brother Charles had had her committed in 1938.

In 1933 he began an increasingly intense relationship with Emily Hale, whom he had known in America in his last spell at Harvard. They never married because he could not contemplate divorce. He enjoyed, too, a long friendship with the philanthropist Mary Trevelyan, who wanted to marry him.

During the Second World War he served as an air raid warden in London. *The Four Quartets* appeared in 1943 and the topical references and sense of shared suffering in his war-time poems increased his popularity.

Eliot lived from 1946 to 1957, with his friend and unofficial archivist and manager, the editor and critic John Davy Howard, at Carlyle Mansions. In 1957, at the age of 68 he married 30-year-old Valerie Fletcher, who had been his secretary, in a secret church wedding at 6.15 in the morning; a marriage that was to bring the contentment that had for so long eluded him.

The couple moved to the Kensington apartment. Eliot was awarded the Order of Merit in 1948, the same year as he was awarded the Nobel Prize for literature. After his death, his widow would prove to be a fierce, highly protective guardian of his work and papers, and editor and annotator of his letters.

Eliot died at his Kensington home in 1965. At his request, his ashes were taken to St Michael and All Angels Church, East Coker, in Somerset, a village from where his Eliot ancestors had left for America and which he commemorated in the *Four Quartets*. Two years after his death he was given his place in Poets' Corner, **Westminster Abbey**.

---

* *A plaque commemorates Bertrand Russell.*

Emerson, Ralph Waldo (1803–1882)

Philosopher, lecturer and essayist

63 Russell Square, Bloomsbury WC1B 5BB (gone: now Imperial Hotel)

Emerson first visited London in 1833. Thirty years of age and not yet the writer he was to become, he was still enduring the effects of the death of his wife Ellen two years previously. He arrived by boat from Boulogne and stayed at these 'good chambers', as they had been recommended to him.

He attended the funeral of William Wilberforce at Westminster Abbey, where he saw the Duke of Wellington, the one man living in Britain 'whom I cared to behold'. In Highgate he called on Samuel Taylor Coleridge 'a short, thick old man, with bright blue eyes and a clear complexion'. They discussed religion and art and compared Coleridge's own visits to the continent with that which Emerson had just taken.

Emerson travelled to Scotland, visiting the then not well-known historian Thomas Carlyle, 'full of lively anecdote, with a streaming humour'. They struck up an occasionally strained friendship that lasted until Carlyle's death in 1881. They talked of books and walked in the hills. On his way back to London Emerson visited William Wordsworth in the Lake District.

His biographer, Daniel Koch, writes that, 'Emerson's experience helped him to get his life back in order. He returned to Massachusetts in an improved mental state and with a new set of plans'. These were to embrace his second marriage two years later to Lydia (Lidian) Jackson, and within 14 years his writings had made him a name on both sides of the Atlantic.

Emerson returned to Britain during 1847 and 1848 on a lecture tour, calling on Thomas and Jane Carlyle at their Chelsea home. The two men walked for some miles – Hyde Park, Buckingham Palace, St James's and The Mall, and at Trafalgar Square passing both the newly erected Nelson's Column and the new National Gallery, relocated in 1838. They visited Emerson's radical publisher John Chapman at 142 Strand (gone), where Emerson lodged on his final visit.

Fort, Charles (1874–1932)

Writer and researcher into unexplained phenomena

39 Marchmont Street, Bloomsbury WC1N 1AP Ⓟ

Fort was born in Albany, New York State, but spent most of his life in the Bronx. His was not a happy childhood as his grocer father was authoritarian and physically abusive. Fort, who was largely self-taught, had early ambitions to be a naturalist and he collected sea shells, minerals, and birds.

Up to this point Fort's life had been varied: at 18, he travelled extensively in the western United States, Scotland and England, but became ill in Southern Africa. Back home Anna Filing, a childhood friend, nursed him and they married in 1896. She was quite unlike him, not a reader but a lover of the cinema and parakeets.

Writing short stories allayed neither his depression nor solved financial problems, but an uncle's modest legacy in 1916 and money from one of his two brothers a year later allowed him to write full time. He worked as a journalist and wrote ten novels which, though well reviewed, did not sell well.

His interest developed into the study of anomalous phenomena, sometimes now called 'Fortean' and 'Forteana'. This describes an interest in events that seem to challenge the boundaries of accepted scientific knowledge, like, most commonly, poltergeists. In 1919 his book, *The Book of the Damned*, came out and this and his later work earned him a cult following, which was strengthened by his extensive correspondence with those who wrote to him.

Charles Fort's Marchmont Street home
(Terry Philpot)

The Forts had first come to London in December 1920 to further his research at the then library of the British Museum. They took a small furnished flat at 15 Marchmont Street (gone) for six months, and returned the following year to live at No 31, where they stayed for seven years. Fort would rise at 8am, work, eat at midday and then make his way to the British Museum, returning at about 5 o'clock, having minutely read newspapers, astronomical journals and scientific periodicals. After an evening meal Fort and Anna might go to the cinema or walk in Hyde Park (he would listen to orators and debaters at Speaker's Corner). He viewed the night skies on his walks and at home sometimes (according to his wife) 'would throw open the windows and stand gazing at the stars. That was his delight for a long, long time'. From 1924 and 1925 poltergeists were allegedly active in the flat, with unexplained loud bangs and pictures falling from the walls.

By the time they left for the USA early in 1928 Fort's health was poor and his eyesight worsening. Distrusting doctors, he never consulted them, but in May 1932, when he collapsed, he was rushed to Royal Hospital in the Bronx. Hours before he died, likely of leukaemia, his publisher visited to show him the proofs of his latest book, *Wild Talents*. His 60,000 notes were donated to the New York Public Library.

Some of Fort's books remain in print, the monthly magazine *The Fortean Times* was founded in 1973 to investigate Fortean phenomena (in 2017 it had a circulation of 13,600) and he has influenced science fiction.

Hutton, Barbara (1912–1979)

Heiress, socialite and philanthropist

Residence of the American ambassador
Winfield House, Regent's Park NW1 4RT

Aged 24 Barbara Hutton was living near Marble Arch, married to Count Haugwitz-Reventlow, and worried about threats of kidnapping against her son Lance. Hutton was one of the richest women in the world, thanks to various family legacies, not least that from her grandfather, Frank Winfield Woolworth, founder of the retail chain. Seeking security and a larger home away from the city centre but within easy reach of it, she purchased St Dunstan's, a white stucco Regency villa, built by 25-year-old Decimus Burton, from Lord Rothermere, the newspaper magnate. In 1936 it was partly destroyed by fire.

She gained permission from the Crown Estate Commission, which owned the lease, to demolish the villa and for the present red brick Georgian-style house to be built on the site, to be re-named for her grandfather and his Long Island estate.

The ground floor is laid out as originally planned but the front entrance was added in 1954. A reception hall runs nearly the depth of the house to the French doors that open to the terrace. The house today contains family rooms, including a dining room, a state dining room and staff offices.

There were parquet floors, 18th century French paneling and marble bathrooms. Several thousand trees and hedges were planted, a ten-foot high steel fence erected and the property was protected by a modern security system. The house contained some of the couple's art collection, including two Canalettos (now in the National Gallery in Washington), Louis XV furniture, Persian carpets and Chinese *objets d'art*.

Two years after the couple moved in the outbreak of war brought disruption and when the marriage failed, Hutton returned to the United States. In war-time California she assisted the war effort by selling War Bonds, funding the Free French and donating her yacht to the Royal Navy. After the war she moved to Paris, the Dominican Republic, Mexico and Tangier and finally back to her home country. On these travels she acquired five more husbands after Reventlow, who was her second. She gave lavishly – both philanthropically but also to complete strangers – and spent extravagantly, not least on palatial homes, yachts and jewelry.

Winfield House was commandeered during the Second World War and used by an RAF barrage balloon unit and also as an air crew reception centre for recruits being screened as prospective RAF pilots. Later it became an American Officers' Club. A flying bomb exploded 40 yards from the house in 1944, killing one cadet and injuring 20 others, while the roof was damaged by other actions.

Buckled floorboards, peeling walls, broken windows, dangling wires and the parquet floor ruined by moisture greeted Hutton when she came back at the end of the war. It was this that caused her to donate the house to the US government for a token dollar so it could be repaired and used as the official residence of the American ambassador. President Harry Truman accepted her 'most generous and patriotic offer'.

The house, standing in 12½ acres, has been enriched by gifts over the years of antique furniture, paintings, porcelain, china, glass, chandeliers and *objets d'art*.

Hutton was never the 'lucky girl' pictured by the press. She passed through marriages and multiple other relationships and was often intoxicated in public. When her third husband, Cary Grant, visited the house in the early 1980s, he said: 'I just remember a beautiful young girl who never saw a day of happiness'.

Her son's death in 1972 in an air crash was devastating, and by the time of her own death her extravagance had brought her close to bankruptcy. Hutton died, at the age of 66, in the Beverly Wilshire Hotel, Los Angeles.

The first ambassador to live at Winfield House was Winthrop Aldrich, who, with his wife, moved there in January 1955. This preceded an extensive refurbishment that included an extension to provide space for cloakrooms and the enlargement of the reception hall.

Later ambassadors also changed the house: John Hay Whitney, who came in 1957, rebuilt the greenhouse and added two extensions. He and his wife left 70 paintings. The flower beds were empty and for the Whitneys' first ball they were filled with 5,000 artificial tulips, while 500 guests were entertained on the terrace and the lawn on Independence Day.

Maxim, Sir Hiram (1840–1916)

Inventor

57d Hatton Garden, Holborn EC1N 8EG ℗
Sandhurst Lodge, 382 Streatham High Road, Streatham, Lambeth SW16 6HP (gone: now Tesco)

Maxim was born of English and Huguenot descent at Brockways Mill, near Sangerville, Maine. He ended up a British citizen with a knighthood, and someone whose name is synonymous with the devastatingly lethal weapon that he invented. He called himself 'a chronic inventor' and there was not a piece of machinery that he came across that he did not want to improve. Maxim's father Isaac, a farmer and wood-turner, also toyed with the ideas of developing an automatic gun and a flying machine.

The family lived in a clearing in a dense forest with more bears than people roundabouts, but Maxim was also a good scholar, well read, and interested in geometry and astronomy.

The Hatton Garden premises where Hiram Maxim invented his eponymous repeating gun (Terry Philpot)

He set off for Canada, after being sent to work for little money for long hours at the age of 14, and kept himself by doing casual work as a bartender, cabinet-maker and mechanic. Maxim avoided serving in the American Civil War and as the war came to an end was working in an uncle's engineering works in Massachusetts, acquiring knowledge of draughtsmanship and continuing technical and scientific studies. He devised what he called a 'density regulator' to equalise the illuminating value of coal gas.

In 1867 he married Louisa Jane Budden, an English immigrant, with whom he had a son and two daughters. However, 11 years later he bigamously married 15-year-old Helen Leighton, with whom he had a daughter. A few years later when Helen discovered his deception and informed his wife, Maxim left but supported Leighton and the child.

By 1873 he was senior partner at his own New York gas and steam engineering company, Maxim and Welch. Five years later he became chief engineer to the United States Electric Lighting Company where he was involved in developing machines and arc and incandescent lamps. This led to his building up an even coating of carbon on lamp filaments by 'flashing' them in hydrocarbon gas, an invention critical to the electric lighting industry.

Maxim's inventions led him to be made a member of the Légion d'honneur and in 1881 he went to work in Europe. He was joined by Sarah Haynes, 14 years his junior, his American secretary and lover and, after his divorce in 1888, his wife. It is said that even after the marriage he would visit brothels and was sexually interested in young girls.

It was not long before Maxim moved to London, opening a workshop in Hatton Garden in 1884. Turning to gun making, he formed the Maxim Gun Company that year and set about designing a fully automatic gun. He saw off competition by patenting every conceivable device connected with the firing mechanism. His was a single barrel, fully automatic weapon that fired ten rounds a second. He refined it to meet different conditions.

The British Army adopted the gun in 1889 and the Royal Navy in 1892. Manufacturing of its last version, the Vickers machine gun, only stopped in Britain in 1963. By this time the gun had been used in many countries, including Germany and Russia, having killed tens of thousands of people.

Maxim then set his sights on flying and between 1889 and 1894 designed a steam-driven test rig. Technically this did fly because in a trial at Bexley in Kent, in July 1894, the runner wheels were lifted off the rail track. However, it proved unworkable because of its excessive weight. A later version inspired HG Wells' *The Argonauts of the Air*.

After a merger with the Nordenfeldt Company in 1888, when he moved to Sandhurst Lodge, the company became part of Vickers Sons and Maxim, of which Maxim became a director. He retired from the board in 1911.

Maxim was a great salesman, travelling the world, including twice to Russia, and demonstrated his wares before many heads

Sir Hiram Maxim, aged 72, four years before his death

of state. He and his younger brother, Isaac (who called himself Hudson), an explosives engineer, fell out, engaged in a feud and vilified one another. Isaac had his brother arrested in New York and prosecuted for bigamy in October 1898, but Hiram was acquitted.

Maxim was 6 feet tall, well built with a good head of hair – jet black in early life, snow white in his later years – and took fastidious pride in his appearance. He was also jealous of other inventors, like his brother Isaac and his rival Thomas Edison.

In 1900 he became a British citizen and was knighted the next year. That winter was spent at a sanatorium in Nice, as he suffered from bronchitis. His design and manufacture of inhalers for use in London was the practical result.

Maxim died of bronchopneumonia and heart failure at his Streatham home in November 1916.

Miller, Lee (1907–1977)

Photographer

21 Downshire Hill, Hampstead NW3 1NT P

Born in Poughkeepsie, New York State, Miller was raped at the age of seven, which left her with a life-long trauma and medical problems. Damaged and traumatised, her resulting bad behaviour got her expelled from a large number of schools in the Hudson Valley, but at 18 she undertook a series of courses in lighting and design at the École Medgyès pour la Technique du Théâtre in Paris in 1925.

Miller's time studying at New York's Art Students League was cut short when a chance encounter launched her career as a fashion model of both sportswear and sophisticated gowns. But this itself led to the art form with which she is forever associated: photography. Working with some of the most noted photographers of the day, she picked up a detailed knowledge of their work. Her fashion modelling work in the USA came to an end after a scandal which arose when she endorsed sanitary towels. Off she went to Paris in May 1929, still only 22 years of age.

In the French capital Miller became the lover, pupil and model-muse of Man Ray, the most renowned photographer of his time. She then became a

Lee Miller

photographer in her own right, as part of the Surrealist movement. She also starred in Jean Cocteau's film *Le Sang d'un Poète* in 1930. Two years later favourable reviews greeted her first photographic exhibition, and she left Man Ray and returned to New York to establish her own studio. In 1933 *Vanity Fair* referred to her as 'one of the seven most distinguished living photographers'.

But a year later Miller gave up her studio to marry an Egyptian businessman named Aziz Eloui Bey, whom she had met in Paris. They lived in Cairo and she became interested in desert travel, eventually producing more than 2,000 photographs of rock formations, buildings and oasis villages.

Longing for Paris she returned in 1937 and fell in love with Roland Penrose, the Surrealist painter. They moved to London and lived in the Hampstead house until 1949. They travelled together – in France Picasso was so taken with her looks that he painted four different portraits of her – to the Balkans and Egypt.

When war came in 1939 they were living back in London, where she worked for *Vogue* and photographed extensively during the Blitz, capturing the surreal landscapes the bombing produced. This work produced *Grim Glory: Britain Under Fire*, published in 1941, and four years later *Wrens in Camera* came from her work with the Women's Royal Naval Service.

She became an accredited war correspondent and followed the American advance through Europe, including the liberation of Paris, the siege of St Malo and the fighting in the Vosges. Her shocking images of the liberated camps of Buchenwald and Dachau helped to alert the world to the realities of Nazism.

In post-war Europe Miller worked in Austria, Hungary and Romania and was given enthusiastic welcomes in London and New York. She returned to work for *Vogue* but the loss of hope for international unity and a better world caused a debilitating disillusion and she became depressed and drank excessively. However, by the late 1960s Miller took on another persona – as a gourmet cook.

Miller and Penrose's son Anthony was born a few months before the couple married in 1947. They moved to Farley Farm in Sussex, where they entertained friends from the art world, and after 1954 she gave up all professional engagements. It was at the farm that she died of cancer in 1977 and her ashes were scattered in the farm's garden.

Plath, Sylvia (1932–1963)

Poet

23 Fitzroy Road, Primrose Hill NW1 8TP *
St George the Martyr, Queen Square,
Bloomsbury WC1N 3AH
18 Rugby Street, Bloomsbury WC1N 3QZ
3 Chalcot Square, Primrose Hill NW1 8YB **P**

Plath was born in Boston and *The Bell Jar*, a dark novel and her only attempt in that genre, is partly set in New York, so it may not be surprising that when she first came to London in September 1955 she took to the city with unbounded relish. 'I'd rather live in London than anywhere in the world', she exclaimed.

In London Plath went to the theatre to enjoy plays as different as Terence Rattigan's *Separate Tables* and Samuel Beckett's *Waiting for Godot*. She liked Soho's restaurants and cafés, became entranced with London's policemen and took tea at the American ambassador's residence, Winfield House. She found her reading came alive in what she observed: 'You remember all the Dickens you read when you were little and suddenly you go to London and you recognise scenes you have seen before and this is simply, I think, a sort of literary influence. I was immensely excited by the historic sense of London … and again by the look of it – something about all the taxi cabs being black and rather like large, impressive hearses.'

Plath had a Fulbright scholarship to study at Cambridge and there she met the poet Ted Hughes at a party in 1956, where they passionately kissed. She slept with him at his flat at the multi-occupied Rugby Street, which he was to memorialise in his poem of the same name. There was far more than physical passion in the relationship, as Plath described in a BBC interview in 1961: 'We kept writing poems to each other. Then it just grew out of that, I guess, a feeling that we both were writing so much and having such a fine time doing it, we decided that this should keep on.'

In June, four months after they met, they were married at St George the Martyr, the Anglican Church, in Bloomsbury, with only Plath's mother Aurelia in attendance and Hughes wearing his one utility suit. Plath remembered 'the dust & grease and carrot peels of Rugby Street on my wedding night', spent in a single bed. They honeymooned with a summer in Benidorm by way of a stay in Paris, and in October she returned to her studies in Cambridge.

When the couple moved to the USA in June 1957, Plath taught at her *alma mater*, Smith College, Northampton, Massachusetts. But teaching encroached on her writing time and energy. In the middle of 1958, they moved to Boston and then toured the USA and Canada. While in the USA Plath received treatment for her mental illness. She was not 21 when she had made her first recorded attempt to commit suicide. There were to be others.

On Plath and Hughes' return to London in December 1959 they took a small, unfurnished flat in Chalcot Square at a weekly rent of three guineas (£3.15). Their circle of friends grew: John Lehmann, the editor of *The London Magazine*, and Karl Miller, the literary editor of *The Spectator*. Supper with **TS Elio**t at his flat in Kensington Court Gardens, which Plath thought a 'rather drab' building, was also attended by Stephen and Natasha Spender, an evening peppered with intellectual gossip about the lives of DH Lawrence, Virginia Woolf, WH Auden and Igor Stravinsky. A month later Eliot was present at a cocktail party given by Hughes' publishers Faber and Faber, of which Eliot was a director. Spender also attended, along with fellow poets WH Auden and Louis MacNeice.

Plath's adopted city inspired her poem *Parliament Hill Fields*, where her miscarriage in February 1961 is poignantly caught as she reflects:

> On this bald hill the new year hones its edge.
> Faceless and pale as china
> The round sky goes on minding its business.
> Your absence is inconspicuous;
> Nobody can tell what I lack.

Plath attended lectures at Bedford College, Regent's Park, a park she thought 'beautiful' and to which she would take her daughter Frieda, who was born in April 1960. That October, too, *The Colossus*, her first poetry collection was published. She studied Italian through Berlitz, took in a Picasso exhibition, and even managed to attend the last day of the *Lady Chatterley's Lover* trial at the Old Bailey.

However, the Plath-Hughes living quarters were cramped. What they dreamed of, she said, was 'a house where I can shout out to Ted from one end to the other and he won't be able to hear me'.

Desire for a country life and improved finances took them to the cottage they bought in 1961 in North Tawton, Devon. The let of their Chalcot Square flat was taken over by the Canadian poet David Wevill and his wife, Assia.

The Devon idyll did not last long. In January 1962 Plath gave birth to their son Nicholas, but by then had found out that Hughes had been having an affair with Assia Wevill before they moved. Hughes may also have been physically abusive to Plath. Betrayal, loneliness and isolation stalked her, and Hughes found living together difficult, not least because of his wife's mental illness.

She missed so much of what she had loved about London. That October Plath wrote to her brother Warren: 'I miss brains, hate this cow life, am dying to surround myself with intelligent, good people. I loved living there and never wanted to leave.'

Primrose Hill was 'slummy', she said, but even so the freehold of a house in Fitzroy Road, her favourite street, was £9,250. She moved in December with her children to the two-floor maisonette. That Plath was now, as she said, the happiest she had been for months must have energised her because despite the two small children she would rise at 4 o'clock each morning and write what became the *Ariel* poems.

The love affair with Hughes may have soured but not the one with London. It was 'the one city in the world I'd like to live in, with its fine doctors, nice neighbours, parks, theatres and the BBC', she told her mother, who urged her to return to the USA.

The Bell Jar was published in January 1963 but, on February 11, deeply depressed, Plath gassed herself in her kitchen. She had sealed the doors with tape, opened a window and seen that one-year-old Nicholas and 2½-year-old Frieda were asleep in their room upstairs, safe in high-sided cots. She placed two cups of milk and some bread and butter next to them. She was 30 years of age.

One of her last poems was *Nick and the Candlestick* ('Your son's eyes … would become/ So perfectly your eyes') and refers to the son who did not know the cause of her death until the 1970s.

A few weeks before her death, Plath had written: 'When I came to my beloved Primrose Hill, with the golden leaves, I was full of such joy.'

---

* *A plaque commemorates a former resident, the poet W B Yeats.*

Robeson, Paul (1898–1976)

Singer, actor and political activist

**The Chestnuts, Branch Hill,
Hampstead NW3 7LT** 🅟
12 Glebe Place, Chelsea, Kensington and Chelsea SW3 5LB

Ironically, given that he moved to London in 1928 believing that racism was less of a problem than in his home country, the next year Robeson was excluded from the Savoy Hotel in the Strand because it operated a 'colour bar'.

Born in New Jersey, university educated and the son of a former runaway slave who was a Presbyterian minister, Robeson was already known to British audiences. He had performed in Britain (having lived at Glebe Place from 1924 to 1926) before he and his family settled for a decade from 1928 (the year that his son Paul Jnr was born), living in Hampstead from 1929 to 1930. He had married Eslanda (Essie) Goode in 1921, who later became his manager and author of a 1930 biography, *Paul Robeson, Negro*. In 1922 he toured Britain in a melodrama named *Voodoo* and in 1925 starred in *Emperor Jones*. Robeson first sang *Ol' Man River* three years later in London in the city's premier of *Show Boat*.

In 1930 there was his first-time, much-acclaimed Othello, a role he was the first black actor to play since **Ira Aldridge**. This was part of several country-wide stage and concert tours. In London he recorded many songs and made two of his most notable films: *Song of Freedom* (1936) and *The Proud Valley* (1939).

Living in Britain was a formative influence in Robeson's life. He met students, including African Londoners, and became interested in African culture and languages (he was said to speak 20 languages). He became patron of the West African Students' Union and claimed to have 'discovered Africa' in London. He met anti-colonialists, like the future Indian prime minister Jawaharlal Nehru, as well as MPs and working class leaders. Communism appealed to him, as did the USSR, which he visited in 1934.

Robeson's political principles were such that he distanced himself from his 1934 film *Sanders of the River*, as he saw it as a glorification of British imperialism. To find a theatrical *milieu* that better suited his ideological outlook he acted at Camden's Unity Theatre (gone), known for its working class and left-wing associations. He played in Welsh mining villages and included folk songs and political songs, often in languages like Russian and Chinese, in his repertoire.

He gave support to Jewish refugees and the International Brigades in Spain. His most implacable statement was when he said in London in 1937: 'The artist must take sides. He must elect to fight for freedom or for slavery. I have made my choice. I had no alternative.' That year he was voted the most popular radio singer in Britain.

An affair with the actress Peggy Ashcroft nearly led to divorce, which Essie wanted but which Robeson was advised would adversely affect his career. He went back temporarily to the USA for a revival of *Showboat* and, with the end of the affair in 1932, the couple came back together again but the marriage never fully recovered.

In 1939 the Robesons returned to the United States and, now one of the most famous performers in the world, he continued on Broadway and elsewhere, refusing to appear before segregated audiences. Robeson remained active in liberal and anti-colonial organisations. Having given support to the Allies in war-time, he took extensive tours in Europe to entertain troops immediately after the war.

Robeson's defence of the USSR and attacks on the Korean War, as well as his general political stance and opinions, had him tailed by the FBI and called before the House Un-American Activities Committee. His passport was confiscated by the State Department in 1950. A National Paul Robeson Committee was formed in Manchester in 1954 and in other places in the UK and worldwide. He broadcast, by telephone link, to a meeting in 1957, in

Paul Robeson in 1942 (Gordon Parks)

St Pancras Town Hall, Euston Road, a short walking distance from the Unity Theatre. In 1958 Robeson's passport was returned. This allowed him that same year to come back to Britain where he sang at both the eisteddfod in Ebbw Vale and **St Paul's Cathedral** before 4,000 people, raising funds for the defence in the South African treason trials, where one of the 156 defendants was Nelson Mandela. He was also the first black person to read the lesson in the cathedral. The following year he played Othello in Stratford-upon-Avon.

He continued to appear at peace and disarmament meetings in the UK and returned on tour to Europe, the USSR, Australia and New Zealand.

Robeson died in 1973 in Philadelphia after more than a dozen years of semi-retirement.

Stewart, Donald Ogden (1894–1980)

Screenwriter, novelist and humorist

103 Frognal, Hampstead NW3 6XR*

Stewart, the son of a judge, born in Columbus, Ohio, and educated at Yale, had already established himself as a highly successful screenwriter – he had won an Oscar for *The Philadelphia Story* in 1940 – and a wit when he settled in London in 1950. He spent the next 30 years of his life in the capital, where he died.

He served in the Naval Reserve in the First World War. Said to be 'bespectacled and prematurely balding, insecure and obsessed with money and success', he started off as a journalist on *Vanity Fair* when living with his widowed mother in New York's Greenwich Village. Stewart was a member of the renowned Algonquin Round Table, known for its wit and repartee, and he grew close to members Dorothy Parker and Robert Benchley.

He had found fame in 1924 with *A Parody Outline of History*, a satire on HG Wells' book, and success again with *Mr and Mrs Haddock Abroad*, the year he met his first wife Beatrice Ames. Other books followed and his 25 films during the 1920s and 1930s included standards like *The Barretts of Wimpole Street*.

Stewart became a socialist after reading the British writer and future Labour minister John Strachey's *The Coming Struggle for Power*. He joined the Hollywood Anti-Nazi League that included many well known stars, writers, producers and directors like Frederic March, Walter Wanger, Clifford Odets, Sylvia Sidney, Oscar Hammerstein, Eddie Cantor and Scott Fitzgerald, with whom Stewart became friendly. He also joined the Anti-Fascist Refugee Committee and the Motion Picture Artists Committee to Aid Republican Spain, but his wife did not approve of his political activity.

Of joining the American Communist Party, he wrote: 'I didn't want to stop dancing or enjoying the fun and play in life. I wanted to do something about the problem of seeing to it that a great many more people were allowed into the amusement park. My new-found philosophy was an affirmation of the good life, not a rejection of it'.

In 1937 he met the widowed Ella Winter, whom he was to marry in 1939 after he and his wife (at her insistence) divorced. Winter had a son, Peter, and Stewart had two sons, Donald and Ames.

Winter described him thus: 'Tall and slender and very graceful, with blond hair and blue eyes that very often held a puckish look like that of a wise and naughty child. Humorous and gentle, shy and warm-hearted.'

She and Stewart remained loyal members of the Communist Party, even when it accepted the Nazi-Soviet Pact.

He continued to work on films like *The Prisoner of Zenda*, *That Uncertain Feeling*, *The Philadelphia Story* and *A Woman's Face*. With America's entry into the war Stewart and Winter worked for the Office of War Information, often scripting propaganda programmes and documentaries, while still working as a Hollywood screenwriter.

However, in 1950 a pamphlet was published naming 151 people in the entertainment industry, including Stewart, claiming that they had been members of subversive organisations before the war. All were blacklisted until they appeared in front of the House Un-American Activities Committee and renounced their past. Winter and Stewart left for London, where they rented this Hampstead house, which had been the home of the first Labour prime minister. Their friend Katherine Hepburn helped renovate the house, coming, it was said, every day for six weeks with a packed lunch from the Connaught Hotel.

In his new country, Stewart wrote for British television and, under a false name (as those blacklisted had to do), wrote films including *Summer Time* (1955) and *An Affair to Remember* (1957). He died at his home in August 1980 and Winter died two days later.

---

* *A plaque commemorates Ramsay MacDonald, the first Labour prime minister.*

Vane, Sir Henry (1613–1662)

Governor of Massachusetts Bay Colony, politician and author

Vane House, 65 Rosslyn Hill, Hampstead NW3 5UD
(gone: now North Bridge House Senior School) P **

From his house in Hampstead Vane was taken for his trial and execution on Tower Hill in 1662, despite a general pardon of the Commonwealth supporters by Charles II. Vane had been an early and increasingly prominent republican, so much so that his wish to practise his religion freely led him to go to the American colonies when he was 22. A year later he was governor of Massachusetts Bay Colony.

Born into land-owning gentry in Essex, at Westminster School Vane seems to have undergone a religious conversion concerned with 'a more Godly life'. His father – Sir Harry – found him posts with English European ambassadors. Charles I viewed him favourably, although preferment at court was thwarted by his father's enemies. A growing disenchantment, indeed, alienation from the Church of England caused him to emigrate to the colonies in 1635.

Vane may have dressed in the Stuart style – long hair and fashionable clothing – but the colonists took well to the 'young gentleman of excellent parts' and his rejection of the old country in 'obedience of the gospel'.

He settled in Boston 'to enjoy the ordinances of Christ in their purity'. Vane worked to resolve disputes to create Christian unity, and his success was such that in March 1636 he became a freeman of the Massachusetts corporation, and a commissioner for military affairs. In May he was elected as governor, 'a wise and godly gentleman', as his supporters had come to see him.

His policies increased orderliness in the city, and he secured peace with the Pequot but failed to do so with the Narragansetts.

Sir Henry Vane (John F Kennedy Library, Boston)

Vane purchased Rhode Island as a refuge for separatist settlers, one of whom was **Roger Williams**, with whom he became close friends.

His failure to stand above religious dispute brought his governorship to an ignominious end, finding himself on the losing side against John Winthrop, his deputy governor, and others. Vane's wish to resign was then held against him as he was seemingly abandoning his post. He stayed only because the Boston church urged him to do so, but when Winthrop was victorious in the election Vane, facing banishment with his confederates, left the colony in August 1637.

Initially leading a quiet life on the family estates in Essex, in 1640 he married 16-year-old Frances Wray and became a member of the Long Parliament. Here he advocated religious freedom and succeeded John Pym as speaker in 1643. In that year, too, he negotiated the Solemn League and Covenant with the Scots that they support the Parliamentarians in their disputes with the king. Vane's strong republicanism led him to membership of the Commonwealth's Council of State from 1649 to 1653. In Parliament he was also instrumental in securing the prosecution of Thomas Wentworth, Earl of Strafford, which resulted in Charles I's dismissal of him from the post of treasurer of the Navy.

It was at Vane House that he very probably entertained leading parliamentary figures like Oliver Cromwell, John Milton, John Pym, Thomas Fairfax, John Hampden and Algernon Sidney.

In the Civil War Vane proved an able administrator, managing the Commons for Cromwell. However, as a believer in the sovereignty of Parliament he opposed Cromwell's dismissal of the Rump Parliament (of which he was a member) in 1653. This led him to withdraw from Parliament and turn to writing theology. He served a brief prison term in 1656 for criticising Cromwell's Protectorate, which he saw as authoritarian. In 1659 he helped the army overthrow Cromwell's successor, his son, Richard in 1659.

However, in 1662, two years after the restoration of the monarchy, Vane was exempted from the amnesty for those who had served the Commonwealth, and was arrested at his home in Hampstead to stand trial for treason. He pleaded 'Honour, Justice, Reason and Conscience' and 'the principles of that Righteous Cause' and said that his actions were on behalf of the Parliament, but all to no avail. Only those who were penitent, said the judges, deserved mercy, and he was executed on Tower Hill on 14 June in 1662.

---

* *The plaque incorrectly gives his birth date as 1612.*

Wellcome, Sir Henry (1853–1936)

Philanthropist and pharmacist

Wellcome Collection, 183 Euston Road, NW1 2BE
6 Gloucester Gate, Regent's Park NW1 4HG Ⓟ

Wellcome, who created an international pharmaceutical company and one of the largest charities in the UK, was born in extreme poverty in his grandfather's log cabin in Almond, in northern Wisconsin.

Wellcome's father was an itinerant Adventist preacher who could not make a living on poor farmland and when, in 1861, the potato crop failed, the family (there was another brother) took off in covered wagons to the new state of Minnesota.

Whatever good life the new immigrants hoped for in Garden City was dashed by a bloody Sioux uprising the year after their arrival. Young Henry moulded bullets and helped his uncle, the local doctor, tend the wounded.

Wellcome was ambitious and self-educated when he left school at 14 and wanted to escape from poverty, poor pay and hard work, and the limitations of where he lived. This took him first to Rochester, Minnesota, at the invitation of an English doctor, William Worrell Mayo, whom he had met in Garden City and who then later persuaded Henry to join him in Rochester, Minnesota and to the Chicago College of Pharmacy. Wellcome then went to its Philadelphia equivalent. Once qualified, he became a travelling salesman for two large American drug companies, while also writing for professional journals.

In 1878 he travelled to the forests of Peru and Ecuador to find the bark of the rare native cinchona trees, which he knew was a source of quinine. He wrote an account of his travels, which was acclaimed in Britain and the USA.

In 1880 27-year-old Wellcome went to London at the invitation of a friend and compatriot, Silas Mainville Burroughs, who two years previously had started a business with a franchise to sell the products of John Wyeth of Philadelphia. He wanted Wellcome as a partner. Burroughs was rich, charming and a great salesman, but with a temperament and judgment that were erratic. He travelled the world seeking new markets for their products, while Wellcome set about creating Burroughs, Wellcome & Co.

Wellcome established the company's first factory in Wandsworth, south London, after deciding that the firm should produce its own products for the mass market, and he invented compressed pills or 'tabloids' (the tablet and the ovoid).

The last portrait of Sir Henry Wellcome
(Wellcome Images)

Wellcome returned to the USA with a serious illness (later shown to be an ulcer) in 1885, as a result of which he published *The Story of Metlakahtla*, on the dispossession of the indigenous peoples of America. Upon his return in 1887 he found that Burroughs intended to dissolve the partnership and run the company himself.

The dispute between the two lasted into the next decade with Wellcome eventually winning in the courts, but Burroughs' planned revenge was only stayed by his death from pneumonia in 1895. Wellcome took full control of a company which was now well-known, respected and prosperous.

Wellcome's gifts for publicity propelled the company forward: exhibitions attracted professionals. He embarked on research, wanting to discover new drugs, not just to sell them. The Wellcome Physiological Research Laboratories were founded in 1894 and a year later came the Chemical Research Laboratories, at the head of which was Wellcome's friend, the chemist Frederick Belding Power, whom he had enticed to Britain from the USA.

A tropical research laboratory was created in 1903 at the Gordon Memorial College at Khartoum. A decade later he founded the eponymous Historical Medical Museum in London, the exhibits for which he had begun collecting as a young man. That year, too, the Wellcome Bureau of Scientific Research was founded to investigate tropical diseases. The Wellcome Museum of Medical Science was set up in 1923.

The businesses, museums, laboratories and institutes came together as the Wellcome Research Institution, a part of the Wellcome Foundation, established in 1924. The company's laboratories were the first commercial ones to be licensed for animal research. The laboratories discovered an effective anti-diphtheria vaccine and were the first to mass produce insulin.

However, Wellcome was nothing if not wide-ranging in his interests and funded archaeological research in Africa and Palestine, even directing a dig himself for three years at a late Neolithic site at Jebel Moya in the Sudan. He was also actively interested in medical missionary work.

Wellcome became an obsessive collector – artefacts, pictures, statuary, books, armour, weaponry and plain junk filled warehouses – which trustees, upon his death, found amounted to one million items and had cost more to accumulate than the exhibits in the British Museum and the Louvre. Much was disposed of but the medical items went to the museum in the Wellcome Building, which Wellcome commissioned in 1931.

In 1901 he had married Syrie, the daughter of Thomas Barnardo, creator of the children's charity, with whom he had a son. The marriage was unhappy and they separated in 1910 (the year he became a British citizen) and divorced in 1916, on the grounds of her adultery with the novelist Somerset Maugham, whom she later married. In 1920 Wellcome leased Gloucester Gate but spent little time there, though it was his London home until he died. He was knighted in 1932.

The once gregarious man became reclusive after 1919 and, on his death, his estate faced heavy death duties and a company whose earlier performance was no longer holding up, to the extent that in its first 20 years the Wellcome Trust gave only £1 million for medical research.*

Wellcome underwent an operation for cancer in 1935. The following year he returned to Almond to buy the 14 acre farm which his family had once owned and had to abandon. He died of pneumonia in the London Clinic in July 1936.

---

* *Things changed, however, and by the 1990s the Wellcome Trust was the largest independent investor in British medical research. Eighty one years after the founder's death, with £26 billion in assets, it gave away £723 million in 2017.*

CITY OF LONDON

American Memorial Chapel
St Paul's Cathedral, St Paul's Churchyard EC4M 8AD

The American Memorial Chapel, St Paul's Cathedral
(Graham Lacdao/St Paul's Cathedral)

Behind the High Altar at the very east end of the cathedral is the American Memorial Chapel. It stands on a space rebuilt after the destruction of the Blitz and is dedicated to the American dead who had been stationed in the UK in the Second World War. It was opened in 1958 at a service of dedication attended by the Queen and Richard Nixon, American vice-president.

The dead are named in a large 500-page, leather-bound book; a roll of honour to the 28,000 Americans – from Aaberg to Zingale – which is placed at the heart of the chapel. The book opens with the words: 'Defending freedom from the fierce assault of tyranny they shared the honor and the sacrifice. Though they died before the dawn of victory their names and deed will long be remembered where ever free men live.'

Thousands of those commemorated died in the Normandy landings on D-Day, as well as in training operations leading up to the campaign and in later battles on the European mainland.

In 1959 President **Dwight D Eisenhower** visited the chapel, known also as the Jesus Chapel. He had commanded the Allied troops on D-Day and wrote: 'Each name inscribed in this book is a story of personal tragedy and a grieving family; a story repeated endlessly in white crosses girdling the globe. The Americans, whose names here appear, were part of the price that free men have been forced a second time to pay in this century to defend human liberty and rights. Fittingly, this roll of honor has been enshrined by the Mother Country of all English-speaking democracies in this special chapel of St Paul's, once a target of barbaric attack. Here, we and all who shall hereafter live in freedom will be reminded that to these men and their comrades of all the Allies we owe a debt to be paid with grateful remembrance of their sacrifice and with the high resolve that the cause for which they died shall live eternally.'

The three stained-glass windows show the symbols of every American state, while the wood carvings contain the birds, plants and flowers of America. On one lime wood panel there are a space rocket and stars – acknowledging the space programme being developed at the time the chapel was completed.

In association with the **American International Church**, each November the cathedral holds a Thanksgiving service.

Billy Fiske Memorial
St Paul's Cathedral, St Paul's Churchyard EC4M 8AD

In the crypt of the cathedral, where the Duke of Wellington and Lord Nelson rest, there is a plaque to Billy Fiske, an American who won two Winter Olympic gold medals before dying as a pilot in the Battle of Britain.

Fiske was born in New York in 1911 as William Meade Lindsley Fiske III, the son of a New England banking magnate. Always known as Billy, he was educated first in Chicago and then, when he was 13, went to school in France. It was there, at the age of 16, that he discovered bobsleighing.

Within three years he was driving the US bobsleigh team, then for the only time made up of five men, to victory at the 1928 St Moritz Winter Olympics. At just 16, while reading economics and history at Cambridge, he was the youngest Winter Olympic champion, something not bested until 1992.

At Lake Placid in the 1932 Winter Olympics Fiske was chosen to carry the United States flag during the opening ceremony and with his now four-man team went on to win his second gold medal. He was also a Cresta Run champion. When Fiske decided not to take part in the Nazi-organised Berlin Olympics of 1936, he very probably denied himself the chance of winning his third gold medal. Between the Olympics and the outbreak of war, he helped develop Aspen, Colorado, into one of the world's leading winter sport destinations by building, with a wealthy friend named Ted Ryan, the first ski lift, hiring guides and opening a ski lodge in the then run-down old mining town.

In 1938 Fiske married Rose Bingham, recently divorced wife of the Earl of Warwick, but when war was declared the following year and the United States remained neutral, Fiske was anxious to enlist. He joined the 601 Squadron, based in Tangmere in southern England by using forged Canadian papers and making use of contacts. In his diary he wrote: 'I believe I can lay claim to being the first US citizen to join the RAF in England after the outbreak of hostilities'.

He was one of 11 American pilots fighting with Fighter Command in the Battle of Britain, flying a Hawker Hurricane. Squadron Leader Archibald Hope wrote of him: 'Unquestionably, Billy Fiske was the best pilot I've ever known. It was unbelievable how good he was. He picked it up so fast it wasn't true. He'd flown a bit before, but he was a natural as a fighter pilot.'

The memorial to Billy Fiske, St Paul's Cathedral (St Paul's Cathedral)

But ten days after joining his squadron, in a dog-fight with Stuka dive bombers, a bullet hit his fuel tank. His hands and ankles burnt and his plane badly damaged, he flew his plane safely back to Tangmere. He was 29 when, on 17th August 1940, he died in hospital from surgical shock two days later. He was buried in the churchyard of the Priory of St Mary and St Blaise, in Boxgrove, West Sussex. His coffin was covered in the Stars and Stripes and the Union Jack.

On American Independence Day 1941 Sir Archibald Sinclair, the Secretary of State for Air, unveiled the Fiske Memorial plaque in St Paul's. The inscription reads: 'An American citizen who died that England might live'. Below the plaque is a small box containing Fiske's RAF wings.

Sir Archibald said: 'Here was a young man for whom life held much. Under no compulsion he came to fight for Britain. He came and he fought and he died.'

In 2008 a window in his memory was unveiled in the church at Boxgrove. There is a memorial tablet to him in the Cathedral of St John the Divine, New York.

Penn, William (1644–1718)

Founder of Pennsylvania

All Hallows by the Tower, Byward Street, Tower Hill EC3R 5BJ Ⓟ

In later life William Penn was to spend time in solitary confinement in the Tower of London but was born, the son of Admiral William Penn, within the 'liberty of the Tower'*. A contemporary letter states that his birthplace was 'on the east side of Tower Hill, within a court adjoining to London Wall'.

His father was a Presbyterian, although one who conformed to the established church, and his mother Margaret was a Dutch Calvinist. Penn himself was baptised in the nearby church of All Hallows on 23rd October 1644. He was conventionally educated at home until he was 11 and then entered Chigwell Academy, near Wanstead in Essex, before going to Christ Church, Oxford in 1660.

On one of his visits to Ireland, often made on his father's business, Penn attended Quaker meetings in Cork. His subsequent conversion, which caused a rift with his father (though they were later reconciled), can be dated to about this time, when he was around 22. It also led to an appearance before the magistrate for being part of a 'riotous and tumultuary assembly'.

Penn travelled the country and went to Holland, France, Italy and Germany, preaching to crowds said to number thousands, the debating style developed at Oxford serving him well.

Penn's *No Cross, No Crown*, written while in prison and published in 1689, was the first guide to how Quakers should behave. Most of his more than 40 works dealt with tolerance, a virtue he did not extend to Catholics, calling the Church 'the whore of Babylon', although this was muted when the Catholic James II succeeded to the throne. His difficulties in always applying his principles in the governance of the colony later led James II to say of him: 'I suppose you take William Pen[n] for a Quaker, but I can assure you he is no more so than I am'.

In 1670, Penn was charged with addressing an unlawful assembly in Gracechurch Street, in opposition to the Conventicle Act, but he was found not guilty, having argued in court that the act threatened the rights of Englishmen (it denied the right of assembly to more than five people for any religious purpose not associated with the Anglican Church). The mayor

William Penn

of London imprisoned the jury, an order overturned by the chief justice, which established the independence of juries.**

When Admiral Penn died in 1670, his son became heir to the family estates and acquired the status of gentleman. Two years later Penn married Gulielma Maria Springett, herself from a wealthy family. They had three sons and four daughters. Two years after his wife's death in 1696 Penn married Hannah Callowhill. They had two daughters, one of whom, Margaret, lived into adulthood and four sons, John, Thomas, Richard, and Dennis, all of whom became co-proprietors of Pennsylvania. (The Penn proprietorial rule was later opposed by **Benjamin Franklin**.)

In 1681 Penn received a land grant from Charles II for what is now Pennsylvania and Delaware, giving Penn the chance to escape persecution and create a colony in keeping with his beliefs.

In 1682 Penn reached the small settlement of New Castle on the Delaware Bay. He may have owned the land but insisted on buying it from the existing owners at full value and also compensating the indigenous Lenape people. He wished that the Quakers live free of persecution, while embarking on what he called a 'holy experiment' in how a colony should be governed. He stayed only briefly at New Castle before making his way to Philadelphia, where for the next two years he set about creating the government. To that end he devised a constitution, the Framework of Government, finalised in 1701. This allowed for all to participate politically, whatever their religion or ethnic background, in an atmosphere of religious tolerance and freedom, and where government, whatever its form, should be based on law.

For indigenous people, the charter aimed to 'reduce the savage natives by gentle and just manners to the love of civil society and Christian religion'. He saw the Lenape, whose language he learned, as 'natural sons of Providence'.

There were limits to Penn's democracy: the powers were subject to his (the proprietor's) wishes and he was, he said, a 'palatine', holding power 'far greater than any king's governor in America'.

Penn's life was not solely concerned with the colony: James II sent him to the Netherlands to seek assurances from the Protestant William of Orange and his wife Mary, who would later usurp the Catholic James, on the king's favour of tolerance, which extended to Catholics and dissenters but alienated Tory Anglicans.

He was also made a deputy lieutenant in Buckinghamshire and was engaged in the writing of the Declaration of Indulgence. Penn was close to the king, 'a right-hand man', says a biographer, acting as a commissioner into the regulation of recusancy fines, and as a mediator between the king and Magdalen College, Oxford. Penn was an advocate for James's policies and a conduit for those who wished to deal with the monarch.

When James II went into exile and it was possible (but at that time not immediately certain) that William and Mary would take the throne, Penn, so close to the king, became suspect and vulnerable. Arrested, he was released on bail of £5,000. Fears of a Catholic uprising even had Penn ('Fr Penn', according to his enemies) labelled as a Jesuit. He was deprived of his right to govern the colony. Penn succeeded in showing that he had always promoted tolerance and supported the new regime, and he regained his place in domestic political life, while being restored in Pennsylvania.

His second and last visit to the colony was from 1699 to 1701, when he was forced to abolish the right of the council to sit as a second legislative chamber and to allow the right of the lower counties to secede.

Ill health and financial problems were the companions of his last years. He died on 30th July 1718 at Ruscombe in Berkshire, and was interred in the burial ground at Jordans Quaker Meeting House, near Chalfont St Giles in Buckinghamshire.

Penn's influence combined status with strong convictions, robust advocacy, and a shrewd political alliance, but it also stemmed from how he lived his own life and governed the colony. At his death he had created not only the colony of Pennsylvania that in less than 60 years would become the founding state of the USA, but he had shown freedom of worship and freedom of speech to be two of the irreducible characteristics of a free society.

In 1984 President Ronald Reagan declared William and Hannah Penn honorary citizens of the United States.

---

* The liberty was the area around and including the Tower of London, outside the control of the City of London and the County of Middlesex, and with its own government. It was abolished in 1894.

** A plaque is affixed inside the Old Bailey attesting to Penn's trial.

Williams, Roger (c1606–1683)

Founder of the Colony of Rhode Island and the Providence Plantations

St Sepulchre-without-Newgate, Holborn Viaduct, Holborn EC1A 2DQ

The Great Fire of London in 1666 gutted the church of St Sepulchre, leaving only the outer walls, the tower and porch standing. It also destroyed the baptismal records of Roger Williams, so we do not know his exact year of birth. We do know that he was the third of the four children of James Williams, a merchant tailor, and his wife Alice (née Pemberton) and that he grew up in the parish.*

Williams could read and write and take shorthand and had a gift for languages – he tutored John Milton in Dutch in exchange for refresher tuition in Hebrew. He studied at Charterhouse School (now Charterhouse, Clerkenwell) and in 1627 gained a BA at Cambridge University. As part of his studies Williams was ordained as an Anglican minister.

When his Puritanism blocked progression within the ministry he became chaplain to the politician Sir William Masham in Essex. He married Mary

Bernard, herself a clergyman's daughter, in Essex in 1629 and they had six children – Mary, Freeborn, Providence, Mercy, Daniel and Joseph – all of whom were born in America.

Williams regarded the Church of England as corrupt and false, views which determined that he leave England. With his wife he sailed in late 1630 on the *Lyon* as one of the earliest Puritan emigrants, and in February 1631 landed in Massachusetts.

Williams was no easier a bedfellow to his fellow Puritans than he had been to his fellow Anglicans. Separation of church and state, liberty of conscience and separation from the Church of England to form new congregations in a new Church as dissenters were his underlying principles.

Roger Williams, seeking refuge with Wampanoag tribe when fleeing from a sentence of heresy and sedition

The sincerity of his religious faith was quickly recognised but Williams refused an invitation to join the Boston church, as it made no public repentance for being in communion with the churches of New England.

When Williams found that the Massachusetts magistrates had blocked the request by the church at Salem for him to become its minister, he moved to the Plymouth Plantation, where occasionally he informally assisted the minister and preached. He also began to be interested in the indigenous Nagaransett people and made friendships with tribal leaders.

He believed the king had no right to make native land over to his subjects. His pamphlet of 1632 condemned the king's charters and questioned whether Plymouth could acquire land without purchase. Williams was expelled from Plymouth for what his fellow colonists regarded as extreme views. He returned to Salem, where his brilliance, godliness and kindness were lauded, and he became unofficial assistant to the minister.

Williams continued to fall out with the colonial authorities (it is likely that his pamphlet attacking the king was burned) and his 'erroneous' and 'dangerous opinions' had him removed from his position at the Salem church. He subsequently met followers in his home.

In October 1635 he was convicted of sedition and heresy, and banishment was prescribed. Illness delayed the sentence being carried out and when it was to be enforced Williams had escaped under cover of a blizzard. He was given protection by the Wampanoag tribal leader in their camp for three months in the spring.

In 1636 Williams and others from Salem purchased land from the Wampanoags on what became Rhode Island, with the help of **Henry Vane**. But action by the colonial authorities caused them to move yet again, and the group purchased land on Narragansett Bay where he and 12 'loving friends' established a new settlement. Feeling that God's providence had brought them to their new home Williams called this area 'Providence'. He transferred the land to the community. Providence, too, was the name Williams gave to his third child, the first to be born in the settlement. The colony became a haven for those who suffered intolerance in Massachusetts.

In 1637 it was established that the writ of the settlement's government ran only to civil matters and thus this became the first place where government and religion were separate. Decisions were taken (by men) by majority vote and citizenship for newcomers was thus determined. Williams also gave help to others from Massachusetts who wished to purchase indigenous land and establish their own settlements.

Williams was an intermediary between colonials and settlers, and in the Pequot War in 1637–8, despite his differences with the Massachusetts authorities, at their request he encouraged the Narragansett to join the colonists and so defeat the Pequot. Williams also studied the language and customs of local tribes to such an extent that in 1643 he published *A Key into the Language of America.*

In the midst of the English Civil War Williams returned to England and, against the opposition of the Massachusetts colonists, gained a charter for the Providence Plantations in 1644. Three years later the four settlements in Rhode Island united to form the Colony of Rhode Island and the Providence Plantations. Its tolerance led Jews, Quakers and Baptists to settle there. In 1651 he went back to England again and returned with a patent to make him 'governor for life' over the Aquidneck Island and Conanicut Island.

In 1641 Massachusetts made slavery legal in the colonies and Plymouth and Connecticut followed. Williams opposed slavery and a law was passed forbidding it, but opposition was such that it was widely disregarded.

Williams died in 1683 and was buried on his property in Providence. However, when in later years his house collapsed, the location of his grave was lost. What was not lost was his opposition to slavery, his belief in the rights of indigenous people, toleration of conscience, and the separation of Church and state, all of which have shaped the modern United States.

---

* *The church has other New England connections: John Smith, a founder of Jamestown and leader of Virginia Colony, is buried there and **Pocahontas** is reputed to have worshipped there.*

Chandler, Raymond (1888–1959)

Novelist

110 Auckland Road, Upper Norwood SE19 2BY ℗

RAYMOND CHANDLER 1888-1959 Writer lived here

How did the imagination of an author, who seems to have invented the dives, bars, alleyways, and shady characters of a very different Los Angeles from that of today, flourish within this ordinary suburban house in one of London's most nondescript areas?

In fact, Chandler was born an only child in Chicago, his parents divorcing when he was six due to his father's alcoholism. He never saw or heard from his father again. After Florence, his mother, was received inhospitably by her relatives in Ireland, she and her son moved to Upper Norwood, where her older brother Ernest Thornton had offered them his support. They lived in the house then called Mount Cyra with Chandler's aunt and uncle and grandmother.

Chandler was a day boy at Dulwich College, one of the city's most prestigious schools, into which he was enrolled in 1900, and where he remained for four years. He later acknowledged how his education, especially in the classics, had influenced his writing.

He had his mind on the Civil Service but not before his uncle paid for him to live in Paris, Munich and Freiburg to learn languages in 1905. Two years later he was third in the 800 Civil Service candidates. Beginning work in the Admiralty, Chandler left after six months: he was not taking orders from those he considered his inferiors. For five years he made a not very good living teaching part time at his old school, working as a reporter on the *Daily Express*, and publishing sketches, reviews, essays and poems in the *Westminster Gazette* and *The Academy*.

In 1912 Chandler returned to the USA, his literary ambitions having made no headway in London. It was in San Francisco, where he made money stringing tennis rackets, that Chandler's biographer Tom Hiney believes 'the character of Philip Marlowe was fleshed out in these resolute, if friendless and moneyless, months in Californian boarding houses'.

Chandler studied book keeping and found work as an accountant, before moving to Los Angeles in 1913 to work as a book keeper, his mother joining him the next year. During the First World War he fought for the Canadians in France and, after being wounded, returned to England and learned to fly with the Royal Flying Corps. In 1919, with the rank of sergeant, he went back to America.

In 1924 Chandler married Eugenie Hurlbert Pascal, a divorced woman 18 years his senior. Sacked from his job with an oil company for excessive drinking, the couple lived off his savings while he learned to write crime fiction, which he saw as potentially lucrative.

He was writing stories for pulp magazines – at $350 a story from *Black Mask*, and $400 from *Dime Detective Magazine* – but he struggled financially. In 1939 he introduced the world to Philip Marlowe in *The Big Sleep*. Six more Marlowe novels in 20 years came from Chandler's pen: *Farewell my Lovely* (1940), *The High Window* (1942), *The Lady in the Lake* (1943), *The Little Sister* (1949), *The Long Goodbye* (1953) and *Playback* (1958). The novels are rich in details of place and atmosphere, with intriguing plots and exotic, often mysterious characters. Marlowe is dogged, cynical, wise-cracking and faces life as it comes, and the books are all written in a spare style. Chandler also worked as a Hollywood scriptwriter.

Like his father, Chandler succumbed to alcoholism. After his wife's death in 1954 he attempted to kill himself and was taken to a psychiatric ward. He frequently came to England and befriended Ian Fleming and Natasha Spender. He would have married his agent Helga Greene had he not died of pneumonia, with complications attributable to alcoholism, in La Jolla, California, where he lived.

He claimed to have written his first piece, aged 19, in that house in Upper Norwood. There is no evidence for that but the boy from the London suburbs and Dulwich College saw his books sell in their millions in dozens of languages and turned into cinema classics, creating a Los Angeles as memorable in its way as Dickens' London.

EALING

Adams, John Quincy (1767–1848)

US Minister to London and 6th president of the United States

Little Boston House, Windmill Lane, Ealing W5 4DL
(gone: now Little Boston, 236 Windmill Road)
All Hallows by the Tower, Byward St, Tower Hill, City of London EC3R 5BJ

The War of 1812, when the USA declared war on its former ruler, led to a severe break in relations and the closure of the London legation on 29th July. The conflict stemmed from the UK's efforts to stop trade between the USA and France, while Britain was engaged in the Napoleonic Wars. Armed clashes, blockades, the impressment of American sailors into the Royal Navy, the British supplying indigenous people with arms, talk of a second war of independence, American expansion into the North-West Territories – all these and more caused President James Madison to declare war.

The war ended in 1815 when the Treaty of Ghent, ratified by the Senate, called for the return of all occupied territory, the restoration of the pre-war boundary between Canada and the USA, and the concession of fishing rights to the USA in the Gulf of St Lawrence.

In February 1815, the month of the ratification, John Quincy Adams, son of the former president **John Adams**, and head of the Ghent delegation, was appointed Envoy Extraordinary and Minister Plenipotentiary to London, presenting his credentials that August. He held the post for two years.

A lawyer, Adams had served in his father's diplomatic missions in Europe until he himself became minister in The Hague and Prussia, and then from 1803 to 1808 in the Senate, before becoming minister in St Petersburg.

Adams was no stranger to London and on an earlier visit from The Hague had met Louisa Johnson, whom he married at All Hallows Church in 1797. Although her father was American consul-general in London Johnson was English, the only First Lady until Melania Trump not to have been born in the United States. He was taken by her 'wit, beauty, literary knowledge and taste for music'. However, he was wary of women and somewhat pathological about sex. He was reluctant to marry but did so at his mother Abigail's urging. Although she disliked the Johnsons, Abigail later came to like her daughter-in-law.

Now minister in London, the family at first lived at 67 *Harley Street, Marylebone,* where Adams spent time setting up his office in Craven Street, where, 60 years before, **Benjamin Franklin** had lived. In August 1815, they moved to Little Boston House, set in two acres of land in the present London Borough of Ealing, which they rented from James Clitherow. At this time

there were sons George (14), John (12) and Charles (8), (a daughter, Louisa, had died in St Petersburg). Two more daughters, Mary and Fanny, were to be born after the family's return to America. They moved in part for the boys' education and to remove them from the distractions of urban life. (When Charles became minister to London in 1861, he revisited his childhood home.)

Their furniture, possessions and wines were loaded onto two carts and a wagon, and the servants returned to London in the evening to collect and convey the Adams family to the house in Ealing. In his diary, Adams writes of their new home:

John Quincy Adams

The house we have taken is not large but neat and elegant and fitted up with all that minute attention to comfort which is so characteristic of English domestic life. We have a coach house and stable, dairy, fruit and kitchen garden. After breakfast we walked in the garden and before dinner I rode out to enquire for a school for our sons.

Adams was an energetic man, walking the four miles to his office in what he estimated to be two hours and thirty minutes, passing Gunnersbury Mansion, Turnham Green, Hyde Park Corner and St James's Park. He woke between 5am and 6.30am and had George read five 'chapters' of the French Bible each morning.

His day was devoted to correspondence, reading newspapers and receiving visitors. Two or three times a week he travelled to London on business, the other days walking for one and a half hours with George before dinner. Adams spoke French fluently, was well versed in Latin, and interested in astronomy, literature, history, politics and religion.

The family were active local residents: they attended St Mary's Church (the house allowed the family a private pew). John and Charles were pupils at Great Ealing School (closed in 1908 and demolished), and their headmaster, a Dr Nicholas, became a family friend, while George was privately tutored by his father. George was also taught by George Huxley, father of Thomas Huxley; and the future cardinal John Henry Newman was a classmate who visited the Adamses. Prince Augustus, Duke of Sussex, son of George III, came to dinner and another neighbour was General Charles Dumouriez, a former military hero and member of the French revolutionary government now living in exile.

The family attended local events, like a pony race at Ealing Dean, and Adams met local friends in a dining club in the New Inn (rebuilt 1867) in what is now St Mary's Road and attended a cricket match in Gunnersbury Park (although his diaries are more interested in describing the cold meal served in a tent). A ball, which the Adamses attended, was held to mark the birthday of the Duke of Kent, soon to become father of the future Queen Victoria, who lived in the area and whom Adams met. But Adams also noted the social conditions, poverty and crime in the area.

Adams suffered a severe and painful eye infection, leading to temporary loss of sight and Louisa read to him, sang and took dictation. With her encouragement he began to write poetry. When Joshua Johnson returned to the USA, pauperised through his notorious extravagance, his daughter and son-in-law were saddled with his debtors and unpaid servants.

Adams' diplomatic duties do not appear to have been onerous, his achievements modest: he negotiated a limited trade agreement with Britain but much of his time was expended on helping stranded American sailors and prisoners of war.

Awaiting recall to the USA in 1817, Adams took lodgings at 20 Craven Street, but still kept on Little Boston House for a short time, with all the family moving to No 20 on 28 April. When they left for home later that month Adams recorded in his diary:

> We finally removed this day from Little Boston House, otherwise called 'Nightingale Hall' at Little Ealing where we have resided since the first of August 1815.... I have seldom, perhaps never, in the course of my life resided more comfortably than at the house which we now quit and which I shall probably never see again.

In 1874 General Adam Badeau, US consul-general, lived in the house, which was demolished in the 1930s.

Adams returned to become the eighth Secretary of State and in 1825 followed his father into the White House, serving until 1829. He was elected a member of the House of Representatives from 1831 to 1838 and, like his father, spoke as an abolitionist.

Merton, Thomas (1915–1968)

Monk, mystic, writer, poet and political activist

18 Carlton Road, Ealing W5 2AW

Merton, who was to become one of the most famous Catholic figures and writers in the world, was 13 and a baptised but non-practising Anglican when he came here to live with his Aunt Maud and Uncle Ben. He called it 'a fortress of nineteenth century security'. His aunt was 'an angel' and 'sprightly and charming'. He told Maud he wanted to be a writer.

He had been born in France to two artists, Ruth, an American Quaker, and Owen, a New Zealander, who was often absent during Merton's childhood. In the year of his birth the family returned to the USA to live with Merton's maternal grandparents in New York. When he was six his mother died of cancer and thereafter he and his father lived a peripatetic life, occasionally returning to the USA to see grandparents, but often living in France.

Merton left his father and his new love, the married novelist Evelyn Scott, whom Merton never took to, and came back in 1923 to live with his grandparents and his brother in the USA.

He went back to France but in 1928 his father took him out of his French school and they moved to England, where he was enrolled in Ripley Court Preparatory School, another boarding school, in Surrey, which he found 'a pleasant and happy place' and where he later said fondly that he had gone through 'a religious phase'. The boys, wearing black Eton jackets and stiff Eton collars, were required to attend church and he began to pray, but gave up the practice on leaving school. Into maturity Merton sometimes asserted agnosticism and at other times he seems to have evinced a father in God but a detachment from institutional religion. He lived at Carlton Road during school holidays.

Merton's father was only an occasional visitor to the house. In the Easter break of 1929 Merton travelled to Canterbury where his father was painting, and he spent time walking in the countryside. His father went to France and Merton went back to school. Then Merton heard that his father was ill and living in Ealing. He returned to London and the two took off to Scotland where a friend lent a house to help with Owen's recovery. Owen was found to have a brain tumour, although when Merton visited his father in a London hospital he seemed to be recovering. He went to Oakham School, a boarding school in Rutland, in 1930 and the following year his father died.

Merton's grandfather had said he would provide for him, while Tom Bennett, Owen's doctor and a school friend from New Zealand and now Merton's legal guardian, allowed Merton to live in his London house.

He continued to travel: in 1931 to Rome and Florence and then to see his grandparents in New York, before returning to Oakham. He went again to Florence, to Germany and, after passing entrance examinations for Clare College, Cambridge, through France and then to Italy, finding himself in Rome in 1933. There he visited churches and began an awakening to religion and read the whole of the New Testament.

In 1933 Merton started studying at Clare College but left in 1934 and the next year returned to the USA, to live with his grandparents, where his interest in religion but antipathy to Catholicism continued, and he enrolled at Columbia University. But it was while at Columbia that, in 1938, Merton was received into the Catholic Church. He then taught English at St Bonaventure's College and at this time reading, charity work and other influences made him think about the priesthood.

He resigned as a teacher at the end of 1941 and entered the Cistercian or Trappist Abbey of Gethsemani, near Louisville, Kentucky. He embarked on a life both scholarly and politically engaged, as he was deeply concerned with civil rights and the proliferation of nuclear weapons. At this time Merton became an American citizen. He was ordained in 1949.

At the time of his death in 1968 (while attending a conference in Bangkok, he was electrocuted by an electric fan) he had published more than 70 books, 2,000 poems, and numerous essays, lectures and reviews. His autobiography, *The Seven Storey Mountain* came out in 1948 and sold 600,000 copies in hardback alone. It is one of the great spiritual and autobiographical works of the 20th century.

Hawthorne, Nathaniel (1804–1864)

Novelist

4 (formerly 6) Pond Road, Blackheath SE3 9JL

Hawthorne was already well known as a novelist when the Senate approved his appointment as consul in Liverpool in May 1853. By this time *The Scarlet Letter* (1850) and *The House of the Seven Gables* (1851), which alludes to the witch trials in his native Salem, had established his name.

Hawthorne got the post when his old college friend, Franklin Pierce was elected president. Hawthorne had written his admiring biography. There was no salary but the post was worth $30,000–$40,000 annually (a consul could make $250 a day signing certificates for ships' goods). The educator Elizabeth Peabody, his sister-in-law, estimated he could come out of it with $100,000 after spending. (He would often send private letters and cigars, jewellery and silver by diplomatic messenger, to avoid postal costs and duties.) His wife, Sophia, an illustrator and transcendentalist, looked forward to four years in England followed by a stay in Italy with her husband and their three children. She particularly wanted to see the artistic masterpieces that she knew only from inferior reproductions.

Henry Wadsworth Longfellow gave them a farewell party, attended by **Ralph Waldo Emerson, James Russell Lowell** and others, Longfellow writing of his friend that 'he seems much cheered by the prospect before him'.

In July 1853 the family and two maids set off in the Cunard Line's *Niagara*, with 150 passengers, a cow for milk and a coop of chickens for the 11-day journey. He was, he said, coming back to the 'old home' of his ancestors.

Hawthorne's duties as consul were not arduous and he often left others to carry them out. In fact he was not in Liverpool much, travelling as far away as Warwick, Leamington Spa, Litchfield, Boston and Oxford. He frequently came to London, sometimes to see the minister James Buchanan, who became president of America in 1857. Hawthorne had found London 'detestable' until his good friend, the wealthy wool merchant and literary enthusiast, Francis Bennoch showed him around. He socialised but, surprisingly, did not seek out other writers like Alfred Tennyson or Charles Dickens (when he once saw the former at a gallery in Manchester, he was too shy to approach him), but he did meet the novelist George Eliot, the social reformer Harriet Martineau, and the singer Jenny Lind. He dined at the Reform Club and visited the Haymarket Theatre. Hawthorne compared the civilised manners of MPs to those of US senators. He went to the Crystal Palace and visited **Westminster Abbey**, the National Gallery and the British Museum. He spent six days in Oxford with Bennoch.

Statue of Nathaniel Hawthorne in his home town of Salem, Massachusetts (Elizabeth B Thomsen)

The family came for a three-month visit to London when Bennoch let them have his Blackheath house while he was staying on the Continent. Hawthorne wrote of 'our having found a particularly delightful abode in the neighbourhood of London', set in the 'oasis' of Blackheath, with a 'home-like atmosphere, the household element, which is of too intangible a character to be let even with the most thoroughly furnished lodging-house'.

The house had a library and drawing-rooms, and was 'bright with the recollection of the genial presences that we had known there – its closets, chambers, kitchen, and even its wine-cellar, if we could have availed ourselves of so dear and delicate a trust – its lawn and cosey [*sic*] garden-nooks, and whatever else makes up the multitudinous idea of an English home – he had transferred it all to us, pilgrims and dusty wayfarers, that we might rest and take our ease'.

The great city port of Liverpool was not a tranquil spot but Hawthorne wrote of being 'tossed about by the turbulence of the vast London whirlpool'. He spent much time wandering about the city: 'I had trodden the thronged thoroughfares, the broad, lonely squares, the lanes, alleys, and strange labyrinthine courts, the parks, the gardens and enclosures of ancient studious societies, so retired and silent amid the city uproar, the markets, the foggy streets along the river-side, the bridges'.

Hawthorne reckoned that, with an 'unweariable and indiscriminating curiosity', he had found places that few Londoners had come across. He did so by deliberately losing his way. He also walked across Blackheath at night sensible of the dangers of being garrotted. But during the day he watched cricket being played there, really only enjoyable for an Englishman, he writes, for he found it 'lazy, lingering, tedious, and utterly devoid of pictorial effects'. He watched archers and children riding donkeys, while eating gingerbread and drinking ginger beer (inferior to the American type). An English summer he found incomparable to the weather in the USA or even Italy.

Domestic pleasures overpowered the temptations of going out, thanks to the delights of the garden in Pond Road, which comprised 'a good many facilities for repose and enjoyment, such as arbors and garden-seats, shrubbery, flower-beds, rose-bushes in a profusion of bloom, pinks, poppies, geraniums, sweet-peas, and a variety of other scarlet, yellow, blue, and purple blossoms, which I did not trouble myself to recognize individually, yet had always a vague sense of their beauty about me'. There was 'that prime feature of English domestic scenery, a lawn', converted into a bowling green, on which the family would sometimes play.

Nearby there were other pleasures: Greenwich Hospital; Greenwich Park, where Hawthorne set his watch by dial-plate on the Observatory wall; and Greenwich fair, all noted meticulously in the several notebooks he kept of his time in England.

A Puritan, he sometimes attended open-air services given by a Methodist preacher in the park, finding 'cold and commonplace' the sermons delivered in churches.

While Hawthorne regarded the English as an intolerant race (he was also anti-semitic), he said they did 'adhere closer to the original simplicity in which mankind was created than we ourselves do; they love, quarrel, laugh, cry, and turn their actual selves inside out, with greater freedom than any class of Americans would consider decorous'.

Hawthorne's time in Blackheath was not long and his rest short, but he wrote: 'I had earned this repose by a long course of irksome toil and perturbation, and could have been content never to stray out of the limits of that suburban villa and its garden.'

His term as consul ended in 1857 and the family returned to the USA after touring France and Italy.

Hope, Bob (1903–2003)

Comedian, actor and writer

44 Craigton Road, Eltham SE9 1QG Ⓟ

Leslie Townes Hope was born here on 29th May 1903 to William Hope and Avis Townes, his Welsh wife. His father owned a failing stone-cutting business, the fate of which was partly determined by his drinking; Avis was a concert singer with never enough bookings. The business had been established in Hitchin, Hertfordshire by William's father James and had once been so prosperous that James had been involved in building the Law Courts in The Strand in London and later worked on the Statue of Liberty when it was created in Paris.

Bob Hope in 1978 (Library of Congress)

63

In 1907, when young Leslie was only four, the impoverished William took off to the United States in the belief that he would find a use for his skills as a trained building craftsman. That Christmas he sent for Avis and their sons Leslie, Fred, Ivor and William John (Jack),

William's lot had not improved much for mother and children travelled steerage, as William had done. The family settled in Cleveland, Ohio. In the USA two more sons, George and Sid, were born and a daughter, Emily, who died in childhood. A lack of interest in education, rather than the family's financial situation, saw Leslie never get past eighth grade.

From an early age Leslie loved entertaining and at 12 entered a talent contest to impersonate a fellow south Londoner, Charlie Chaplin. He became a boxer (as Packie East) in the late 1910s. In the early 1920s Hope began in show business as a dancer and comedian in vaudeville, and began informally calling himself 'Bob' in 1929. He started doing films (like *The Firs* in 1934), theatre and broadcasting, and engaged in a long-running partnership with Bing Crosby. His brother Jack became a moderately successful film and television producer. Hope became an American citizen when he was 17.

When Hope died at his home in Palm Springs, he was still one of the most famous and richest entertainers in the world.

HACKNEY

Poe, Edgar Allan (1809–1849)

Poet and short story writer

Manor House School, Stoke Newington Church Street, Stoke Newington N16 0JL (gone: now 172) Ⓟ

Poe's was an unsettled childhood even before he was taken to London by his adoptive parents at the age of six. Born in Boston to poverty-stricken parents David and English-born Elizabeth (Eliza), who were travelling actors, he was left as an infant in the care of his paternal grandparents in Baltimore, Maryland, along with his older brother Henry.

After the boys' sister Rosalie (or Rosie) was born at the end of 1810, both parents were suffering from tuberculosis, and there are claims that the two older boys were placed in the care of an old Welsh woman. In the summer of 1811 David disappeared never to be seen again, and at the end of the year Eliza died.

A well-to-do woman named Frances (or Fanny) Allan, wife of a Scots émigré John Allan, had visited Eliza in her last illness. The Allans had no children of their own and became Edgar's effective adoptive parents at their home in Richmond, Virginia, where they had two slaves. (Poe seems to have been pro-slavery, and retained affectionate memories of the two slaves and the small black community he encountered.) Poe took as his middle name the couple's last name at baptism. However, while devoted to Frances, Poe had a largely fractious relationship with John.

John Allan's business hit hard times and, seeking the prosperity that London seemed to offer, in June 1815 he took his wife and son across the Atlantic, along with Frances' sister and companion Anne Moore Valentine, and the older of the two slaves, known only as Thomas. On arriving in Liverpool, the party made for Scotland to visit Allan's relatives. They were there for two months before going to London to take lodgings in Southampton Row,

Edgar Allan Poe in 1848, a year before his death

Holborn, later finding a permanent home in the same street at number 39 (gone). They all caught cold in London's damp and inhospitable climate.

Poe was to write of this time of 'how fondly do we recur in memory of those enchanted days of our boyhood when we first learned to grow serious over *Robinson Crusoe*'. Poe referred to Defoe's 'faculty of identification – that dominion exercised by volition over imagination which enables the mind to lose its own ... individuality'.

Poe was enrolled in a boarding school in Sloane Street, Chelsea, where his father was billed for a 'Separate Bed' (that is Edgar did not have to share a bed with another child), a 'Seat in Church', and William Mavor's *English Spelling Book* and Fresnor's *Geography*. In June 1818 his father said that he could read Latin 'pretty sharply'. (Back in the USA, in his early teens Poe was reading Ovid, Virgil and Cicero, while excelling as a boxer and a swimmer, ironic given his later chronic ill health, exacerbated or even caused by alcohol.)

In July of 1817, the 'enchanted days' came to an end when he was enrolled at the Manor House School, situated in a street where Daniel Defoe had once lived. Stoke Newington was a leafy village of fine houses and an old church. In his autobiographical short story, *William Wilson*, published in 1839, Poe describes the area as 'a misty-looking village' on the edge of London.

Poe suffered a life-long inner emptiness stemming from his sense of abandonment and lack of love. His imagination was fuelled by his early experiences – the adults in his life, his mother on her death bed, his disappearing father, the choppy Atlantic crossing, where he was schooled and lived, his fear of the dark and of death, his early fascination with cemeteries – which all fired the Gothic, macabre aesthetic which was to mark his work. This began in his early teens and was expressed especially in stories like *The Fall of the House of Usher*, *The Murders in the Rue Morgue*, and *The Pit and the Pendulum*.

Poe continued with his Latin and took dancing lessons. Rev John Bransby, the head teacher of Manor House School, was a disciplinarian and remembered Poe as 'a quick and clever boy and would have been a very good boy if he had not been spoilt by his parents; but they spoilt him and allowed him an extravagant amount of pocket money, which enabled him to get into all manner of mischief'. Poe was also, he said, 'intelligent, wayward and wilful'.

Bransby was not pleased to recognise himself in one of the characters in *William Wilson*. Poe refers to the school as having numerous floors and rooms 'and no end in its windings'. In fact, Manor House was plain and functional, and he took some architectural details from The Laurels opposite. He was to tell a friend later in life that his school days had been 'sad, lonely and unhappy'. But John Allan said that 'Edgar is growing wonderfully and enjoys a reputation as both able and willing to receive instruction'. Later he describes his son as 'a very fine Boy and a good scholar'.

Frances was unhappy and homesick. Allan was down to his last £100, and his business, Allan & Ellis, was failing. When the firm was wound up and its debts settled Allan decided to leave England and return to the United States to try his hand as a farmer or planter. Poe left the school in May 1820 and on 8th June the family left Liverpool on the *Martha*, arriving six weeks later in New York to take a steamboat to Richmond.

His American life was to be marked by excessive drinking, moving from place to place, poverty and general instability. In 1827 he published his first poems, then found his fiancée, Elmira Royster Shelton, was engaged to someone else. He got himself discharged from West Point military academy in 1829, after enlisting in 1827, and moved to Baltimore, where he started writing stories. By 1835 Poe was editor of Richmond's *Southern Literary Messenger*, making a name as a critic. He married his cousin Virginia Clemm (when he was 27 and she was 13 years old), to whom he appears to have been an affectionate husband until her death at the age of 24.

Other journalistic jobs followed and in 1845 his poem *The Raven* brought him fame, which enabled him to attract large crowds to lectures and to make money.

Poe had unsuccessfully been entangled with other women after Virginia's death, and then became engaged to Elmira Royster, by now a widow. Whilst travelling from Richmond (where they later intended to marry) to Philadelphia and New York, he disappeared in Baltimore for five days, and was eventually found in a bar being used as a polling station. He died aged 40 of causes unknown (syphilis, heart failure and alcohol have all been cited) and is buried in Baltimore.

Pocahontas (c1596–1617)

Algonquin princess

London Road, Brentford TW8 8AP (now the site of the Royal Mail Sorting Office, 50 London Road) *
Banqueting House, Whitehall, Westminster SW1A 2ER
St Mary-le-Bow Church, Cheapside, Holborn, City of London EC2V 6AU

On marriage, Pocahontas became Rebecca Rolfe and known as that during the year she spent in England. She is buried in the church at Gravesend where she died when unable to accompany her husband back to Virginia.

Her birth name was probably Matoaka but her father called her by the name by which she is known, Pocahontas, which has been translated as 'little-wanton', or 'playful one'.

Her wider fame rests on her saving Captain John Smith** in 1607, when he was captured by the Powhatan, a tribe within the Algonquin, in December 1607. He said that when he was laid across a stone and was about to be clubbed to death she threw herself across his body. He wrote: 'Pocahontas, the King's dearest daughter, when no entreaty could prevaile, got his head in her armes, and laid her owne upon his to save him from death.'

Pocahontas was a frequent visitor to James Fort, Virginia colony, turning cartwheels when naked and playing with the English boys. Smith said that at her own risk she provided the colonists with food. As he was to explain much later, 'during the time of two or three years, she next under God, was … the instrument to preserve this Colonie from death, famine and utter confusion'.

When Smith went back to England in 1609, after being injured in an accident with gunpowder, fighting between the indigenous people and the English recommenced. Between that year and 1612 Pocahontas may have married Kocoum, an indigenous American who may have been her father's bodyguard.

In April 1613, Captain Samuel Argall detained Pocahontas as a hostage to end the Powhatan's attacks on the colonists and to force the return of English

A well-known portrait of Pocahontas attired for her visit to London. The inscription refers to her Christian baptism (National Portrait Gallery)

prisoners and weapons. When the Powhatan capitulated, nearly a decade of peace came about.

Pocahontas was living in the chaplain's house, when held prisoner, and converted to Christianity (she took Rebecca as a baptismal name). She also fell in love with the recently widowed John Rolfe, a tobacco farmer, who was about 11 years her senior. He had arrived in the colony in May 1610 by which time only 70 of the original 600 colonists remained after the ravages of famine and armed clashes.

In seeking permission from the governor to marry, Rolfe described his future wife as 'one whose education hath bin rude, her manners barbarous, her generation accursed, and … discrepant in all nurtriture from my selfe'. In April 1614 they were married in Jamestown and their son Thomas was born the following year.

The marriage brought peace between the colonists and the Powhatan, with one settler writing that 'we have had friendly commerce and trade not only with Powhatan but also with his subjects round about us.'

For the Virginia Company, though, the married couple were a first class example to would-be migrants and investors that the colony was not a harsh place with few amenities and unfriendly natives. Rebecca was a Christian, friendly, of noble birth; she spoke English, dressed fashionably, and carried herself with dignity. In short, what distinguished her from the English men and women, whom the company courted?

Thus, in June 1616 the Rolfes and their son and perhaps a dozen Powhatan arrived in London via Plymouth. They first put up in an inn, the Bell Savage, Ludgate Hill, opposite where Cannon Street Station now stands, which was destroyed in the Great Fire of London.

Smith wrote to King James I to ask that Pocahontas be treated respectfully, for otherwise 'her present love to us and Christianity might turn to … scorn and fury, and England might lose the chance to rightly have a Kingdom by her means.'

She was accepted into the heart of London society: the queen received her at Whitehall Palace (gone); the bishop of London held a dinner in her honour at Lambeth Palace; and, with a companion, Tomocomo, a Powhatan shaman, she met the king at a masque hosted by the playwright Ben Jonson at the Banqueting House, Whitehall, Westminster (though the King was so self-effacing she did not know who he was until afterward); and her portrait, engraved by the Dutch artist Simon de Passe, shows her as a finely clothed grand lady of the time. While in London, Rebecca is said to have worshipped at the Church of St Mary-le-Bow, Cheapside, where Smith was also a parishioner.

However, London's air caused Rebecca respiratory problems, and so the family moved in the autumn to a villa in the then small village of Brentford in Middlesex. Here John Smith made a visit and, as she had believed that he had died after leaving Virginia, Rebecca said to him: 'your Countriemen ... lie much', but she wanted to them to call one another 'father' and 'childe', and 'so I will bee for ever and ever your Countrieman'.

Ben Jonson met her at an inn, which he referred to in *The Staple of News* and which may have been the Three Pigeons in Brentford, which he frequented. Opposite the villa was Syon Park, home to the 8th Earl of Northumberland, father of George Percy, one of the first of the 150 Jamestown colonists and for a short time governor of Virginia, who left for England in 1612 and whom the Rolfes would almost certainly have known.

The Rolfes were due to set sail for Virginia in March for he was now secretary of the colony, but for Rebecca the trip was 'sore against her will'. She may have been suffering from tuberculosis or pneumonia for she became too weak to travel. She was put ashore at Gravesend, Kent, where she died on 21st March. She was buried in the chancel of St George's Church where there is a life-size bronze.

Rolfe was afraid of taking their son to sea and left him with relatives. Thomas later emigrated to the land of his birth, married and raised his own family.

---

* A memorial plaque to Pocahontas has been set in the wall of Syon House opposite the site of her former home.
** Smith died in London in June 1631 and two years later was buried in the south aisle of St Sepulchre-without-Newgate Church, where he is commemorated by a stained glass window. A statue stands in the churchyard, a replica of that in Jamestown, Virginia.

ISLINGTON

Paine, Thomas (1737–1809)
Writer and revolutionary
Angel Square, The Angel EC1V 1NY (gone) P

'The rights of man' is a phrase which has now entered the language (if now controversially, given its gender specificity), but the book whose title gave it its currency was written in the inn which then stood on the site of the building on the junction of High Street, Islington, and Pentonville Road.*

An inn had been here since end of the 16th century and by the time Tom Paine stayed here to write his book in 1790 The Angel was the largest of a row of coaching inns along the High Street.

Paine was born in Norfolk and had been an excise man in Grampound in Cornwall and Lewes in Sussex, but had emigrated to the American colonies in 1774, with the help of his friend **Benjamin Franklin**. He came to know Franklin through a mutual interest in science and the American thought him 'an ingenious, worthy young man' in the letter of introduction which he had given Paine.

In his new country Paine had inspired the American patriots of the Revolutionary War with his pamphlet, *Common Sense* ('Written by an Englishman') in 1776, that advocated American independence from colonial overlords, and his series of pamphlets, *The American Crisis*, published between 1776 and 1793. It was Paine who allegedly coined the term 'United States of America'.

Thomas Paine in 1792

John Adams said of *Common Sense*: 'Without the pen of the author of *Common Sense*, the sword of Washington would have been raised in vain', while the historian GM Trevelyan opined that 'it would be difficult to name any human composition which had the effect at once so instant, so extended and so lasting.'

For much of the 1790s Paine lived in France, deeply involved in the French Revolution, of which *The Rights of Man* was partly a defence. It was also a book that laid out social reforms. Apart from arguing for a written constitution, a national assembly (like that of the USA), and the abolition of aristocratic titles and privilege, Paine proposed family and maternity allowances, benefits for newlyweds, universal education, old age pensions, and pensions for those unable to work through disability, all to be paid for by progressive taxation.

The book was published in 1791 and by leaving England Paine avoided standing trial, which led to his conviction *in absentia* in 1792 for seditious libel on the British writer and politician Edmund Burke, to whose book, *Reflections of the Revolution in France*, Paine's had been a rebuttal.

In 1792, despite not speaking French, Paine was elected to the French National Convention but, with the Girondists and Robespierre as his enemies, he was arrested in December of the next year and imprisoned in Paris, to be released in 1794. He returned to the United States, where he lived a quiet life engaging in his scientific pursuits, and died seven years later.

---

* *There is a plaque set in a memorial. The sculpture, unveiled in 1991, is inscribed with four of Paine's most famous sayings: 'These are the times that try men's souls'; 'My country is my world and my religion is to do good'; 'Lay then the axe to the root and teach governments humanity'; and 'It is necessary for the happiness of man that he is mentally faithful to himself'. Another claim has been made that the book was written in the Old Red Lion in St John Street, Islington (where there is also a plaque).*

Albright, Madeleine (1937–)

US secretary of state

Princes House, 52 Kensington Park Road, Kensington W11 3BW

The earliest memories of the woman who, in 1997, was to become her country's first female Secretary of State, were of London and the English countryside, of bomb shelters and blackout curtains, and being taken by parents to see the steel barriers being erected at the seashore to deter German invasion.

For the then Marie Jana Korbelová was nearly two years old when, ten days after the Nazis entered her native Prague, her parents, Josef and Mandula Korbel brought her to London. They left Prague on 25th March 1939 on the Simplon Orient Express to Greece, from where they took a boat to England. They settled first in a dreary and cramped boarding house in London before moving to a two-bedroom flat on the second floor of this then four-year-old, redbrick apartment block.

Marie's family was soon to be joined by her cousin, Dáša Deimlova, aged 11, the daughter of her father's sister. She arrived on the *Kindertransport* and Josef met her at Harwich, from where they travelled by train to Liverpool Street Station. Dáša and Marie shared a room in Princes House.

Princes House was home to a mixed group – British, Polish, Czech, Spanish, German and Canadian. Josef was a diplomat and the Czechs in the house included the family of Josef's friend, Prokop Drtina, who had been private secretary to the Czech President Edvard Beneš at the time of the Munich conference.

Marie's mother remembered:

> We were living in a foreign country but surrounded only by Czech people, without making friends with the English, except for a very few … English people have a different temperament than those coming from Central Europe. It was pleasant to be there as only temporary guests. That was what we wanted and what they wanted as well.

Josef, who tried to make contact with friends, acted as an adviser to Beneš's government-in-exile, while Marie and her mother spent many hours in nearby parks (mainly Ladbroke Square Gardens). The apartment had a phone and a radio, which fascinated Marie because when she heard her father broadcasting, she thought he was *in* the radio.

When the air raid siren sounded during the Blitz all residents went to the cramped cellar, which was divided into several small rooms and one larger one to accommodate about two dozen people at any one time, and

71

occasionally more when nearby buildings had to be evacuated. They sipped tea and coffee and shared snacks of bread and biscuits waiting for the all-clear from the air-raid wardens. 'In the morning when the all-clear sounded, we burst into the street or climbed onto the roof to survey the damage,' wrote Albright.

With the entry into the war of the USA in 1941, the family and their friends felt sure that the Axis powers would be defeated.

In 1944, now with a baby sister, Katherine, Marie moved with her parents to share a four-bedroom house with a Czech couple, the Goldstückers, at 22 Stompond Lane, Walton-on-Thames, Surrey. Dáša was away at school in Wales, while Marie went to a local private school. Chickens were kept in the back garden and vegetables grown. The adult Albright remembered pushing her sister in her pram and taking the ration book and shopping list to a nearby grocery.

The family lived there for more than a year and witnessed the coming of the V-1s, 'doodlebugs', when Josef was an air-raid warden. One V-1 fell just a few streets from their house on 19th June – altogether 18 fell on the town.

In all this time, Marie and her family attended Mass (she converted from Catholicism to Episcopalianism upon marriage in 1959). But what she did not know until she was 59 was that her parents were Jewish and had converted to Catholicism from Judaism in 1941. She learned, too, that a dozen relatives, including three grandparents, had been murdered in the Holocaust.

The Korbels returned to Prague in 1945, where Josef was appointed ambassador to Yugoslavia, and soon after this Albright changed her name to Madeleine. However, the family were forced into a second exile when the Communists staged a coup in Prague in 1948.

Marie went to school in Switzerland, while her mother, sister and now a brother, John, went back to London, where she eventually joined them in a cramped rented apartment. At the end of 1948 the family departed for the USA on *SS America* and settled first on Long Island and then in Denver, Colorado. Marie became a US citizen in 1957. Her father became a distinguished academic.

American Food Store

2 Ladbroke Grove, Kensington W11 3BG

Until 2008 the owners ran a Post Office and newsagents. When that closed after 38 years they decided to indulge their love of American food and open this unique shop. Lucky Charms, A&W Root Beer, Twizzlers and Nerds were obvious choices although, of course, available in many places in London and elsewhere. But there are now a thousand items from candies to sodas; Betty Crocker to Duncan Hines; and cake mixes to cranberry sauce and cornbread.

Very often what passes for American food elsewhere is significantly different from the real thing: for example, Cheerios in UK shops are all sugar, while the American version is sugarless.

And in case there is any doubt about the patriotism of the shop, there is a range of Stars and Stripes plates, cups and napkins, and lapel badges.

Bell, Alexander Graham (1847–1922)

Inventor of the telephone

57 West Cromwell Road, Kensington SW5 9QS
115 Jermyn Street, St James's, Westminster W1Y 4UH (gone)
Royal Society of Arts, 8 John Adam Street, Charing Cross, Westminster WC2N 6EZ

Edinburgh-born Bell was 15 when he first came to London to stay with his grandfather, Alexander Bell, a well-known elocutionist. After teaching at Somerset College in Bath, in 1867 he returned to London to be assistant to his father who, also a notable elocutionist, was continuing his own father's work.

Having developed a skill for teaching deaf people, Bell graduated from London University in 1868. When his parents emigrated to Canada in 1870 he went with them and worked with deaf people in Boston and Northampton in Massachusetts, and in Hartford, Connecticut. In 1873 he was appointed to the chair of vocal physiology and elocution at Boston University and the next year became an American citizen.

Alexander Graham Bell

His interest in perfecting instruments of use to deaf people led him to develop ideas for a telephone. Bell had been in his 20s when he began his early experimental work. He had conceived of the theory of the telephone when staying on holiday with his parents in 1874 and in about October of that year he produced his ear phonautograph, which made use of the human ear (with its eardrum). He became more and more involved in experimental work with his assistant Thomas Watson. On 2nd June 1875, Bell's first membrane diaphragm telephone transmitter produced speech sounds.

After further tests in March the next year and January the following year, his patents became the fundamental telephone patents. They were tested 600 different times in 18 years.*

Bell's invention had a long genealogy, stretching back, through many elaborations, to Robert Hooke in 1667 with his acoustic string telephone, with sounds sent by mechanical vibrations over a taut extended wire.

A few days after setting up the Bell Telephone Company, he married Mabel Gardiner in 1877. She was deaf from early childhood and they had two daughters, Elsie and Marian, and two sons, Edward and Robert, both of whom died in infancy. The Bells came to Jermyn Street on what was supposed to be part of their year-long honeymoon in Europe but such was his energy and professional dedication that he would use the opportunity to pursue business interests and make contacts.

In late 1877 the couple took up residence in the large house in West Cromwell Road ('the less aristocratic end' wrote Mabel) at a rent of £225 a year. They had moved from rooms in Half Moon Street, off Piccadilly, and the Alexandra Hotel (gone). While here Bell went to lecture at the Physical Science School in Kensington. Mabel reported in a letter: 'Alex says the lecture was a complete failure as he was tired before he began and feeling faint and ill. The lecture began at three and [he] was sick all afternoon but felt better in the evening.'

In October that year, Bell was invited to speak to the Society of Telegraph Engineers at a meeting at the Institute of Civil Engineers in Westminster. He returned so full of what had happened that he sat down to write a letter to his parents, telling them: 'The hall was crammed and numbers were turned away. I am told that the principal scientific men of London were present.'

In November 1877 Bell demonstrated the telephone at the Society for the Encouragement of the Arts, Manufactures and Commerce (the Royal Society of Arts). He spoke to telephones placed elsewhere in the building, as well as in a nearby hotel and in the society's print shop in Fleet Street, Holborn.

The Times commented: 'If any proof were wanting of the universal interest that this remarkable instrument is exciting, it was shown by an assembly of the members which not only filled the hall and staircases of the building, but overflowed into the street outside.'

At about this time, and probably later, Bell had rooms at the Buckingham Palace Hotel, Buckingham Gate, Victoria (gone). In January 1878, he gave a demonstration to Queen Victoria at Osborne House on the Isle of Wight. 'Most extraordinary', she exclaimed, sufficiently impressed to order a pair of telephones.

Bell was forced to defend his patents in a letter to *The Times* in July 1878, when accused of seeking a telephone monopoly. His letter was sent from 115 Cannon Street (gone) in the City of London. There are claims that the first long-distance call in the UK was made from this address but evidence is lacking. The following month Europe's first telephone exchange opened in London.

Bell also worked on a telegraph system, and in February 1875 the Bell Patent Association was formed, becoming the American Telephone and Telegraph Company in 1885, now AT&T, the world's largest telecommunications company.

In the early 1880s Bell switched his interests to developing the photophone, whereby a light beam would allow the transmission of speech signals from one place to another. He came to regard this as his greatest invention but the radio made it obsolete.

In January 1915 Watson received the first transcontinental call from 333 Grant Avenue in San Francisco from Bell at 15 Dey Street in New York.

Bell was ceaselessly inventive and experimented with spectrophones, phonographs, telephonic probes, kites, aeroplanes, hydrofoil boats and air conditioning. He was also interested in sheep breeding, longevity and eugenics.

He was proof of his own belief: 'There cannot be mental atrophy in any person who continues to observe, to remember what he observes, and to seek answers for his unceasing hows and whys about things.'

Bell died at his home on Cape Breton Island, Nova Scotia, Canada. Telephone traffic throughout the USA was silenced for a minute at 6.25pm on 4th August 1922, when he was buried.

---

* *The history of Brown's Hotel, Mount Street, Mayfair, claims that Bell demonstrated the phone there. However, there is no contemporary record or mention in Bell's notebooks to confirm this.*

Benn, Caroline (1926–2000)

Education reformer and writer

12 Holland Park Avenue, Kensington W11 3QU 🅿

The then 23-year-old Caroline DeCamp met 24-year-old Anthony Wedgwood-Benn at tea in Worcester College, Oxford in 1948, where she was attending a summer school and he was reading PPE. Nine days later he proposed to her on a park bench on Magdalen Bridge, the day before she was due to return home to Vassar College, New York, where she was studying. He later bought the bench from the local authority and installed it in front of their west London home.

In June 1949 they married in Cincinnati and she was to be his main confidante for more than 50 years, someone with whom he tested his ideas and who gave him both support and constructive criticism. It was to be a long-lasting marriage, which produced four children and ten grandchildren, as well as one of the longest political partnerships in British history.

Caroline was born in Cincinnati into a wealthy family and was radical from an early age, having voted for Henry Wallace, the Progressive Party candidate, in the 1948 presidential elections.

She gained a degree in 1951 in Jacobean drama at University College, London. The next year she and Tony moved to the house in Holland Park Avenue. While his political interests ranged from parliamentary reform to public ownership, and from industrial democracy to colonial freedom, her abiding interest was comprehensive education, which seemed not very different from the high schools she was used to in her native country, and she was one of the founders of the Campaign for Comprehensive Education. In 1970, with Brian Simon, she co-wrote *Halfway There*, a study of the progress of the comprehensive ideal in the UK, and in 1997, with Professor Clyde Chitty, produced *Thirty Years On*. She also wrote a biography of Keir Hardie, published in 1992.

When Tony Benn left the BBC upon election to Parliament, the fact that all their children were at private schools was incompatible with the couple's political outlook and upheld a system with which they were in profound disagreement, as well as undermining the Labour policy of comprehensive schools. Thus, Stephen and Hilary left Westminster under school for the nearby and renowned Holland Park Comprehensive School, and Melissa and Joshua followed in due course. Caroline would become a governor of the school for 35 years, as well as a member of the Inner London Education Authority (where Stephen later served, as Hilary followed his father into the House of Commons) and the board of Imperial College, London, president of the Socialist Education Association, in addition to tutoring for the Open University and at Kensington and Hammersmith Further Education College.

She was diagnosed with cancer in 1995 and died five years later. Though Tony remained politically active, a popular speaker and oversaw the publication the last three volumes of a sequence of ten diaries, it was said that he 'never fully recovered his cheerful demeanor'.

The year Caroline died marked the 50th anniversary of his election to Parliament. When he retired the next year he claimed that it would allow him 'more time for politics', words he attributed to his late wife.

With old age, Tony could no longer keep up the large family home – where for their golden wedding anniversary Caroline had appeared wearing the red-striped dress she had worn when sitting on the park bench in 1948 – and he moved to a warden-assisted flat nearby. There he died in 2014 surrounded by their family.

Douglass, Frederick (c1817–1895)

Abolitionist, author and diplomat

5 Whitehead's Grove, Chelsea SW3 3HA (gone: now Nell Gwynne Court) ⓟ

Frederick Douglass

Douglass made two visits to England, Scotland and Ireland (he never visited Wales) but the first one, from 1845 to 1847, was the most significant of his life. He arrived as a fugitive from slavery – he had fled the USA through fear of recapture – and he returned a free man after some British supporters paid $700 (£150) to his slave owner, Hugh Auld, for his liberty.

Douglass was well known before he ever arrived because his book, *Narrative of the Life of Frederick Douglass, an American Slave**, published in 1845, had become widely known, with French, Dutch and German translations. So much so that he calculated that what he earned from the book – he had gone to Ireland partly to meet the publisher who would bring it out there – would meet the expenses of his trip.

He arrived in Liverpool and visited most of the great cities like Belfast, Glasgow, Edinburgh, Bristol, Leeds, Manchester and Newcastle, as well as smaller towns. In Dublin he shared a platform with Daniel O'Connell, the Irish nationalist, and Douglass's own oratory earned him the title 'the black O'Connell'. In Scotland he visited the home of Robert Burns, as well as mounting his 'Send back the money' campaign to have the Free Church return donations from Southern slave owners.

Douglass was much taken with Britain, comparing the lack of prejudice he experienced with the institution of slavery in his own country. (In fact, there were protests against him as a black man.) When he came to London in May 1846 Douglass stayed at the modest Chelsea home of British abolitionist George Thompson.

Born in Maryland to a black mother and possibly a white father, Douglass spent 20 years as a slave. His escape in 1838 was not his first – he had tried twice before. After successfully escaping, he married a free black woman, Anna Murray, who had helped him to escape north. When they settled in Massachusetts the man born Frederick Augustus Washington Bailey took the name by which he was ever after known. They had five children and were married for 45 years until she predeceased him. (After his wife's death, Douglass married Helen Pitts, a white suffragette.) In Massachusetts he worked for the Massachusetts Anti-Slavery Society.

In Britain he gave lectures in public halls, private homes, chapels and churches. Often his audience numbered thousands, filling some of the great speaking venues, like the vast Freemason's Hall, Great Queen Street, Covent Garden. Douglass commonly addressed more than one meeting a day; sometimes his theme was temperance or world peace, often it was to arouse people to knowledge of the realities of slavery and to urge public support for its abolition.

He addressed the London Peace Society, the Complete Suffrage Association, the National Temperance Society, and the British and Foreign Anti-Slavery Society. He deplored one person holding another in bondage as a chattel and the physical cruelty, not only of back-breaking work but of actual torture, and the breaking up of families – when young, he had been forcibly separated from his grandmother and mother. But Douglass also deplored the forced ignorance resulting from not allowing African-Americans even the most rudimentary education, although he himself had been taught to read the alphabet by the sympathetic wife of one of the masters. This led him to a life-long reading habit.

He visited Parliament and also met people like Hans Christian Andersen in London; John Bright of the anti-Corn Law agitation, who would later write an introduction to the third edition of Douglass's autobiography in 1882; and Lord John Russell who was about to start his first term as prime minister after Sir Robert Peel, whom Douglass also met.

In his London reception address at Finsbury Chapel, Islington, Douglass said:

> I have on my back the marks of the lash; I have four sisters and one brother now under the galling chain. I feel it my duty to cry aloud and spare not. I am not averse to having the good opinion of my fellow-creatures. I am not averse to being kindly regarded by all men; but I am bound, even at the hazard of making a large class of religionists in this country hate me, oppose me, and malign me as they have done – I am bound by the prayers, and tears, and entreaties of three millions of kneeling bondsmen, to have no compromise with men who are in any shape or form connected with the slaveholders of America. I expose slavery in this country, because to expose it is to kill it.

He returned to the USA to carry on his agitation and to that end founded the *North Star*, the first abolitionist newspaper. He also became more fully involved in the fight to obtain the vote for women. In the Civil War, in which three of his sons fought, he served as a Union recruiter. He also became the first African-American nominated (against his approval) for the vice presidency for the Equal Rights Party in 1872. He served as US minister in Haiti from 1889 to 1891.

---

* *Douglass published two other autobiographies, the last of which was* The Life and Times of Frederick Douglass *published in 1881 (revised 1892).*

Epstein, Sir Jacob (1880–1959)

Sculptor

18 Hyde Park Gate, Kensington SW7 5DH Ⓟ
25 Queen's Gate, Kensington SW7 5JE

Epstein grew up in New York's largely Jewish Lower East Side, where he was taken by its teeming street life, which he used to sketch from an early age. He studied at the Art Students League and then at night school, while earning his keep by working in a bronze foundry. Later, the money he made from illustrating Hutchins Hapgood's 1902 book *The Spirit of the Ghetto* allowed him to move to Paris and spend six months at the École des Beaux-Arts and then to study at the Academie Julian.

He turned from painting to sculpture in 1899–1900 but this did not prevent him receiving many painting commissions for some years after and his work being publicly displayed.

Epstein moved to London in 1905 and a year later married Margaret Dunlop. They lived first in 219 Stanhope Street, near Camden Town (gone) and then moved to the Stamford Street Studios, Fulham (gone), where they remained until 1908. Epstein became a British citizen in 1910. In Paris between 1912 and 1913 he met Picasso, Modigliani and Brancusi, then moved back to England where he lived and worked near Hastings in Sussex from 1913 to 1916. In 1913 he became a founding member of the London Group, English artists opposed to the traditions of the Royal Academy but also an alternative to the New English Art Club. Associated with **Ezra Pound** he never joined the Vorticists. That year, too, he enjoyed his first solo exhibition at the Two-One Gallery in the Adelphi, the Strand.

The Epsteins were forced to leave Sussex for 23 Guilford Street, Bloomsbury (gone) when their foreign name aroused war-time suspicions. He also lived and worked in Loughton in Essex. Epstein was conscripted into the 3rd Battalion of the Royal Fusiliers, known as the Jewish Legion, in the First World War but suffered a breakdown and was invalided out, without ever leaving the country.

Most of Epstein's later work was exhibited at the Leicester Galleries, also in London. He had a one-man show in his native New York in 1927.

Two years later he moved from the Bloomsbury house to Hyde Park Gate, where he lived to the end of his life, while he worked in nearby Queen's Gate. (Earlier he had a studio in Cheyne Walk, Chelsea, and in the First World War had worked from a garage in Lamb's Conduit Street, Holborn, as well as in Hastings).

Epstein was also a fashionable artist, creating portraits for **Elsa Lanchester**, Joseph Conrad, Sibyl Thorndyke, Ramsay MacDonald, Albert Einstein, Chaim Weizmann, George Bernard Shaw and Haile Selassie as well as, after the war, Sir Winston Churchill.

He led a complicated private life. While still married to Margaret Epstein he had five children with other women. His wife's tolerance – she brought up his first and last children and allowed his lovers to live in the family home – had its limits. In 1923 she shot and wounded Kathleen Garman, herself an artist, with whom he had four children, one of whom died in infancy. Epstein paid Garman's hospital bills and persuaded his lover not to press charges, in order to avoid scandal. Margaret died in 1947 and he married Garman in 1955, having been knighted the previous year.

Epstein created a new understanding of what could be the subject of public art and he is particularly known for large, muscular subjects. But some of his work, using nudes, depicting pregnancy and displaying sexuality, brought charges of indecency and caused public outrage as early as 1908.

In London his *Memorial to WH Hudson* (Rima) (1925) can be seen in Hyde Park, and *Night and Day* (1928–9) adorns the entrance of Transport for London at St James' Underground Station, 55 Broadway; while *Madonna and Child* (1950–52) is in Cavendish Square, off Oxford Street. His statue of the South African statesman Jan Smuts stands in Parliament Square. Cathedrals (famously, *St Michael and the Devil*, in Coventry) show his work and he was responsible for the striking tomb of Oscar Wilde at Père Lachaise Cemetery in Paris.

Gardner, Ava (1922–1990)

Actress

Flat 3, 34 Ennismore Gardens, Knightsbridge SW7 1AE Ⓟ

Gardner was born into poverty, the youngest of the seven children of a sharecropper in North Carolina. From then until her death 67 years later in this spacious luxury apartment a stone's throw from Harrods, she became one of the world's most famous film stars, acquiring along the way three famous husbands: the actor Mickey Rooney, the singer Frank Sinatra and the band leader Artie Shaw.

She was known for her sensual beauty and her tumultuous private life. She was tempestuous, volatile, easily bored but also witty and courageous, with a zest for life: someone who enjoyed people but valued privacy. She engaged in numerous well-publicised affairs, but she also made a number of highly ranked films.

Although she won praise for her acting, Gardner denigrated her talent, saying typically in an interview in 1985, 'Listen, honey, I was never really an actress. None of us kids who came from MGM were. We were just good to look at.'

Her outspokenness got her into trouble. When she arrived in Australia to make *On the Beach*, she said: 'I'm here to make a film about the end of the world, and this sure is the place for it.'

Ava Gardner in *The Killers*, the film that first established her

Gardner came to London in 1968, partly to escape long-drawn-out actions for alleged payment of back taxes, but also for a private life of comparative anonymity. Always an independent woman, she was one of the first stars to escape the clutches of Hollywood by not living there. She lived first in a large house in Alexander Square, South Kensington, which she sold in 1972 for this five bedroom apartment. 'I love the history and grandeur of my little London retreat; some say it is too big for me alone, but I love the space', she said of her last home. Two years after she moved to London, she appeared in *Tam-Lin*, the first of 11 films made when she was living in her adoptive country. Her last film was *Regina Roma*, in 1982. There was also television work.

Gardner had intended to be a secretary, but on a trip to New York, Larry Tarr, her brother-in-law and a professional photographer, sent a portfolio to MGM who put her under a seven-year contract in 1941, when she was 18. Mainly small roles in a string of films led to her finding stardom at 24 in *The Killers* (1946), her breakthrough that enabled her to be seen as more than a beautiful woman, a label which, though, she never wholly escaped. Later notable films included *Showboat* (1951), when her voice was dubbed; *The Snows of Kilimanjaro* (1952); *Mogambo* (1953), for which she won an Oscar nomination; *The Sun Also Rises* (1957); *On the Beach* (1959); and *Night of the Iguana* and *Seven Days in May* (both 1964).

Her marriages to Rooney and Shaw lasted only a year before separation and then divorce. She was married to Sinatra from 1951 to 1957, but their marriage was marked by public rows, a separation in 1953 and reconciliations. However, they remained close all her life and after their final split he sent her a large bouquet each birthday, the long-dead flowers kept until the next bouquet arrived.

Gardner's final years were a sad decline, worsened by smoking and heavy drinking, which she never gave up. Pneumonia caused her to seek treatment in the United States, where Sinatra met all her expenses. Back in London she had a stroke, affecting her left side, which left her left arm partly paralysed, but she continued to work on her posthumously published memoir, *Ava: My Story*.

Gardner died of bronchial pneumonia at her home a month after her 67th birthday, with her friend and long-time housekeeper Carmen Vegas and her beloved Welsh collie Morgan by her bedside. On hearing of her death, Sinatra broke down and blamed himself for not visiting her. At her wish she was buried with her parents in North Carolina.

Gellhorn, Martha (1908–1998)
War correspondent and writer

72 Cadogan Square, Knightsbridge SW I X 0ED*
31 South Eaton Place, Belgravia, Westminster SW I W 9EL
20 Chester Square, Belgravia, Westminster SW I W 9HS

Touring Europe in her teens, Gellhorn gave London short shrift – the food was appalling, the hotels poor, and the weather even worse. She caught a train to Cornwall. This inauspicious introduction to the capital did not prevent her, however, from making her home in a top-floor apartment in Cadogan Square for the last 28 years of her life.

Gellhorn, who claimed to have lived in 40 homes during an adventurous life, covered every major conflict in 60 years. Born in St Louis, Missouri to wealthy parents, her journalistic career began after she dropped out of Bryn Mawr College, Pennsylvania, later moving to Paris to become a foreign correspondent. There she had a long affair with the French writer and economist Bertrand de Jouvenel, whom she would have married had his wife agreed to a divorce.

Back in the USA in 1934, Gellhorn travelled the country, officially to document the effects of the Depression, but in 1936 she met Ernest Hemingway in a bar in Key West, Florida, whom she would marry in 1940. Her first experience as a war correspondent was in 1937 when she travelled with Hemingway to Spain during the Civil War.

There was no reconciling Hemingway's wish for a wife at home (and in bed) and her wish for professional freedom. She left him during a row at London's Dorchester Hotel in 1945. They divorced a year later and she resisted every attempt to link their names (to her detriment) in later life.

Gellhorn was in China during the conflict with the Japanese and in Czechoslovakia when the Nazis invaded, while she covered the USSR's attack on Finland in 1939. She reported the Second World War, including the bombing of London and the D-Day landings and was forever marked by visiting Dachau at its liberation. Twenty-one years later she was in Vietnam, and in Jerusalem she covered the trial of Adolf Eichmann. An impassioned Zionist, she went to Israel in 1967 to report the Six Day War. After that she filed reports from El Salvador, Nicaragua and the US invasion of Panama in

1989 when she was 81. 'Journalism is education for me', she said. 'Writing is payment for the chance to look and learn.'

While she lived in many places, including Europe, Cuba, Mexico and Kenya, she purchased her 'little sewer' in South Eaton Place in 1946 to begin what became a permanent life in London, punctuated with much travel. When she was 42, she adopted baby Alessandro from an orphanage in Italy. She named him George Alexander Gellhorn but he was known as Sandy. They had an uneven relationship but were reconciled late in her life. After she married compatriot Tom Matthews, journalist and writer and former executive editor of *Time*, in 1954 at Caxton Hall, Westminster, they lived for a time in his set in *92 Albany, Piccadilly*, and then in Chester Square. However, finding it difficult to work in the house Gellhorn took an apartment at *215 Ashley Gardens, Victoria*.

Gellhorn was especially close to one of Matthews' four sons, also Sandy, who became her executor. She and Matthews divorced in 1963 and she moved to 39 Chandos Court, Caxton Street, Victoria (gone). In 1970 she moved to Cadogan Square. The upper floor served as a study, and she had friends nearby, while others visited. She enjoyed what London had to offer and liked to walk along The Embankment and in Kensington Gardens. She would often spend weeks, even months at Catscradle, her cottage in Gwent.

Gellhorn's last substantial piece of reporting was about the plight of street children in Brazil when she was 87. As she herself said, her body was becoming older than her mind, and there was much pain in her last 10 years. She reviewed thrillers for *The Daily Telegraph* and audio-novels for *The Observer* when she could no longer read.

The New York Times called Gellhorn 'a cocky, raspy-voiced, chain-smoking maverick'. Her biographer, Caroline Moorehead, talks of her 'restless energy, always on the move'. She suffered, too, says the same source, 'a degree of loneliness, self-doubt and a sense of failure'. Cantankerous she could be, but, with deep convictions, unending curiosity, and tall and elegant, she had a gift for friendship that embraced **Eleanor Roosevelt**, HG Wells and Leonard Bernstein.

In her last 20 years she gathered 'my chaps' – young men and women, often writers, journalists and people in publishing, who would visit. Friends came for drinks in the late afternoon or evening, often for hours but this rarely turned into dinner.

Gellhorn developed ovarian and liver cancer. On the day she died, she phoned a friend to discuss the Bosnian war and the harassment of Bill Clinton, and apologised for not being able to visit that week. She had put her affairs and papers in order, her flat was, as ever, tidy, and tulips stood on the side when on 15th February 1998 she swallowed what was thought to be a cyanide capsule. 'Death is nothing', she told her friend, the novelist and actress Betsy Drake. 'The only fear is the manner of dying.'

Gellhorn's ashes were scattered on the Thames on an outgoing tide 'for my last travels'.

---

* A plaque will be erected on the building later in 2019.

Harte, (Francis) Bret (1836–1902)*
Author
74 (now 72–74) Lancaster Gate, Bayswater W2 3NH Ⓟ

Harte enjoyed fame in his day both in his native USA and Europe. He was born in Albany, New York State, of English and Dutch descent, with an English grandfather who was a Jewish merchant and a founder of the New York Stock Exchange. Harte was only 19 when he went to California, determined to turn his hand to writing. This was the literary making of him, for whatever came later he remains best remembered for his tales about the Gold Rush, which had taken place only a few years before his arrival, with their cast of miners, prostitutes, bankers and gamblers. There is nothing romantic about his work, which often exposes hypocrisy, greed and corruption by sheriffs, bankers and politicians but finds virtues in the social outcast.

Bret Harte in 1902, the year of his death

He had left school at 13 and was familiar with the world he portrayed for he worked (or he said he did) as a journalist, teacher, printer, gold miner, and as a Wells Fargo messenger, protecting valuable stage coach shipments, while all the time writing poetry. In 1862 Harte entered an unhappy marriage with Anna Griswold with whom he had two sons and two daughters. They spent only 16 of their 40 married years actually together.

In California he employed **Mark Twain** as a writer and they became friends. Twain was to say, before they fell out with each other, that he learned his craft from Harte.

In 1870 Harte's widely published poem, *Plain Language from Truthful James* (also known as *The Heathen Chinee*), a rebuttal of racism against the Chinese immigrants, brought instant fame and he went east to pursue a literary career that among other things gained him a $10,000 annual contract from *The Atlantic Monthly*.

However, Harte's writing declined, he overspent, his funds diminished, and interest in his work, by publishers and the public alike, waned. He sought a new readership in Europe, leaving the USA in the summer of 1878 never to return. As US consul in Germany he became one of that country's most popular authors. He then landed the same position in Glasgow in 1880 but seems to have done little there, leaving business to be carried out by others and spending so much time in London that he sent 562 letters and telegrams to his Glasgow office. Five years later Harte secured the London posting and the capital became his home for the rest of his life. In all this time he had financially supported his family in the USA, though he never visited them and when Anna came to London to visit him, he refused to see her.

The *Oxford Dictionary of National Biography* says that even before he went to England, 'with local fame came mannerisms at odds with his uncouth subject matter. So transformed, Harte would not have been out of place in a London club in Pall Mall; he wore elegant clothes and affected a nasal voice.'

In Europe Harte wrote prolifically and in London he turned his pen to writing plays, which were more lucrative than short stories and gained the patronage of Marguerite Van de Velde, the wife, then widow, of a Belgian diplomat. It was at their house in Lancaster Gate that he spent most of his time. He also developed a gift for successful parody: Thackeray, Disraeli, Conan Doyle and Kipling were among his targets. He had an additional income from journalism, but it was never enough: at his death he left his wife his copyrights and £360.

Harte died in Camberley, Surrey, of throat cancer at the country home of his patron and is buried in the churchyard of St Peter's Church, Frimley.*

He never lived to see the long-running West End hit *Salomy Jane* based on his work, or the many silent films that were adapted from his Gold Rush stories.

---

* *His gravestone gives his birth date as 1837.*

James, Henry (1843–1916)
Novelist and short story writer

13 De Vere Mansions, 34 De Vere Gardens, Kensington W8 5AQ 🅟
21 Carlyle Mansions, Cheyne Walk, Chelsea SW3 5LS
3 Bolton Street, Piccadilly, Westminster W1J 8BA (gone)

James knew Europe well by the time he settled in London in 1876, at the age of 34. And he had also written three books – *A Passionate Pilgrim and other Tales*, *Transatlantic Sketches*, and *Roderick Hudson*. He had come to Paris in November 1875 as correspondent for the *New York Tribune*, and there began another novel, *The American*. Here he met fellow writers Gustave Flaubert, Ivan Turgenev, Edmond de Goncourt, Alphonse Daudet and Émile Zola.

New York-born, James had visited London for long stays with his parents as a boy and in 1869 in uncomfortable and dreary lodgings at 7 Half Moon Street, Piccadilly (now incorporated into Flemings Hotel). In December 1876, with $1,350 (which would see him allright for a year) from the *Atlantic Monthly*'s serialisation of *The American*, he settled in 3 Bolton Street, Piccadilly (gone) where he was to live until 1886.

He was to write later: 'I took possession of London. I felt it to be the right place.' At the time he wrote to his brother, the philosopher William James: 'I have done with 'em, and am turning English all over.' His letters of introduction, including one from **Henry Adams**, remedied the fact that he hardly knew a soul. Now James could count TH Huxley, Richard Monckton Milnes, and the anthologist FT Palgrave as friends, and he met William Gladstone, Alfred Tennyson and Robert Browning.

In 1877 he returned to the French capital for three months but otherwise James was in London occupying himself with prolific writing of both journalism and novels. Early in 1878 his *French Poets and Novelists* came out and *Daisy Miller* appeared in the middle of the year, as well as, later that year, *The Europeans*. 'I have certainly become a hopeless, helpless, shameless (and you will add, a bloated,) cockney' he joked to William.

James published prodigiously because he wanted to set aside money to support the writing of his ambitious *The Portrait of a Lady*. This he began in mid-March 1880 in Venice and London, having completed *Washington Square* the month previously, and he finished it at the end of August 1881.

Though London was his home, James's travelling did not cease: from October 1881 to May 1882 (during which time his mother died) he returned on a long-delayed visit to his home country, now a celebrity; and in the autumn of 1882 went off to France for six weeks, which resulted in *A Little Tour in France* (1884).

He was forced to return to the USA later that year due to his father's illness but he arrived in December too late for the funeral. A few years later another stay in Venice produced the *Aspen Papers* and soon after that James was writing in Switzerland, Italy (again) and Paris. His London

Henry James' 70th birthday portrait by John Singer Sargent

circle had widened yet further to include the critic Edmund Gosse, **John Singer Sargent**, his compatriot novelist Constance Fennimore Woolson and the illustrator Gerald du Maurier, whom he would visit in Hampstead.

He wrote to a friend at this time: 'I shall never marry ... I am both happy enough and miserable enough, as it is, and don't wish to add to either side of the account', and there is good reason to believe that he was gay, but chaste. The unmarried state suited his literary work but did not diminish his gift for friendship and socialising. In late 1884 his sister Alice came to live near him so that he could take care of her, with her recurrent and disabling illnesses.

After *The Bostonians*, which he began in London in the summer of 1883, James took to researching at London's Millbank Prison (gone) for *The Princess Casamassima*, his first novel with no major American characters.

After his American publisher went into liquidation, causing him financial loss and the need to borrow $1,000 from his brother, in November 1885 he took a long lease on the fourth-floor apartment in De Vere Gardens to which he moved the following March.

James turned to the theatre when his fiction was not producing the income he needed, sometimes dramatising his own novels (like *The American* which ran at the Comedy Theatre, but for only 70 performances), as well as short stories for the *Yellow Book*. But his foray into the theatre effectively ended dramatically when his *Guy Domville* at the St James Theatre was greeted with (as he related) 'hoots & jeers & catcalls of the roughs, whose *roars* (like those of a cage of beasts at some infernal zoo) were only exacerbated (as it were) by the conflict'.

He returned to fiction but was deeply affected by the deaths of friends in the years ahead, not least Alice, who, tended by James, died of breast cancer on 6th March 1892, while almost two years later Fennimore Woolson seems to have committed suicide in Venice.

Short stories, in the *Chap-Book of Chicago* and *The Atlantic*, were published, as was *The Spoils of Poynton* in 1897, while cycling became a hobby. This is when James began to live in a country home in Rye in Sussex, renting first at Playden, and then, in February 1897, the Vicarage. He returned to London to complete *What Maisie Knew* but came back to lease Lamb House in September of that year.

He purchased the freehold of the flat in De Vere Gardens in 1899 but gave up the lease in 1902 and took rooms at the Reform Club, 105 Pall Mall, as a London base. Despite success, even then James could complain to a friend of economic crises. Short stories, a novella and a novel preceded *The Wings of a Dove*, *The Ambassadors* and *The Golden Bowl*, all written by 1904.

In August 1904 James set sail for the USA, 22 years after his last trip, visiting his brother's family, fellow novelist Edith Wharton, and New York, Philadelphia, Washington, the South, St Louis, Chicago, Los Angeles and San Francisco. Eleven months later he returned to Rye.

Despite a uniform edition of his novels appearing in the USA, a play performed in Edinburgh, travel essays and much other writing, in 1908 the money he made from his pen was the lowest for a quarter of a century.

James was not in good health: he had minor heart problems, he was overweight, he suffered nervous collapse and had digestive problems, and suffered relapses and depression. In 1910 he sailed to the USA with William, who had been staying with him, but William died a week later. In August 1911 James came back to England, settling in London to avoid the winters in Rye.

In 1912 he received an honorary doctorate from Oxford and the following year took a flat at Carlyle Mansions, Cheyne Walk, Chelsea, to which he moved in the new year. When he was 70 friends subscribed to have his portrait (now in the National Portrait Gallery) painted by Sargent, unsmiling, detached, aloof and almost Olympian, which was at variance with the complex and very human person he was.

James continued to write, while giving patriotic support for the UK when the First World War broke out. He became a British citizen in 1915. Ill and increasingly isolated, he suffered a stroke in early December 1915, in which month he was awarded the Order of Merit. He died at Carlyle Mansions in February 1916. His funeral was held at Chelsea Old Church and his ashes were buried in the family plot in Cambridge, Massachusetts.

Kauffer, Edward McKnight (1890–1954)
Dorn, Marion (1896–1964)

Designers

139 and 141 Swan Court, Chelsea Manor Street, Chelsea SW3 5RT Ⓟ

Kauffer had an early start in life when, on leaving school, aged 12 or 13, he became a helper to a scene designer for the grand opera in Evansville, Indiana. By the time he was 17 he was a painter and also left home to join a troupe of travelling players. Three years later Kauffer was working in a San Francisco bookshop and signed up for formal artistic training at the Mark Hopkins Institute of Art.

He adopted the name of a patron, Professor Joseph E McKnight, who helped him study in Paris, where he arrived in 1913 and where the next year he married a compatriot Grace Ehrlich, a concert pianist. The First World War forced them to London, where, as Edward McKnight Kauffer, he soon mixed in artistic circles. He found post-war fame as a poster artist, having, in the year of coming to London, designed posters for the Underground Electric Railways Company.

His work combined Japanese woodcut print and the influence of van Gogh as well as of Futurism, Vorticism and Fauvism. He also produced art work for leading commercial companies and created a street sign, in the Cubist style, for the Poetry Bookshop in Bloomsbury, titles for **Alfred Hitchcock**'s film *The Lodger*, graphics for the British Empire Exhibition of 1924, posters for the Empire Marketing Board, illustrations for Curwen

Press's books and for Francis Meynell's Nonesuch Press. From 1927 to 1929 Kauffer had a spell as a designer at the WS Crawford advertising agency. But Kauffer remained attached to his early painting as a water colourist.

Kauffer came to love his adopted land, where he enjoyed the perceived tradition and calm. He was part of the various artistic groups, like the London Group and Roger Fry's Omega Workshops. He had a gift for friendship and spent time with the poet **TS Eliot**, artist Roger Fry, photographer Man Ray and the writers Aldous Huxley and Marianne Moore.

His success increased with the decades: in the 1930s, he produced work for the Orient Line and Shell-Mex, and a photo-mural in Brighton's art deco Embassy Court, as well as branching out into designing theatrical sets and costumes, including for ballet. In 1936 he became an honorary (being American) royal designer for industry.

While Kauffer and his wife had a daughter, Anne, in 1920 the marriage was failing and from 1923 he and the San Francisco-born textile designer Marion Dorn lived at 17 John Street, Adelphi, Charing Cross (gone), moving in 1931 to Swan Court, Chelsea. In the summer of 1940 they reluctantly left England, at the urging of the US embassy. They married in New York in 1950.

Dorn had been educated at Stanford University and had married her former tutor, the artist Henry Varnum Poor in 1919, when they lived in New York, but the marriage ended the year she began living with Kauffer, whom she had met that year in Paris.

She worked as a graphic and textile artist, extending to the design of interiors, wallpapers and decorative panels and, from 1928, designing carpets for the Wilton Royal Carpet Factory. In the 1930s she switched to woven and printed fabrics. Her work appeared in Claridge's, the Berkeley and the Savoy, as well as limited edition, fine art products. Her eponymous design consultancy was formed in 1934. Dorn's work was widely exhibited in London, Paris, New York and her home city.

Her clients included Noel Coward and Graham Sutherland, but as well as private and corporate clients, there were public commissions as varied as the carpet for the diplomatic reception room at the White House and the moquette seating for the London tube train carriages. In 1957 she was made an honorary fellow of the British Society of Industrial Artists.

Kauffer's inventiveness with poster and book illustration continued in New York but he never had the career in the USA that he had enjoyed on the other side of the Atlantic. He died in New York in October 1954. Dorn lived in retirement in Tangier in Morocco where she died on 28th January 1964 and is buried.

Kennedy, John F (1917–1963)
35th president of the United States
Kennedy, Joseph (1888–1969)
United States ambassador
14 Princes Gate, Knightsbridge SW7 IPT ℗ *

None of the Kennedy family spent very long at the 36-room palatial house in Kensington, a gift to the US government in 1921 by **JP Morgan**. John F Kennedy lived there for the shortest time, and Joseph Kennedy's tenure as US ambassador was a short and not very happy one, lasting only from 1938 to 1940.

The ambassador liked the residence's external appearance – with red geraniums, white daisies and blue forget-me-nots in flower boxes – but was less enamoured with the décor. He wrote to one of President Roosevelt's sons, Jimmy: 'I have a beautiful blue silk room and all I need to make it perfect is a Mother Hubbard dress and a wreath to make me Queen of the May.'

Joseph Kennedy had arrived in 1938 via Plymouth and Rose Kennedy came in late March with five of the couple's nine children: Joe Jnr and Jack were both at Harvard; Rosemary was in a special school; and Eunice was to escort Rosemary when the term ended**. To make room for them all, Rose displaced 26 servants from their upper floor bedrooms. The parents made available a rack of bicycles for the children on the large marble terrace in the garden.

Six-year-old Edward and his 12-year-old brother Robert, who ran the elevator in the ambassadorial residence, went to Gibbs School, 134 Sloane Street, Chelsea. Bobby was good at maths but gave up Latin. When a boy called Cecil in Teddy's class picked on him and stretched his patience to be good, he got his father's permission to be involved in a fight.

Rosemary went to a Montessori school in Hertfordshire and Jean, Eunice and Patricia went to the Sacred Heart Convent in Roehampton. A contemporary described them as 'like birds of paradise, bringing a glamour and

The Kennedy family at Hyannis Port, in 1931 (the year before Edward was born). L–R: Robert Kennedy, John F Kennedy, Eunice Kennedy, Jean Kennedy (on lap of) Joseph P Kennedy Sr, Rose Fitzgerald Kennedy (behind) Patricia Kennedy, Kathleen Kennedy, Joseph P Kennedy Jr (behind) Rosemary Kennedy. (Richard Sears/John F Kennedy Presidential Library and Museum, Boston.)

worldliness that contrasted with the attitude of the dour daughters and displaced European aristocrats and English girls in tweed'. Eunice was said to have a 'rather alarming piety', posing histrionically when praying. But she also chased the ball aggressively and when she shouted when playing field hockey she was informed that nice girls in England did not behave like that. Kathleen, who was educated at the independent girls school Queen's College in central London, and was also an energetic sportswoman, was launched into society and became 'debutante of the year' 1938.

Teddy Kennedy was a particular public favourite, walking his dog Sammy or wearing a Puritan costume. He was photographed at the opening of a zoo, where he patted a zebra who clamped its teeth on his arm. 'I thought I was being eaten by a zebra', he exclaimed.

Kennedy Sr took up his post four days before German troops were ecstatically received in Vienna as Hitler incorporated Austria into the Greater Germany. Czechoslovakia's fate was sealed seven months after that.

The embassy at *4 Grosvenor Gardens*, near Victoria Station, was also a grand house, though that year the embassy was moved to 1 Grosvenor Square (MacDonald House)***, where there were 200 diplomatic staff.

The ambassador made no pretence, like previous holders of his post, to adopt the manners of an English country gentleman. Greeting visitors with his feet on the desk and constantly chewing gum did not win him admirers. However, the press wrote admiringly of his refreshing, authentic unconventionality and one tabloid called him 'The USA's Nine-Child Envoy'. Being American and having a charming family, high society still welcomed them, while the ambassador formed a close relationship with politicians and diplomats, not least Neville Chamberlain, the prime minister, whose own life and personality could not have been more different. (Kennedy and Winston Churchill shared a mutual dislike.)

When Kennedy presented his credentials, as new ambassador, to George VI at the Court of St James, he refused to wear the traditional court dress, which included knee breeches. To be photographed in those, he told the Foreign Secretary Lord Halifax, would 'ruin' him in America. He wore a tailcoat and long trousers and apparently Queen Mary disapproved.

In 1938, when Kennedy and Rose spent a weekend at Windsor Castle, he said to his wife: 'Rose, this is a helluva place – a long way from East Boston'.

In March 1939 the whole family, who were Catholics, went to Rome to attend the coronation of Pius XII, as the ambassador was designated the president's representative (with the exception of Joe Jnr who was stuck in Madrid at the tail end of the Spanish Civil War).

Jack Kennedy, like Joe Jnr, had attended the London School of Economics in 1935 for courses after his time at the college-preparatory Choate Rosemary Hall, Connecticut. In July 1938, at the end of his sophomore year at Harvard, he came back to London to work at the embassy, where Joe worked as secretary to their father, but, more importantly for Jack, to enjoy the social life to which, as an ambassador's son, he easily gained entry. The aristocracy embraced him and regattas, lunches, dances, dinners, balls and races pushed work into the background. In August the family went to the south of France, taking a villa. London and the developing European crisis fired young Jack's imagination as he returned to his junior year at the end of August.

Joe, Jack and 19-year-old Kathleen were at the Commons after the declaration of war on 3rd September 1939 to hear Chamberlain, but the ambassador was an isolationist, who favoured the Munich agreement and urged his president **Franklin Roosevelt** to keep the United States out of the war. Kennedy believed that when war did come, Britain would be defeated. An anti-Semite, he appeared indifferent to the fate of Germany's Jews and told one friend that 'I'd sell a hundred Polands down the river rather than risk the life of one British soldier.'

When Churchill became prime minister in 1940 and as Hitler made further incursions into Europe, the ambassador announced that he'd not stay more than 30 days after the bombing started, and rented a 70-room mansion in Sunningdale, Berkshire. Cowardly, malevolent and pigeon-livered were only three of the charges made by British civil servants.

When the Blitz came Kennedy shocked Britons and Americans in London alike in announcing his return, with his family, to the USA for an indefinite period. All left with the exception of the ambassador and Rosemary, to whom he was devoted, because she was doing well at school. The children in the States sent records of them singing to shorten the distance but eventually Kennedy left on 23rd October 1940. Against his instincts, Kennedy backed Roosevelt for his third term and after the election resigned as ambassador. He then campaigned against his country's entry into the war. Jack served with distinction and was later to return to London as president.

The Kennedy family was never united again. In 1943 Kathleen (or Kick) married the Marquess of Hartington, heir to the Duke of Devonshire, but was widowed four months later when he died on active service in Belgium. She died in an air crash in 1948 with her romantic partner the 8th Earl Fitzwilliam. Joe, too, died in the war, as a pilot, in a flying accident in Suffolk.

---

*   *There are two plaques: one to John Fitzgerald Kennedy, the other to **Junius S Morgan** and **John Pierpont Morgan.***

**   *Jean Kennedy Smith, in her memoir, states that all the children, except Joe and Jack, travelled together.*

***   *No 1 is now 1–3 Grosvenor Square and offices. It was extensively reconstructed reusing almost all the stone, most of the salvaged bricks, replicating the oval room and reusing elements where possible, refurbishing and reusing the old metalwork to the ornate entrance doors and metal railings of the light well. The façade was, according to the architects, carefully reconstructed to its previous glory.*

Losey, Joseph (1909–1984)

Film director

29 Royal Avenue, Chelsea SW3 4QE ℗
60 Queen Anne Street, Marylebone, Westminster W1G 8HP

Joseph Losey had spent 15 months in Italy, France and England, when, in 1953, he first settled in London. By then, at the age of 44, he had had three careers: in pre-war New York theatre and radio, and in Hollywood films.

He had switched from studying medicine to theatre, first as a critic and then as a director but the middle class, mid-west Episcopalian who became a Marxist left his native country because of FBI surveillance on his communist activities. Losey's political thinking was partly influenced by the East German playwright Berthold Brecht, whom he had met in 1936 and who supervised Losey's direction of **Charles Laughton** in 1947 of Brecht's play *Life of Galileo*, in Los Angeles and New York.

Summoned before the House Un-American Activities Committee, Losey renounced Stalinism and ceased political activity but also went into exile in England. Unlike others who fell foul of McCarthyism, Losey's work was often avowedly political, like his *The Living Newspaper* documentary theatre, and documentaries for progressive educational foundations. Yet his animated cartoon *Pete Roleum and his Friends* in 1939 was a plug for American oil interests.

Losey came to London in poor health, plagued by a shortage of money, and with a broken marriage and a son back home. His stay was initially by virtue of never-to-be-guaranteed permits. One person who befriended him was his fellow exile Carl Foreman.

Living at first in Queen Anne Street, his earliest work in Britain – minor TV work and low-budget B movies – was under a pseudonym as he was blacklisted. Losey also made documentaries for the Crown Film Unit, the Post Office and British Transport Films. *Time without Pity* in 1957 was the first British film under his own name. Rank gave him a £1 million contract for three films but lack of their success ended the deal. However, in 1960 *Blind Date* and *The Criminal* and, in 1963, *The Damned*, boosted his reputation in Britain and France.

While he never made films in the USA again, Losey never gave up his American citizenship (although in 1968 he had the short-lived idea of seeking British naturalisation). His stays in England were long: from 1953 to 1975 and from 1983 to 1984, living in France from 1975 to 1982. Britain was largely his base and he often used British actors, but he was a truly European director. His most renowned collaboration was with the English dramatist Harold Pinter, who scripted *The Servant* (1963), *Accident* (1967), and *The Go-Between* (1971). Other films made in Britain were *King and Country* (1964), *Modesty Blaise* (1966), *Boom!* (1968) and *Secret Ceremony* (1968).

Though his 'Pinter' films differed in subject matter, they were linked by themes reflected elsewhere in Losey's work: power relations, class and sexuality. He created a personal genre that spanned popular and arthouse cinema.

His films made overseas included *The Assassination of Trotsky* (1972), *A Doll's House* (1973), *Galileo* (1975), *The Romantic Englishwoman* (1975) and (in France) *Mr Klein* (1976), *Les Routes du Sud* (1978), *Don Giovanni* (1979) and *La Truite* (1982).

The high regard which Losey gained from critics, the public and fellow actors and directors still did not avoid the strain and stress of large numbers of projects often abandoned for financial reasons.

Large and physically imposing, Losey suffered from asthma and drank heavily in later life. He married four times and had two sons, born 19 years apart, with his first and third wives. He had donated his archive to the British Film Institute before his death from cancer on 22nd June 1984 at his Chelsea home, where he had lived since 1966. He was cremated at Putney Vale crematorium.

Morgan, Junius Spencer (1813–1890)
Morgan Snr, John Pierpont (1837–1913)
Financiers
14 Princes Gate, Kensington SW7 1PT Ⓟ*

In 1853 John Pierpont Morgan travelled on his own to London, arriving at Southampton and then travelling to Manchester to meet his parents, Junius and Juliet, who had come from the United States via Liverpool. When Morgan arrived at Southampton, a private railway car was attached to the train to take him to London. In London they stayed at the Ellis Hotel, St James's Street (gone), visited **St Paul's Cathedral** and attended services at **St George's Church**, Hanover Square. At the Bank of England 'I held 1,000,000 pounds in my hands', the son boasted. They went to Germany and Paris, and when back in London took lodgings at 38 Jermyn Street, Piccadilly (gone), the next day seeing Queen Victoria and

JP Morgan in 1903

Prince Albert at a military camp at Cobham, Surrey. The family had ten days in Scotland before returning to America on 23rd July.

Junius had come to London in 1854 and stayed for 23 years, when he entered the firm of **George Peabody**, succeeding as its head ten years later when he renamed it JS Morgan & Co. In 1874 he had leased Princes Gate (he purchased it sometime between 1857 and 1859) and it was here that John Pierpont came with his family in July 1871 to stay with his parents. A fortnight later they travelled to Paris and then to Pau, Germany and Austria, Rome, Cairo and in the autumn he sailed home.

Later, when John Pierpont Morgan was in England for almost a year he often stayed at Dover House (gone), the Georgian lodge and family home in Roehampton, which stood in 92 acres of woodlands, ornamental gardens and pasture, with greenhouses, stables and barns and grazing cattle. There he held his famous Fourth of July parties. Work in the London office at 22 Old Broad Street (gone) in the City of London never got in the way of the dinners and parties as part of the London season, and opera in the Royal Opera House, Covent Garden. He holidayed in Scotland and the Lake District, Egypt and Italy.

JP Morgan was married twice (his first wife died four months after their marriage). With his wife, Frances Tracy, he had four children: Louisa, John Pierpont Jnr, Juliet and Anne. When John Pierpont Jnr arrived in London in 1898 his father gave him and his wife Jane use of 13 Princes Gate. In 1904 he purchased No 14 and joined the two townhouses. According to the family's biographer, Ron Chernow: 'The original house now had the magnificence of a great museum and was resplendent with oils by Velasquez, Rubens, Rembrandt and Turner – export duties kept Pierpont from taking the collection to America'.

Every evening, whether John Jnr was resident or not, servants would place periodicals and warm milk by his bed and adjust the reading light. He and Jane had two boys, Junius Spencer Jnr and Henry Sturgis (both born in London) and three girls, Jane and Florence, while Alice died at a young age. There were family prayers and the reading of Dickens and Thackeray and strolls in nearby Hyde Park. The girls' lives were restricted – they never went to school but had private tutors, and their father believed that higher education made young women less feminine. They were not allowed to talk to strangers and came to see their upbringing as a suffocating round of social duties.

Life was a gilded cage. The liberal statesman Earl Grey and Florence Nightingale were neighbours, while the writers Rudyard Kipling, **Henry James**, Sir James Barrie and **Mark Twain** came to dinner. Jane had been reluctant to come to London but it soon reminded her of her native Boston and she became a convinced Anglophile. Her husband saw England as a second home, so much so that he expressed a dewy-eyed patriotism. In

February 1898 he donned a cocked hat and took a sword to accompany his wife to be presented to the Queen in the throne room of Buckingham Palace, something unknown for Americans, let alone industrialists.

John Jnr inherited the house in 1913 and, during the First World War, loaned it to the Council of War Relief for the Professional Classes, who used it as a maternity home. In 1921 he gave the house to the US government and it became the residence of the ambassador to the UK until 1955, when the official residence moved to **Winfield House**.

* *There are two plaques on the building: one to the Morgans and the other to* **John F Kennedy***.*

Pound, Ezra (1885–1972)

Poet

10 Kensington Church Walk, Kensington W8 4NB ℗
5 Holland Place Chambers, Kensington W8 4LS
48 Langham Street, Fitzrovia, Westminster W1W 7AR

Pound, born in Idaho and one of the most revolutionary poets of the 20th century, lived in London from 1908 to 1920, which were to be formative years, not least due to the characters and life of the city he absorbed into his work. He chose the city because it was home to WB Yeats, whom he revered and with whom he struck up a friendship. He believed, too, that London had a literary culture in which he could thrive.

Ezra Pound's home in Kensington Church Walk

Helped with a monthly £4 allowance from his father, Pound moved around a bit in his new adopted home, taking lodgings for a while, then moving to Langham Street, which features in his *Pisan Cantos* written four decades later. He did not stay in either place long because a year after his arrival he went to live in Kensington Church Walk, his home until 1914. He lived in a top floor bed-sitting room and extolled his landlords, Mr and Mrs Langley, as positively the best that England can produce at ANY level.

To this house came a veritable roll call of early 20th Century writers: Ford Madox Ford, William Carlos Williams, DH Lawrence and **Hilda Doolittle** (to whom Pound had been engaged), and his compatriot Robert Frost, then living in Beaconsfield, who once found him in the bath. Another visitor was the artist Henri Gaudier-Brzeska. Pound offered them tea, lit the gas fire and expounded his wisdom, often in several languages. It was not far to walk to 80 Campbell Hill, where Ford, founder of the *English Review* lived, and where Ford and his common law wife Violet Hunt, held salons.

Ezra Pound in 1917 during the London years

In 1912 Pound coined the phrase 'imagism' to describe clarity, precision and economy in poetry, dubbing Doolittle 'HD Imagiste', and in 1914 he was a founder of the Vorticists. All of these were signs of his radical advocacy of artistic innovations in literature, painting, sculpture, and music.

The years in Kensington Church Walk were productive ones for the poet as he produced *Persona* and *Exultations*, both in 1909, and *Ripostes* three years later. He promoted James Joyce and **TS Eliot**, assisting his fellow American financially. In 1917, Pound encouraged Eliot to publish a critique, *Ezra Pound: his Metric and Poetry*. In 1922, by which time he was in Paris, Pound edited Eliot's *The Waste Land*.

But while creative, Pound could also be violently oppositional. Unsurprisingly, given their contrasting outlooks and styles, he took against the Georgian group, who numbered Robert Frost, John Masefield and Rupert Brooke. He challenged one of them, Lascelles Abercrombie, to a duel, accusing him of 'stupidity [which] carried beyond a certain point becomes a public menace'. His opponent chose unsold copies of their own books as weapons, a joke that even Pound appreciated.

Pound would study at the British Museum Library in the day and write in the evening. His *Spirit of Romance*, published in 1910, was based on lectures he had given at the London Polytechnic the previous year. One of those attending was the novelist and friend of Yeats, Olivia Shakespear, and her artist-daughter Dorothy Shakespear. Pound and Dorothy married in 1914, moving to Holland Place Chambers, and her independent means helped him continue to avoid the inconveniences of regular work. Though lacking formal musical training Pound served as music critic of the *New Age* when in London.

It was at a concert that he met American violinist Olga Rudge, with whom he began a life-long relationship when in Paris, and two years later they became parents of a daughter, Mary. This caused a long separation between Dorothy and Pound during which time she became pregnant with a son, Omar, whom Pound regarded as his own.

In 1916 he produced *Lustra*, most of which had been written in Kensington Church Walk. It is often regarded as the best fruit of Pound's London years, with translations from Chinese and Provençal, along with manifestos, epigrams and love poetry. It also shows great humanity towards those of whom he writes.

In 1920 the Pounds left for four years in Paris, but returned to Italy (he had come to London from Venice). As that decade darkened with the rise of fascism Pound's political sympathies were firmly with Mussolini and Nazi Germany, influenced by banking and high interest rates and a few big Jews, as his *Canto 52* puts it.

In the war he broadcast for the fascists for Radio Rome, often lacing what he had to say with virulent anti-semiitism. He was arrested by the victorious American forces and held in an army prison camp, and, after being judged mentally incompetent to be tried for treason, Pound was incarcerated in St Elizabeth's psychiatric hospital in Washington DC until 1958. London remained in his deeply disturbed and malevolent mind: in his *Pisan Cantos* he recalled the teashop in Holland Street, Mrs Langley and the bells of St Mary Abbots (the latter less kindly – he blamed their tolling for his state of mind) and meeting **Henry James**. The poems received the Bollingen Prize in 1949, to much outrage.

Pound was released in 1958, giving the fascist salute upon arrival in Italy, where he spent the rest of his life, sometimes with Dorothy (who later moved back to London), and at others with Olga.

He returned to London in 1963 for Eliot's funeral and died in Venice two days after his 87th birthday.

Sargent, John Singer (1856–1925)

Portrait and landscape painter and muralist

31 and 33 Tite Street, Chelsea SW3 4JP Ⓟ

Sargent, who died the most famous portrait painter of his day, was an American who spent little time living in his native country (and then only in his mature years) but was nonetheless attached to it, his American relatives and his New England ancestry. Born in Florence to American parents, both from wealthy families – his father's were in shipping, his mother's merchants – much of Sargent's childhood was spent travelling in Europe. His parents had come to Europe when their first-born had died and, while intending to return to the USA, became expatriates.

He did not visit the USA until he was 21 years of age, and while he made his home in London from 1885, he was a cosmopolitan, and, like his mother drawn to travel. At home in Italy, France and Germany, Sargent also visited the Holy Land between 1905 and 1906.

Sargent studied at Florence's Accademia di Belle Arti before, at the age of 18, entering a Paris studio as a student and then assistant, where he remained until 1878. He lived in Paris until his move to London in 1885 and during that time he exhibited his first portrait at the Paris Salon, and had also travelled in Spain, Morocco and the USA.

He took his own studio in 1883 at 41 Boulevard Berthier (he twice painted a portrait of his friend Claude Monet) but his move to London was, to an extent, forced: his portrait *Madame X* was shown at the Salon in 1884, causing a scandal and alienating many of Sargent's admirers, who considered it risqué, with the subject in a low-cut, nearly sleeveless dress.

In London Sargent was a founding member of the New English Art Club, but before his move he had exhibited at the Royal Academy (he was made an associate in 1894) and the Grosvenor Gallery. Three years after settling in London he had a one-man exhibition at the St Botolph Club in Boston, Massachusetts, and an exhibition later in New York.

Sargent enjoyed summers in the English countryside with parties of male friends, who included **Henry James**, which inspired landscapes, figure studies, river scenes and still lifes. He took over The Studios at No 33 Tite Street from **James McNeill Whistler** in 1886 and moved to No 31 in 1901, meaning he had two studios, where he painted until his death.

It was his showing at London's Royal Academy of his *Carnation, Lily, Lily, Rose*, painted between 1885 and 1886, which established Sargent's British reputation, as well as showing the influence of Impressionism on his work. That reputation became such that his sitters would include the actress Dame Ellen Terry; the art dealer Asher Wertheimer and his family; and the writers Robert Louis Stevenson, Coventry Patmore and Henry James, as well as Sargent's famous Sitwell family group. As well as James, other Americans sought his brush, like **Lady Jennie Churchill**; while on trips to

John Singer Sargent's home in Tite Street (Terry Philpot)

America he received commissions from **Theodore Roosevelt** (when president) and the Rockefellers and Vanderbilts. Among his students was the young Vanessa Bell.

Sargent was a man who valued his privacy and independence: he may have memorialised the establishment but he was never one of its number, and in 1918 refused the presidency of the Royal Academy. He did not, however, refuse all honours – there were several honorary degrees and the Légion d'honneur in 1889, the French Order of Merit and, in 1909, the Belgian Order of Leopold. His American citizenship, which he never renounced, precluded the offer of a knighthood.

However, while his fame as a portrait painter endures, Sargent had given up the genre, of which he had grown tired, by 1910, save for the occasional portrait (most importantly that of James for his sitter's 70th birthday in 1913). Instead he devoted himself to landscapes, and painted murals in the Boston Public Library and, later, a decorative scheme for the Boston Museum of Fine Arts.

He had visited the Western Front in the First World War at the government's invitation and it was an official commission that produced *Gassed* (1919), said to be the best work of war art, which is now in London's Imperial War Museum.

Sargent was a striking-looking man, over 6 feet tall, with dark hair and a full beard. Even in his studio he wore well-cut, bespoke suits and smoked cigars, and was, according to his friend and fellow artist Sir William Rothenstein, possessed of a 'gargantuan appetite'. Immensely sociable and a keen mimic yet, as Cynthia Asquith, wife of the prime minister and diarist, recalled a 'curiously inarticulate man, he used to splutter and gasp, almost growl with the strain of trying to express himself; and sometimes, like Macbeth at the dagger, he would literally clutch at the air in frustrated efforts to find, with many intermediary "ers" and "ums", the most ordinary words'.

Apart from a brief romance in Paris, there were never any close relationships with women, and while there has been discussion that he was gay, of this there is no evidence, although he did execute an unusually large number of works of naked men. He was, though, deeply attached to friendship and family, and especially to his two sisters. One, Violet, had six children, and when Sargent's father died in 1889 he assumed the role as head of the family.

Professionally, his great energy produced 1,200 oils, 1,000 water colours, three cycles of murals and countless drawings.

Sargent was preparing to travel to Boston to complete the installation of the library murals, when he died of a heart attack in his sleep at 31 Tite Street. There was a memorial service at **Westminster Abbey** and burial at Brookwood Cemetery, Woking in Surrey.

Thompson, Sir Benjamin, Count Rumford (1753–1814)

Soldier, physicist and inventor

168 Brompton Road (formerly 45 Brompton Row), Knightsbridge SW3 1HW **ⓟ**

Some Americans receive knighthoods, a title they can use if they are British citizens, but few, if any, also become counts of the Holy Roman Empire. Thompson achieved both but then Thompson, who was born in Woburn, Massachusetts, was an unusual man who led a very varied and unusual life.

He attended school in rural Massachusetts and would sometimes walk to Cambridge to hear lectures. He took lessons from the local minister and showed an aptitude for algebra, geometry, astronomy and mathematics. At 13 Thompson was apprenticed to a merchant in Salem and later to a doctor. At 16 he was carrying out experiments on the nature of heat.

His prospects were few until he married a widowed heiress named Sarah Rolfe, who had been left property in Concord, New Hampshire, by her late husband. She persuaded the governor to appoint her new husband as a major in the state militia.

Thompson was opposed to the colonists' revolt against the British and recruited loyalists, which led to the family home being attacked and to him fleeing behind British lines, leaving his wife and daughter, also called Sarah, to whom he never returned. He became an adviser to General **Thomas Gage**, serving as a lieutenant-colonel of the King's American Dragoons.

His position allowed him to experiment with gun powder. The result of his work being published in a learned journal was a trip to London at the end of the war, acclaimed as a scientist.

In 1785 Thompson was in Bavaria, where he would spend 11 years, as an *aide de camp* to the Prince-elector Charles Theodore. He became minister for the army and undertook its reorganisation, as well as doing the same for workhouses. He invented a soup named after him and established potato cultivation in the principality. There were other experiments and the creation of the Englischer Garten in Munich, which is today one of the world's largest urban parks.

Thompson's former compatriots seem to have forgiven his betrayal because in 1789 he was elected a foreign honorary member of the American Academy of Arts and Sciences although, 10 years earlier, aged 26, he had been elected a member of the Royal Academy. Two years later he was made a count of the Holy Roman Empire, taking his title from Rumford, New Hampshire, where, ironically, he had been married.

His scientific work continued as he devised a way of measuring heat as a solid substance and investigated the insulating properties of various materials, including fur, wool and feathers. His further work on heat was important when, later in the 19th century, the laws on the conservation of energy were established. Thompson invented a percolating coffee pot, a kitchen range and the double boiler. He modified the design of chimneys and cooking stoves, fireplaces and industrial furnaces, and kilns producing quicklime. He also worked on the measurement of light.

He returned to London in 1798 and the next year, with Joseph Banks, created the Royal Institution.

Sarah had died, and in 1804 he married Marie-Anne Lavoisier, herself a chemist of noble birth and widow of the chemist Antoine Lavoisier. They separated after three years but Thompson continued his scientific work in Paris until his death.

Twain, Mark (1835–1910)

Writer and humorist

23 Tedworth Square, Chelsea SW3 4DR Ⓟ

Samuel Langhorne Clemens, who became Mark Twain in 1863, grew up in Hannibal, Missouri, and could claim English and Scots-Irish descent. His belief that 'when I stand under the English flag, I am not a stranger', expressed on his last visit to London in 1907, testifies to his affection for England. The feeling was mutual.

He made several trips to Britain and Europe before that last trip and in 1900 he was in London when he declared himself an anti-imperialist. It is said that it was on this visit that he cabled the Press Association, on hearing that an American newspaper had reported him as being gravely ill: 'The report of my death was an exaggeration.'

Twain came in 1872 hoping to gather material for a book which

Tedworth Square, where Mark Twain stayed on his last visit to London (Terry Philpot)

was never written. Whether this was due to 'too much dining – too much sociability', as he remarked in his journal, we do not know, but he did keep a detailed diary and wrote a spoof guidebook, which remains unpublished.

He gained a ticket for the reading room of the British Museum (now situated in the British Library), and told an audience:

The Library at the British Museum I find particularly astounding. I have read there hours together & hardly made an impression on it. I revere that library. It is the author's friend. I don't care how mean a book is, it always takes one copy. And then, every day that author goes there to gaze at that book, & is encouraged to go on in the good work. And what a touching sight it is of a Saturday afternoon to see the poor toil-worn clergymen gathered together in that vast reading-room cabbaging sermons for Sunday!

In September, a month after arriving, Twain wrote to his wife Olivia (Livy) of his amazement at the reception he had received – applause when his name was read out from a guest list for a dinner in the City of London. He wrote that:

> … when he came to my name along with the rest, there was such a storm of applause as you never heard. The applause continued, & they could not go on with the list. I was never so taken aback in my life – never stricken so speechless – for it was totally unlocked-for [*sic*] on my part. I thought I was the humblest in that great titled assemblage – & behold, mine was the *only* name in the long list that called forth this splendid compliment.

That November, when about to return home, the Lord Chancellor told Twain that 'when affairs of state oppress him & he can't sleep, he always has my books at hand & forgets his perplexities in reading them!'

This was perhaps surprising. Twain was only 37 and while he had published several short stories by this time, there were only two short story collections, a book of essays and two volumes of non-fiction, *Innocents Abroad* and (that year) *Roughing It*. *The Gilded Age* did not appear until the next year and *The Adventures of Tom Sawyer* a year after that, while *The Adventures of Huckleberry Finn* was not published until 1884.

In May 1873 he sailed from New York, this time with Livy and their 14-month-old daughter, Olivia, known as Susy, together with Clara Spaulding, his wife's childhood friend. (The couple were to have three daughters, two of whom predeceased him, as did his 18-month-old son Langdon in 1872.)

In July the party went to Edinburgh, 'fleeing thither for rest and refuge', as Twain later expressed it, and then to Ireland. Back in London, he visited a gallery given over entirely to the works of Gustave Doré. He described *Christ Leaving the Praetorium*, a large work which the artist had just completed, as 'the greatest work of art that I have ever seen.' However, Twain's seriousness was offset by his humour for he produced a sketch of gallery employees too eager to sell engravings to visitors. In October, to public demand, he began a series of lectures.

In 1899 he was in London twice, both times seeking treatment for his daughter Jean's ill health. In the middle of 1900 Twain stayed as a guest of Hugh Gilzean-Read, a newspaper proprietor, at his home, Dollis Hill House, Dollis Hill Lane, Brent (gone: ruins in what is now Gladstone Park). Twain spoke of the 'paradise' of Dollis Hill and wrote that he had 'never seen any place that was so satisfactorily situated, with its noble trees and stretch of country, and everything that went to make life delightful, and all within a biscuit's throw of the metropolis of the world'.

Livy died in Florence in 1904 and Twain came back to London for the last time in 1907, now one of the most famous authors in the world. He arrived at Tilbury where, he said, the stevedores greeted him with 'a welcome which went to the marrow'. His daughter Clara said of the Tedworth Square house that her family 'loved that cosy little house and the entire surrounding region' and remembered her father rising at four or five in the morning to write.

While here Twain was given an honorary degree by Oxford University, remarking: 'I never expected to cross the water again, but I would be willing to journey to Mars for that Oxford degree.' When he was in Oxford he told one student, a maharajah: 'I like the degree well enough, but I'm crazy about the clothes! I wish I could wear 'em day and night … If there's a dearth of Maharajahs any time in India, just cable me, sir, and I'll take the next train.'

He was not joking about his fondness for the gown for he would often wear it at home, and even did so when his daughter Clara married in 1909.

One other honour bestowed on him was honorary membership of London's Beefsteak Club. Told that only three other men had been so honoured and that one was the Prince of Wales, Twain responded: 'Well, it must make the Prince feel mighty fine'.

Before he left for the USA, Twain attended a banquet held in his honour, in Liverpool, given by the Lord Mayor, with a Member of Parliament proposing the toast.

Thirty five years after his first visit to England, with an honorary doctorate in his pocket and civic acclaim in his memory, the former printer, steamboat pilot, gold miner and journalist, whom the novelist William Faulkner would call 'the father of American literature', set sail for home for the last time.

Welch, Elisabeth (1904–2003)

Singer, actress and cabaret artist

1 Ovington Court, Ovington Gardens, off Brompton Road, Kensington SW5 1LB Ⓟ

Welch, born in West 23rd Street, New York, of indigenous, African-American, Scottish and Irish ancestry, came to London in 1933 and died there aged 99.

She began singing in a Baptist church choir and early on set her sights on becoming a professional singer, making her debut when she was 22 in an early black Broadway show, *Runnin' Wild*. In this she sang *Charleston*, which introduced a new dance. That decade, too, she appeared in a variety of New York shows but made very few sound recordings.

In 1929 Welch went to Paris where she appeared at the Moulin Rouge with her fellow black American Josephine Baker and in other cabarets. In 1931 she sang *As Time Goes By* in cabaret, a decade before it became popular through *Casablanca*. Back in New York she sang Cole Porter's *Love for Sale*.

Welch's first London role was in an all-black revue in which Porter saw her and asked her to appear in his *Nymph Errant* in 1933. (Ivor Novello saw her in *Nymph Errant* and gave her a part in his *Glamorous Night*.) Before she opened in Porter's musical she appeared in London in *Dark Things*, and sang *Stormy Weather*, with which she would always be associated. After that Welch made London her permanent home and in 1933 moved to an apartment in this block, where she lived until 1936. That was the year that her husband, an American musician named Luke Smith, whom she had married in 1924 and separated from in 1928, died.

Elisabeth Welch in her Kensington home in 1975
(Allan Warren)

As an interpreter of popular songs – from George Gershwin to Noel Coward – in the 1930s she became one of the first artists to appear on television and also made films, often as a singer, including two with **Paul Robeson**. Her film career lasted until 1979 when Derek Jarman cast her in *The Tempest*, in which she sang *Stormy Weather* and played the Goddess.

During the Second World War her affair with David Astor was put paid to by his mother **Nancy Astor** objecting to Welch being black. Welch entertained the armed forces, appearing with John Gielgud, Michael Wilding and Edith

Evans in Gibraltar and also touring the Middle East. In the post-war years she was frequently in West End revues, one-woman shows, and on radio and television, even once appearing in *Aladdin*, and in the Royal Variety Performance in 1979 and 1986.

She was on stage in New York in 1980 and again in the city in 1986. This was when her one-woman show earned her an Obie Award. A Tony nomination came for her part in *Jerome Kern Goes to Hollywood*. When she was 93 she sang *Stormy Weather* for a television documentary.

Welch died at the age of 99 in the entertainers' retirement home, Denville Hall, in west London, to which she had moved four years previously, and where her ashes were scattered in the garden.

Whistler, James Abbott McNeill (1834–1903)

Painter

96 Cheyne Walk, Chelsea SW10 0DQ
(formerly 2 Lindsey Row) Ⓟ *
31 and 33 Tite Street, Chelsea SW3 4JP
74 Cheyne Walk, Chelsea SW3 5TT (gone)

James McNeill Whistler in 1885
(Library of Congress)

Whistler, born in Lowell, Massachusetts, and his brother William, were the only two of the five sons of their well-to-do parents to survive infancy. He was nine when the family moved to Russia where his father was appointed engineer of the Moscow-St Petersburg railway. Young Jimmy began taking drawing classes at the Imperial Capital of Fine Arts in St Petersburg, which determined him on painting, when he had hoped to follow his father in graduating from West Point and then become an architect or engineer.

In 1849 Whistler lived in London with his half-sister Deborah and her husband the etcher and surgeon Francis Seymour Haden at their home at 62, Sloane Street, Chelsea (gone). Haden encouraged his young relative, taking him to the Royal Academy and introducing him into the artistic and scientific circles of South Kensington.

Whistler's father died of cholera and the family went back to the USA, less provided for than when they had left, and James and William spent two years at school in Connecticut. He excelled at drawing (in 1852 he published his first work, the lithographed title-page to *United States Military Academy: Song of the Graduates*) but after two years had to leave because he failed at chemistry.

By late 1854 Whistler was in the drawing division of the US coast and geodetic survey, Washington, DC, where he etched topographical plates and maps, but left the following February.

He had taken up portrait painting and a relative, Thomas Winans, paid for him to study art in Paris in September 1855, while his half-brother George supported him by buying his etchings and pictures. Here he studied at the École Impériale et Spéciale de Dessin, entered the studio of Charles Gleyre, and, living for four years in the Latin Quarter, became friends with English artists and the illustrator and novelist George du Maurier.

Whistler left the French capital for London in 1859, living again with the Hadens and later taking rooms in Newman Street, Fitzrovia, with du Maurier. In the first two years he made etchings of the Thames (*The Thames Set*). In 1862 he met the poet Algernon Charles Swinburne, with whom he became intimate, and whose theory of art for art's sake had a profound influence on him.

He made an extended stay in the south of France, and in 1865 exhibited at the Royal Academy. In 1866 he leased the house in 96 Cheyne Walk and Anna, his mother, came to live with him and there he painted her famous portrait, *Arrangement in Grey and Black*. He held his 'Sunday breakfasts here for fellow artists' and lived here until late 1878. However, recognition eluded him (he failed to be elected to the Royal Academy) and family relationships worsened when, in 1867, the friendship of Haden and Whistler ended.

In 1870 Whistler fathered James Whistler Hanson (who later became his secretary), with a parlour maid Louisa Hanson. Seven years later, Maud Franklin, an artist and his model, gave birth to Maud McNeill Whistler Franklin, who may not have survived infancy. The couple had another child, Ióne, who was probably born in 1877.

An exhibition at the gallery at 148 Pall Mall, which Whistler took on a year's lease in 1874, was so well received that his portrait painting was compared to Velázquez, to which Whistler responded, 'Why drag in Velasquez?'

Whistler came to be seen by a younger generation, among them Walter Sickert, as a leader in modern painting. One of these, Mortimer Menpes, described him as 'slight, small-boned, and extremely dainty'.

He was also an art critic, who often took fellow critics to task, but when, in 1877, *Nocturne in Black and Gold: the Falling Rocket* was exhibited at Grosvenor Gallery, it provoked the wrath of the critic John Ruskin, who denounced the work as 'a pot of paint thrown in the public's face'. Whistler sued and in 1878 the jury awarded him damages of only one farthing (he had asked for £10,000).

Whistler had moved to 31 Tite Street in 1878 and lived there for a year because in 1877 he had his friend the architect EW Godwin design the White House, 35 Tite Street (gone) that would be both studio for his growing practice of portrait painting, a home and a place to entertain. However, the debts created by the project and the cost of the libel action caused his bankruptcy and the loss of the White House after only a year. Schemes to make money had failed and he had been forced to sell work for less than it was worth. Oscar Wilde bought some household effects and art at an auction.

Whistler's relationship with Wilde gained public attention through the humorous telegrams they exchanged in *The World* in 1883. However, Whistler's affection for Wilde frayed when he resented his role as spokesman for the aesthetic movement in England and America. By the time they were neighbours again in Tite Street (Whistler was then at the *Tower House, 46 Tite Street* from 1888 to 1889), the relationship was acrimonious and ended when Whistler accused the playwright of plagiarism in an article in *Truth* in 1890.

In 1879 Whistler moved to Venice for 14 months and in 1881 moved to 33 Tite Street, where he lived until 1884**. In 1888 Whistler married Beatrice Godwin, widow of his architect friend and herself an artist and designer. They lived in Paris and travelled in France and then settled in the Tower House in 1888, which they left in 1889 and moved to 21 Cheyne Row. Six years later they moved to St Jude's Cottage Hampstead (gone), where Beatrice died of cancer in 1896.

Whistler was garlanded (in 1892 he was made officer of the Légion d'honneur); there were banquets in his honour in Paris and London; and exhibitions were held in London, Paris, Munich, New York, Philadelphia and St Petersburg.

After Beatrice's death her younger sister, Rosalind Birnie Philip, became Whistler's secretary, ward and executor. He spent much time travelling – in 1900 to Holland, Dublin, Gibraltar, Algiers, Tangier, Marseilles and then Corsica, where he stayed until the following May.

In April 1902 Whistler moved from Paris to lease 74 Cheyne Walk in May, where he lived with Birnie Philip. He died at his home in 1903 of heart failure.

---

* A statue of Whistler stands in Cheyne Walk.

****John Singer Sargent** took over No 33 from 1886 to 1925 and also lived at No 31 from 1901 to 1925, where he died. The stone plaque on No 31 is to Sargent.

McMillan, Margaret (1860–1931)
Pioneer of nursery education and socialist propagandist
McMillan, Rachel (1859–1917)
Health visitor and educationalist
51 Tweedy Road, Bromley BR1 3HN ℗

The only two surviving children of Scottish immigrants, Margaret and Rachel were both born in Westchester County, New York State. They came to Scotland with their mother, Jane, following their father's death, when they were about five and four years old, respectively. Their early education was in Inverness and after that, to prepare herself for a career as a governess, Margaret spent time in boarding schools in Frankfurt am Main, Geneva and Lausanne. She returned to work as a governess in the English shires.

After leaving school, Rachel spent three years teaching at the Ladies College, Coventry. But, in 1877, when her mother and grandfather died, she came home to nurse her widowed grandmother for 11 years. In Edinburgh she was drawn into involvement, through some cousins, with local socialists. In 1888 she became a junior superintendent of a hostel for working young women in Bloomsbury, London.

Margaret came to live with her sister in London and worked as a volunteer in the settlement movement. She also trained for an abortive career as an actress. She had been drawn to socialism when a governess and now both sisters attended socialist meetings, became members of the Fabian Society and met Keir Hardie, William Morris, George Bernard Shaw and others.

Caroline Steedman says in her entry on Margaret in the *Oxford Dictionary of National Biography* that, despite her fame for her later work with children (which tended to be lauded after her death), her 'main importance now lies in her successful career as a female political propagandist, her original theory of agency and childhood, and the light that both these factors throw on the relationship of the personal and the political in late nineteenth-century British socialism, and on ethical socialism itself'.

In 1893 both sisters moved to Bradford, although Rachel did not stay. After working in 1895 as secretary to the Women's Industrial Council in Liverpool, she returned to the capital to qualify as inspector of nuisances. The next year she joined Kent County Council as a peripatetic teacher of hygiene, essentially pioneering what became health visiting, a job she did until 1913.

In Bradford Margaret joined the Independent Labour Party, taught adult education, worked for Robert Blatchford's *Clarion*, spoke at meetings (an unusual thing for a woman then) and in 1895 published her only novel, *Samson*. She was also elected to the local school board. This brought her face-to-face with the plight of children: the neglect, poverty and preventable illnesses. She wrote pamphlets for parents about hygiene, while campaigning for school medical inspections, school clinics and school meals.

In 1903 Margaret was back in London to live with Rachel, who was renting the house in Bromley. Here left-wing luminaries like Prince Kropotkin, the Lansburys, Margaret Llewelyn Davies, and the Countess of Warwick came to tea. Margaret's journalism continued and she taught for the newly founded Workers Educational Association, while also lecturing for the Ethical Society.

Margaret, shocked by the conditions she had seen in Bradford, now faced them in London, and took on the part-paid and part-voluntary job of manager of a group of Deptford elementary schools in 1903. She also campaigned for the medical inspection of school children. Rachel gave her financial support, as did the wealthy, Virginia-born politically radical soap manufacturer Joseph Fels so that she could open an experimental school clinic at Bow, east London. This led to the Deptford Clinic opening in 1910, out of which grew the Camp School (an open-air nursery school) in 1911, which the sisters ran together. These endeavours put equal emphasis on children's physical and intellectual development.

In the Camp School, children had to be exposed to 'the great healers, earth, sun, air, sleep and joy'. To that end Margaret took especial interest in the design and layout of the buildings so, for example, 'the walls at either end shaped in butterfly form to catch all the sunshine possible'. Maximum light and ease of access to the outside would be ensured by roof lights and movable walls.

Margaret referred to the nursery school as 'a place where living things are taken care of so that at least they spring up into things of beauty and colour and perfume. Those who do all this culture work will be cultured. The little gardeners themselves, not the flowers or the vegetables or the trees, will be the glory of the garden'.

Rachel became exhausted by the strains of her work at the Camp School and of nursing Margaret though illness, and this stress led to her premature death in 1917 at her Deptford, south London, home.

Only much later, and particularly through her biography in 1927, did Margaret attribute much of her thinking and educational philosophy to her sister: it was she who had conceived of the health centre and Camp School.

Margaret memorialised Rachel when she founded the Rachel McMillan Training College for teacher training. Steerman remarks: 'Rachel McMillan's interest for modern times must be the way in which she emerged from a traditional and sheltered background of helpful Victorian girlhood to pursue a career in the new forms of social and health care work that emerged at the end of the nineteenth century.'

Created a Companion of Honour in 1930, Margaret died at the Bowden House Nursing Home, Harrow on the Hill, then Middlesex, in 1931. The sisters are buried in the same grave in Brockley Cemetery, south London.

SOUTHWARK

Harvard, John (1607–1638)

Benefactor of Harvard University

St Saviour's Church (now Southwark Cathedral), London Bridge SE1 9DA

John Harvard's statue at Harvard University, an idealised representation as it is unknown what he looked like

Harvard was baptised on 27th November 1607 at St Saviour's Church, Southwark. Robert, his father, was a butcher and, with his second wife Katherine Rogers, from Stratford-upon-Avon, had nine children, of whom Harvard was the fourth.

Robert, whose business was in Pepper Alley, held a number of important posts in the parish, including those of vestryman, churchwarden, overseer of the poor and a governor of the parish grammar school, which his son probably attended.

However, in the summer of 1625, when Harvard was 17, Robert died of the plague. It devastated the family for his half-sister from his father's first marriage and two brothers also died. Harvard had already seen the death of four other siblings and half-siblings and only his mother, his brother Thomas and himself survived to come into a comfortable legacy. The death of his mother's subsequent well-to-do husband added to the family's fortune.

His father's legacy opened up new possibilities for Harvard, whose education had not continued after the grammar school, and he entered Emmanuel College, Cambridge, in late 1627, supported by his own financial resources.

He gained a BA and then an MA and by 1637 his mother and surviving brother had died, leaving him the main heir to assets estimated to be £2,000 in cash, rental properties and an inn, the Queen's Head, in his native parish.

Emmanuel was a college specifically for the education of preaching clergy and it was also a stronghold of Puritanism, which is why Harvard had chosen it. Thus, he was the now ordained Rev John Harvard, when in 1636 he married Anne Sadler in Lewes, Sussex, the daughter of the vicar of neighbouring Ringmer. (However, no record of his ordination has been found in either England or the USA.)

It was Emmanuel, too, that in the 1630s and early 1640s sent 35 emigrants to New England. The Harvards were to follow in their wake, living first in London. In 1637 they set off for New England and by August the couple were one of maybe 150 families living in Charlestown, across the harbour from Boston, Massachusetts, where Harvard became a freeman. However, less than a year later, in 1638, Harvard died. He made a death bed bequest to the 'schoale or Colledge' at Cambridge recently undertaken by the Massachusetts Bay Colony of his library of more than 400 volumes, on subjects sacred and secular, and £800. It was in gratitude that the institution is now known as Harvard University.

Southwark Cathedral

Memorials

London Bridge SE1 9DA

The Cathedral and Collegiate Church of St Saviour and St Mary Overie, to give it its full title, dates from 1905, incorporating St Mary Overie, dating back to at least the 12th century and probably earlier.

In the nave there is a memorial tablet to **Sam Wanamaker**, the actor, whose tablet is next to that of Shakespeare, whose Globe Theatre on Bankside he recreated.

Oscar Hammerstein II, a regular visitor to the cathedral, left £2,000 on his death to support two choir boys at the cathedral who are still known as the Hammerstein Chanters. The plaque was unveiled in 1961 by Hammerstein's second wife, Dorothy.

In contrast to the theatre and the 20th century memorials, **Mahomet Weyonomon**, chief of the Mohegan tribe of Connecticut, was buried in an unmarked grave in St Mary Overie Churchyard, and there is a carved pink granite boulder monument from the tribal Connecticut reservation in the churchyard to commemorate him (see pp114–116).

A chapel is named for **John Harvard**, benefactor of what became Harvard University, who was baptised in St Saviour's Church. The window in Harvard's chapel is by the American John La Farge, muralist, painter, decorator and stained-glass window maker. It was commissioned and paid for by Joseph Hodges Choate, a Harvard graduate, who became a distinguished lawyer and served as US ambassador to the UK from 1899 to 1905. The main subject of the window is the baptism of Christ, in a style after Poussin, which alludes to the baptism of John Harvard in the church in 1607. The arms of Harvard University are shown upper left and those of Emmanuel College, Cambridge, where Harvard studied, on the right. The centre displays the Royal Arms as they appeared between 1415 and 1603. The window was reconstructed in 1948 after damage by bombing in 1941.

Wanamaker, Sam (1919–1993)

Actor, director, creator of the Globe Theatre

Globe Theatre, 21 New Globe Walk, Bankside SE1 9DT ℗ and 7 Bentinck Close, 76–82 Prince Albert Road, St John's Wood, Westminster NW8 7RY ℗ *

Born in Chicago to first generation Russian-Jewish parents, Wanamaker was young when he set his sights early on theatre, developing a love of Shakespeare.

A method actor, he married a Canadian actress, Charlotte Holland, with whom he had three daughters, one of whom, Zoe, born in New York (and a British citizen in 2000), inherited her parents' abilities and became a well-known stage and television actor in the UK.

Wanamaker first appeared on Broadway in 1941 and fought in the Far East in the Second World War. His post-war stage career was rapid but he came to the attention of House Un-American Activities Committee. He avoided appearing before it as, facing a subpoena, he flew to England to appear in Clifford Odets's *The Country Girl* (*Winter Journey* in London) in 1952.

Wanamaker decided that with HUAC in the ascendant his career would better flourish in England, where he now made his permanent home, working as an actor and director, often of American plays.

One of the first things he did when he came to London was to seek out the site of Shakespeare's Globe. He had expected to find a magnificent memorial. Instead he found what his *ODNB* biographer calls 'only a dirty plaque rammed into the wall of a Courage brewery bottling plant on a back street in Southwark'.

Wanamaker became director of Liverpool's New Shakespeare Theatre, and in 1956 at London's Royal Court Theatre put on a well-regarded production of Berthold Brecht's *The Threepenny Opera*. In 1959 he played Iago with **Paul Robeson** as Othello at Stratford. He also appeared in several big box-office film hits like *Those Magnificent Men in their Flying Machines*, *Private Benjamin*, *The Competition*, *Irreconcilable Differences*, *Raw Deal*, and *Superman IV*.

When the period of the witch hunts had passed he returned to the USA to work but this was largely as a jobbing actor for his career tended to be in run-of-the-mill films and television series. However, this doubled curiously with his emergence as a director of opera, with Michael Tippett's *King Priam* at the Coventry Theatre and the Royal Opera House, Covent Garden, *La Forza del Destino* at Covent Garden, and, to open at the new Sydney Opera House, Prokofiev's *War and Peace*.

But in 1971 Wanamaker did something which made for his most permanent memorial and is forever associated with his name: he set up the Globe Playhouse Trust (later the Shakespeare Globe Trust). A quarter of a century later the replica of the Globe Theatre opened in Southwark.

However, this was far from easy sailing: the local council wanted the land for low-cost housing and some in his own profession regarded him as 'an upstart crow'. It was 'Wanamaker's Folly' which brought with it setbacks, antagonism, pettiness but also his banding together like-minded actors, artists, architects, scholars and funders.

Wanamaker, however, did not live to see his theatre opened by the Queen in 1997, let alone its continuing success as a unique London theatrical experience. He had died of cancer at his Westminster home nearly four years previously.

---

* *A plaque can also be found in* **Southwark Cathedral,** *where in March 1994 his memorial service was held.*

Weyonomon, Mahomet (c1700–1736)

Mohegan tribal chief

Southwark Cathedral, London Bridge SE1 9DA

The memorial to Mahomet Weyomon in the grounds of Southwark Cathedral (Aidan Cusack)

Mahomet Weyonomon was the chief or sachem of the Mohegan tribe of Connecticut, and great-grandson of Uncas, the tribe's founder. In 1735 he attempted to do what Oweneco, his grandfather, had failed to do – to seek the restoration of tribal lands by petitioning George II.

Oweneco had visited England and petitioned Queen Anne about how settlers had taken much of his people's planting and hunting lands. The Queen ordered a commission, which found that the settlers had, indeed, taken lands illegally. While the colonial governor was ordered to restore the land to its rightful owners, the instruction was never implemented. Further encroachments by settlers, who had been sold land by the colonial government, which had claimed that it owned the land, had made the Mohegan subsistence way of life increasingly unviable, and so Weyonomon was delegated again to seek royal redress. The tribe's territory had been contested since 1659 when Major John Mason had been named as the tribe's 'Protector and Guardian'.

Weyonomon was accompanied on his visit by fellow Mohegan 20-year-old Acquont (or Augh Quant) Johnson and three Anglo-Americans from a distinguished Connecticut family: another Major John Mason, his oldest son Samuel and an unnamed son. They lodged in premises in Aldermanbury in the City of London, owned by a Mr Midhurst. The king referred the matter to the Commissions of Trade and Planning who agreed to reopen the case.

However, Weyonomon died of smallpox in August 1736 and although he fled to the countryside, Mason suffered the same fate in December. While Mason, being an Anglo-American, had the right to be buried within the walls of the City of London, this was not a privilege extended to foreigners like Weyonomon. His body was placed in an unmarked grave in the grounds of St Mary Overie (now incorporated within Southwark Cathedral).

The *Daily Journal* for 11 August 1736 reported:

> On Sunday last about one o'clock in the Morning died of the Small Pox, in the 36th Yeare of his Age, Mahomet Weyonomon, Sachem of the Tribe of the Mohegans in the Province of Connecticut in New England. He was Great Grandson to the famous Sachem Uncafs or Onkafs, who took part with the English upon their firft fettling of that Country. He was very decently interred laft Night (from his Lodgings at Mr Midhurst's in Aldermanbury) in St Mary Over's [*sic*] Burial-place.

Isaac Watts, the theologian and hymn writer, to whom Mason had appealed for support, opined that 'tis probable that the affair will end', when told of the deaths. But it did not, for Johnson and Samuel Mason presented a new petition in April 1737 and the Privy Council ordered a new commission. The case persisted until 1772, when the colonialists prevailed.

In the summer of 1737 the king gave £300 to meet the expenses of the party and to pay for the return of the survivors to their home.

The historian Coll Thrush writes that 'although he no doubt was at first mourned deeply among his people, over time the Mohegan lost track of [Weyonomon's] story, just as London seemed to forget that he had ever existed'.

However, when researchers, who included a Mohegan tribal member, discovered mention of the chief in a magazine, interest developed. This led to the Mohegan tribal council and the cathedral commissioning a monument to Weyonomon to be placed in the grounds of Southwark Cathedral. The five-tonne abstract monument is impressive. It was carved by British sculptor Peter Randall-Page from a pink granite boulder, which incorporates Mohegan symbols, from the Mohegan Connecticut reservation. In 2006, Mohegan leaders came to London to hold a ceremony to recognise Weyonomon's death, which included burning sweet grass and sage to bring good spirits and the singing of an Honor Song. The unveiling was carried out by the Queen, accompanied by Prince Philip, in the presence of Mohegan tribal members, including tribal council president Mark, council member Bruce Two Dogs Bozsum and tribal member Shane White Raven Long.

The Queen was presented with a copy of Weyonomon's original petition and a pipe of peace.

In his address, the Very Reverend Colin Slee, Dean of Southwark said:

> We cannot right past wrongs but we can remember them and transform them to inspire better conduct throughout humanity now and in years to come.

Yeardley, Sir George (1587–1627)

Colonial governor of Virginia

St Saviour's Church (now Southwark Cathedral), London Bridge SE1 9DA

Yeardley, like **John Harvard** after him, was baptised in St Saviour's in July 1588.

His father Ralph was a merchant tailor but in 1605 the son became a foot soldier, under Sir Thomas Gates, fighting the Spanish in the Netherlands. When Gates became governor of Virginia, Yeardley went to colonial America to serve him. He set sail in June 1609, survived a shipwreck off the Bermudas, and reached Jamestown in May 1610.

Sickness, starvation and death at the hands of the indigenous people had devastated the town. It was agreed that the settlers could return home and Gates ordered Yeardley to secure it, which he did. In 1616 he became deputy governor of Virginia, returning to England in 1617, and the next year marrying Temperance Flowerdieu (or Flowerdew), with whom he had three children. A month later he was made governor of Virginia and knighted by James I. He was twice more to hold that post during which time, among other things, he relaxed constraints on trade with the local tribespeoples, abolished martial law and the colony enjoyed a brief prosperity. He attempted to provide education for indigenous people by creating a university or college at Henrico. However, the Rev Thomas Lorkin, who was appointed to teach, was unable to find adequate buildings within what was a ruinous settlement.

Yeardley's reform programme failed to gain the support of Virginia's first assembly when he summoned it in July 1619. The power of Sir Edwin Sandys, the assembly's opposition leader, made the programme nearly impossible to implement. Because of Sandys Yeardley was forced into conflicts with the tobacco growers. When in 1621 1,000 unskilled settlers arrived, Yeardley became so exasperated that he resigned the governorship. He stayed on until the arrival at the end of that year of his replacement Sir Francis Wyatt.

Yeardley amassed large land holdings and died in November 1627 at James City and was buried in the parish church.

TOWER HAMLETS

Jefferson, Jane Randolph (1720–1776)

Mother of Thomas Jefferson, 3rd president of the United States

St Paul's Church, 302 The Highway, Shadwell E1 3WD

Jane Randolph was born in February 1720, likely in Shakespeare's Walk, Shadwell, the home of her parents Isham, a Virginia-born mariner and merchant, and Jane Randolph, who was English. She was baptised on the 20th of that month in St Paul's Church, literally around the corner from Shakespeare's Walk. The street was destroyed in the 19th century to make way for Shadwell Basin.

The present church dates from 1820 but the parish was created in the 17th century to serve sailors and residents of the docks.

Shadwell was a growing and thriving place, no distance from the City of London. When Randolph was four the family were living in nearby Whitechapel parish, where her younger brother Isham was born. The year after young Isham's birth the family moved to Williamsburg in colonial Virginia and lived in various places.

Randolph married Peter Jefferson in 1739 and her father provided a dowry of £200, but it was not paid until his death. Upon marriage she moved to her husband's estate, which he had begun to acquire in 1736 from a William Randolph, a likely distant relative of his future wife as she was the grand-daughter of another William Randolph, a 17th century colonist, merchant, landowner, planter and Virginia politician. Peter named Shadwell after his wife's birthplace.

Their first child, also Jane, was born in June 1740 on the estate and the house was built in 1741. Jane was the first of ten children, of whom Thomas, born in 1743, was the third, although he only spent a few years of his childhood at Shadwell. By his death in 1757 Peter had acquired 1,500 acres adjacent to the original land. With other land there were 7,200 acres. Shadwell was one of four farms and Jefferson later named the whole estate Monticello for the mountain it contained. He inherited the estate as the eldest son. The family home, which was largely destroyed by fire in 1770, was, according to Susan Kern, 'a well-appointed gentry house full of fashionable goods'. In 1774 there were 18 slaves on the estate, 12 of them children or adults too old to work.

Jefferson seldom mentioned his mother and one biographer consequently calls her 'a shadowy figure.' But one reference to her came in a letter to Jefferson's uncle William, her brother, a merchant in Bristol in June 1776, when he wrote: 'The death of my mother you have probably not heard of. This happened on the last day of March after an illness of not more than an hour. We suppose it to have been apoplectic.'

Jane, who inherited the land and plantation, died on 31st March 1776, three months and two days before her son set his signature, with others, to the Declaration of Independence.

Jones Jnr, Christopher (c1570–1622)
Captain of the Mayflower

Blackwall Stairs, Blackwall Way, Yabsley Street, Poplar E14
The Mayflower Pub, 117 Rotherhithe Street, Rotherhithe, Southwark SE16 4NF*
St Mary's Church, Rotherhithe, Southwark SE16 4JH 🅟

William Halsall's 1882 painting *The Mayflower in Plymouth Harbor*

There was a 'prosperous wind', in the words of one passenger, when the *Mayflower* sailed to America from Plymouth on 6th September 1620; having picked up more passengers and supplies at Southampton, it began its journey from Rotherhithe along the Thames. The Mayflower public house boasts that the London (then Surrey) passengers and crew set out from here, and the Blackwall Stairs led to the dock from which they sailed. From Southampton there were about 102 passengers and 30–50 crew.

The original plan was to journey with the *Speedwell*, which had passengers from Holland, but that ship had twice to return to port and was unseaworthy for such a voyage. It returned to Holland, with some of its passengers joining the *Mayflower*. This meant the loss of a month's sailing time. At least one keg each of French or Dutch wine was taken in the ship, which had been chartered by the Merchant Adventurers.

Jones was likely born in Harwich in Suffolk, where the ship, of which he became part owner, was made in 1708. He was the son of a mariner and ship owner. Jones himself was a freeman of Harwich, a burgess and a tax assessor, and so a man of means. He moved to Rotherhithe parish, then an area of wealthy merchants, in 1611 and had made several commercial voyages to

Europe in the *Mayflower* before taking the pilgrims. He was twice married and once widowed and had children, who were baptised in St Mary's.

The journey took nearly two months when land was sighted off Cape Cod, Massachusetts on 11th November. The ship anchored at Plymouth Rock due to strong winds, although the original destination had been Virginia.

While still at sea, the passengers decided to write and sign the Mayflower Compact to establish a form of government in their new home. This was to be the first written document of government, a constitution, for what would become the United States.

The plan had been to return immediately after the passengers had disembarked but many of the crew were struck by the illnesses which had beset the passengers. Thus, the ship and crew remained in dock at Plymouth over the winter of 1620–1621, during which time about half of them died.

Jones and the surviving crew returned to London on the *Mayflower* sailing from Plymouth on 5th April 1621 and arriving at Rotherhithe on the Thames on 5th May 1621, more than halving the time it had taken on the voyage out.

Jones returned to his European trading trips and a little more than a year after his return died on a trip back from France on 21st May 1622. He was buried in St Mary's Church (rebuilt 1716), where, in the churchyard there is a memorial stone to him, while a plaque on the church tower commemorates the voyage.

---

* *The Mayflower public house has a descendants' book which visitors can sign.*

Severs, Dennis (1948–1999)

Museum creator

Dennis Severs House, 18 Folgate Street, Spitalfields E1 6BX*

Severs, who was born in Escondido, California, was according to his obituarist, the architectural historian Gavin Stamp, 'a true original, an artist of perverse genius who created a three-dimensional historical novel out of bricks and mortar and timber and the objects he picked up for a song on countless stalls'.

For Severs was the creator of the house named after him, where he lived, a unique house museum, depicting the life of generations of a fictitious family. Ralph Samuel, historian and East End resident, called it 'a magical mystery tour which dazzles the visitor with a succession of scenes more crowded with memorable incident than the mere facsimile of what passes in the museums as a period room'. For Severs himself it was 'a famous time-machine'.

He was the son of Earl and Helen Severs, their fifth son, although the first four, all much older than their brother, had been accumulated from different marriages. He was, he said in *The Space Between*, an unpublished guide to the house, a dreamy and imaginative child, who, at one of his several schools he attended, was seen as somewhere between 'exceptional' and 'mentally retarded.'

Severs was a young storyteller, which gave him credibility with his fellows, but he became obsessed early on with collecting. He remembered with some prescience: 'Down deep, I always believed that one day I would travel past picture frames and into the marinated glow of a warmer, more mellow and more romantic light. There was one such light in particular, one that I saw in the combination of old varnish and paint, and that appealed to me as my ideal. By the age of 11, it was identified as English.'

The Victorian Room (Roelof Bakker)

Stamp wrote of him: 'Dennis was one of those Americans in England who seemed to have arrived from nowhere, to have no past, no roots and who, so irritatingly, could not be placed socially.'

He had visited England in 1965 and 1966 and moved to London a year later, five days after graduating from high school. He abandoned his legal studies when a legacy proved insufficient and turned to running rides in a Victorian landau around Hyde Park and the West End, a business that he closed when a developer purchased his stable in west London. In 1979 he bought the handsome, five-storey, brick town house, built in 1724, and lived there until his untimely death.

The moment was propitious. Spitalfields was run down and threatened by developers, a threat opposed by the Spitalfields Historic Buildings Trust. Having saved the house, Severs set himself an unusual task: not so much renovating it but, as he put it, 'to bring it to life as my home'. He explained:

> With a candle, a chamber pot and a bedroll, I began sleeping in each of the house's 10 rooms so that I might arouse my intuition in the quest for each room's soul.
>
> Then, having neared it, I worked inside out from there to create what turned out to be a collection of atmospheres: moods that harbour the light and the spirit of various ages in Time.

Spitalfields is an ancient, even mysterious place, where history seeps from the walls and successive generations of immigrants have replaced the last –

French Huguenots, Eastern European Jews and now Bengalis – bringing their own stamp and culture, where church has become synagogue has become mosque.

To reflect the atmosphere of the area, Severs invented the Gervais (later Jervis) family, 18th century silk merchants, who had lived in his house for nearly 200 years and, as one writer said, 'whose members had apparently just left each of the rooms entered'. This game of hide and seek Severs saw as 'a still life drama' that was assisted by actual guttering candles and concealed taped sound-effects, which ranged from a baby's cry to a fire being stoked or the winding of a clock. The potter and ceramicist Simon Pettet lived with Severs as his partner from 1983 (he died in 1993) and his work, including a fireplace with Delft-style tiles depicting contemporary Spitalfields residents, can be found in the house.

As Severs himself wrote of 'The Plot': 'The ten rooms harbour ten "spells" that engage the visitor's imagination in moods that dominated the periods 1724–1914. Your senses are your guide.' Each room caught a glimpse of the family's history. The house says that it was its founder's intention that to enter it 'as if you have passed through the surface of a painting, exploring with your senses and imagination a meticulously crafted, 18th century world'. Severs wrote of his creation 'drawing human nature and history together as one'.

This was no 'heritage' venture, not even a museum: visitors have to enter the spirit of Severs' creation and he did not stop short of rejecting those who did not comply.

Two days after Christmas 1999, Dennis Severs, long HIV-positive, died of cancer. He had acquired the house from the Spitalfields Trust and bequeathed it to them.

---

* For visiting times see www.dennissevershouse.co.uk.

Virginia Quay Settlers Monument
Virginia Quay, Jamestown Way, Poplar E14 2DE

This is arguably the most significant place in London in the history of the United States. Jamestown, Virginia and Plymouth Plantation in Massachusetts may attract thousands of tourists each year as the hallowed ground where the first English settlers touched land, but it was from this place, in 1606, that 105 of them embarked on a journey across the Atlantic.

Brunswick Quay, once part of the thriving London docks, was renamed Virginia Quay in the settlers' honour but the monument was not finally completed until 1999. It added to a monument set up in 1951, which itself replaced and incorporated a plaque from 1928. That original marker was set into the wall of the nearby Dockmaster's House on Blackwall Quay and presented by the Society for the Protection of West Virginia Artefacts.

Virginia Quay Settlers Monument (Leutha)

Suffering bomb damage in the Second World War, the house was later demolished and the plaque was set in a new monument put up in 1951 donated by the London Port Authority and unveiled by Walter Gifford, the American ambassador. There was a bronze mermaid surmounting this monument which was stolen but recovered at an auction in about 2007, but not placed back on the monument.

A construction company involved in the area's redevelopment repaired the monument and had the astrolabe (a tool used in 17th century navigation) added. The new monument was unveiled by Philip Lader, the US ambassador.

The free-standing stone and bronze monument, on a rock-hewn base, is made of stones from the old quay capped by a sculptured astrolabe created by the award-winning sculptor Wendy Taylor.

The early colonists settled in Jamestown, Williamsburg, and along the James River and other navigable waters in Virginia during the 17th century. Their flotilla consisted of three small ships: *Susan Constant*, the *Godspeed* and the *Discovery*.

Despite exhaustion and illness resulting from the long voyage, the settlers established Jamestown in May 1607 as the first Virginia English colony (Virginia was then the name for the whole of the east coast north of Florida of what became the USA). An attack by indigenous people necessitated the building of a wooden stockade, but this was just one affliction on the community. By 1609 only 60 of the original 150 settlers remained, decimated by disease, famine and continuing attacks. When Captain John Rolfe joined the colony in 1610 he came with tobacco seeds which thrived in the local climate and Virginia was eventually established as a tobacco-based colony. His marriage to **Pocahontas**, daughter of a tribal chief, in April 1614, brought respite from the conflict with the indigenous people.

The plaque states:

FROM NEAR THIS SPOT/DECEMBER 19 1606/SAILED WITH
"105 ADVENTURERS"/THE "SUSAN CONSTANT" 100 TONS/
CAPT CHRISTOPHER NEWPORT/IN SUPREME COMMAND/
THE "GODSPEED" 40 TONS/CAPT BARTHOLOMEW GOSNOLD/
THE "DISCOVERY" 20 TONS/CAPT JOHN RATCLIFFE/LANDED AT
CAPE HENRY VIRGINIA/ APRIL 1607/ARRIVED AT JAMESTOWN
VIRGINIA/MAY 13 1607/WHERE THESE "ADVENTURERS"/FOUNDED
THE FIRST PERMANENT/ENGLISH COLONY IN AMERICA/UNDER
THE LEADERSHIP OF THE/INTREPID CAPT JOHN SMITH/
EDWARD MARIA WINGFIELD/PRESIDENT OF THE COUNCIL/
THE REVEREND ROBERT HUNT/AND OTHERS/AT JAMESTOWN
JULY 30 1619 WAS/CONVENED THE FIRST ASSEMBLY IN AMERICA.

Whitechapel Bell Foundry (gone)

First Liberty Bell struck here

32–34 Whitechapel Road, Whitechapel E1 1DY*

On 12th June 2017, after at least 447 years of history, the Whitechapel Bell
Foundry closed its doors and left behind these premises which it had taken
in 1738. This was a former coaching inn, The Artichoke, which had been
damaged in the Great Fire of London. When it ceased trading in 1738 Thomas
Lester – Master Founder of the foundry – took over the premises, which are
now Grade II* listed.

The foundry moved from the north side of Whitechapel Road as Lester
needed new space to accommodate extra workshops and storage areas when
bell-founding was undergoing a great expansion.

When it closed it was one
of two bell foundries left
in the UK and the oldest
manufacturing company in
continuous business. In fact,
there is some evidence that
the business may have dated
back to 1420. As this was
72 years before Christopher
Columbus set sail for the USA,
it is appropriate that two of
the foundry's most famous
products are the Liberty Bell
and Big Ben in Parliament's
Elizabeth Tower.

The Liberty Bell in Independence Hall, Philadelphia (Ronan Perry)

Not that this Liberty Bell was the first export to what was then the colonies. Bells went to Christ Church, Philadelphia in 1754. (St Michael's, Charleston, South Carolina, was supplied in 1764.)

In late 1751 the four superintendents of the Assembly of the Province of Pennsylvania were instructed to order a 2,000lb bell from England. Part of the instruction was that the bell should have an inscription, which turned out to be prophetic. It was to read: 'Proclaim LIBERTY Throughout all the Land unto all the Inhabitants Thereof Lev XXV.'

The bell was created by Lester in his new premises and it is recorded that the bell arrived safely in September 1752. However, in March the next year it was reported that it cracked at the first stroke. Unable to return it on the ship on which it had come, it was recast by two 'ingenious' workmen, Pass and Stow. They deemed that Lester's bell was too brittle and modified the alloy by adding 1½ oz of copper to every one pound of Lester's bell.

But the freedom of a bell's tone relies on the metal being brittle. The men recast it again without success and then Lester's correct balance of metal was restored, and it is this bell that now hangs in the Liberty Bell Center, across from Independence Hall, Philadelphia, its former home.

However, in 1753, the clients were still not satisfied and Lester was again asked to recast the bell at a cost of 2d (1p) for each pound. This, though, never happened and Pass and Stow's recasting was hung in the State House Steeple.

The bell was taken to Allentown and hidden for a year in the Zion Reform Church when the British threatened to occupy Philadelphia in 1777 because of the fear that the British would remove the Liberty Bell and other bells and make them into cannon. When the British withdrew, the bell returned to the city in the summer of 1778.

The present bell is cracked, though no one knows how. It is said to have happened in 1835 while being tolled at the death of Chief Justice John Marshall of Virginia. Another story which ties in with that, given the date, is one told in 1911 to a newspaper reporter. Emmanuel Joseph Rauch, then about 86 years of age, said that in 1835, when he was 10, he was one day passing State House Square when Downing, the steeple keeper, invited him and several other boys to ring the bell in honour of George Washington's birthday. After 10 or 12 strokes, Downing and the boys noted a change in the tone of the bell. When the steeple keeper climbed the steeple he found a crack 12" to 15" long. The boys were told to go home.

English hand bell ringing in the USA derives from the Whitechapel hand bells, which were sent to Miss Margaret H Nicholls by Arthur Hughes, general manager of the foundry, in 1902 after she had successfully rung two hand bell peals on a trip to England from Boston. This led to tune ringing being followed by the creation of the New England Guild of Hand Bell Ringers in 1937, and in 1954 by the American Guild of English Hand Bell Ringers.

In 1964 the foundry provided the change-ringing peal of 10 bells in a radial frame for the National Cathedral in Washington DC. In 1997 it supplied North America's first change-ringing peal of 12 bells to Toronto Cathedral.

In 1976, when the USA celebrated its bicentennial, a group from the Procrastinators Society of America mounted a mock demonstration over the bell's defects outside the foundry, with placards proclaiming 'We got a lemon' and 'What about the warranty?' The foundry offered to replace the bell so long as the original was sent back in its original packaging.

Between 1968–1976 the foundry produced about 15 full-size, 2,400 one-fifth size, and 200 one-ninth size replicas of the bell for the Limited Editions Collectors Society of America Inc in Boston. The foundry was also commissioned to cast the 12,446lb Bicentennial Bell for 1976, which is now in Philadelphia with its predecessor. This bears the inscription:

FOR THE PEOPLE OF THE UNITED STATES OF AMERICA
FROM THE PEOPLE OF BRITAIN
4 JULY 1976
LET FREEDOM RING

In 2001, to mark the 250th anniversary of the original bell, the foundry was asked to cast a replica of the Liberty Bell.

The last bell to be cast was given to the Museum of London. The bell patents were sold to White's of Appleton in Oxfordshire, the bell-hanging company with which the foundry had worked for 197 years.

---

* A planning application for the foundry site was to be considered as this book was in press by Tower Hamlets Council. This would demolish a 1980s rear extension to build an hotel, while the Grade II* listed foundry building would not be demolished but used for workshops, offices, a café, and a new foundry.

WALTHAM FOREST

Hitchcock, Alfred (1899–1980)

Film director

517 Leytonstone High Road, Leytonstone E11 4QH **P**
175 Salmon Lane, Limehouse E14 7EU (gone)
Gainsborough Studios, Poole Street, Hoxton, Hackney N1 7BG (gone: now apartments) **P**
153 Cromwell Road, Kensington, Kensington and Chelsea SW5 0TQ

A plaque now marks the place near where Alfred Hitchcock was born on 13th August 1899 and where on the ground floor was the greengrocery and poulterer's run by his father, William. His mother Emma was a dignified, house-proud, lower middle class housewife.

Leytonstone was then a growing suburb on the tip of London where it fades into Essex, boosted by the coming of the Great Eastern Railway only 43 years before the birth of its most famous son. When Hitchcock was seven the electric tram began to replace the horse.

Given the world-wide fame which was to come to him later in life and has long outlasted his death, young Alfred, with an older brother, William, and sister, Ellen, was an isolated little boy, tubby and with few friends. The home was one of strict discipline. When he was five, his father sent him to the local police station with a note. He was locked in a cell for ten minutes and released with the admonition: 'That's what we do for naughty boys'. Oddly, his father would call him 'my little lamb without a spot'.

William was a successful merchant and when Alfie or Fred, as the family called him (he took Hitch in adulthood), was six or seven, he purchased two fishmonger shops and the family lived above one of them, just north of Limehouse Basin at the appropriately named 175 Salmon Lane (gone). Hitchcock recalled: 'I remember my father going to work in a dark suit with a very white starched shirt and a dark tie.'

Limehouse's Chinese community had moved in a couple of decades earlier and the docklands area was rough and tough, with small shops and houses a few steps back from the pavement. Public houses were open from

early morning to past midnight, with gin or a pint of beer to be had for a penny. Drunkenness was rife. All of this, and the coming and going of ships and seamen from abroad, gave colour in contrast to the more monochrome Leytonstone. Hitchcock is known as a child to have read Thomas de Quincey's essay, *On Murder Considered as a Fine Art*, in which de Quincey describes the area, in 1812, as being 'a most dangerous quarter' and 'a perilous region' of 'manifold ruffianism'. Such reading and what he observed about him would have fed the imagination of the young Hitchcock, as did the Catholicism in which he was raised, with its stress on guilt, sin and repentance, as well as mystery and miracle.

Alfred and Alma Hitchcock in 1966 (Frederick Magnussen)

Travel, by ship and train, play a large part in the Hitchcock *oeuvre* and as a child he collected maps, timetables and tickets. He memorised the stations on the Orient Express and Trans-Siberian Express and at eight had travelled from the beginning to the end of the London General Omnibus Company's routes.

Hitchcock was an altar boy and at nine boarded at the Salesian College in Battersea, but only for a week before being sent to the local convent school in East India Dock Road near his home. At ten he was sent to the Jesuits' St Ignatius School at Stamford Hill, Stoke Newington, where discipline was harsh but not more so than was common in other schools in his day.

'I was terrified of the police, of the Jesuit fathers, of physical punishment, of a lot of things. This is the root of my work', he was to say.

The school would have been a long journey, involving bus changes or a long walk between stops. Hitchcock studied Latin, mathematics, physics and English, read Shakespeare and Longfellow and memorised and recited passages.

When he was eight or nine he made his first visits to the cinema, with short-running films like *A Ride on a Runaway Train* and *Hal's Tours and the Secrets of the World*. He must have seen Chaplin's early films released in the UK when he was 14, while Harold Lloyd, Douglas Fairbanks Sr and Mary Pickford were viewed in the dark. He would not have to go far for entertainment as cinemas and music halls aplenty were within walking distance of home. He seems to have read the trade magazines, like *The Bioscope* and the *Kinematograph* and *Lantern Weekly*, from an early age. He would also take the bus and attend sessions at the Old Bailey.

Hitchcock left school at 13 or 14 (the school leaving age then was 12). He enrolled to study mechanics and acoustics and in 1914 went to work as a draughtsman and an advertising designer with WT Henley's Telegraph and Cable Company. That month his father died of chronic emphysema. He enrolled for service with the outbreak of the First World War but, on coming of age, was exempted, although on what grounds is not known. Hitchcock attended night school courses in art and art history and was much taken with the work of **Edgar Allan Poe**, whom he discovered at 16.

In 1920 Hitchcock was appointed to design and illustrate silent movie titles by the Famous Players-Lasky Corporation in their new Islington Studios in Poole Street, a disused power station. It was the most technically advanced studio in the UK.

At the studios he met a film editor named Alma Reville, who had joined the studios in 1921, the same year that Hitchcock began working there full time. She was his almost exact contemporary, born the day after him in the same year. They married on 2nd December 1926 at the Brompton Oratory in Knightsbridge. They leased the two-bedroom, top floor flat of the four-storey house in Cromwell Road, for which Hitchcock designed the furniture. Their daughter Patricia was born here in July 1928. They also later bought a house in the country, in Surrey.

Alma would become an important collaborator in Hitchcock's films, often with a screen credit. His daughter trained as an actress and appeared in three of her father's films: *Stage Fright* (1950), *Strangers on a Train* (1951), and *Psycho* (1960).

The First World War had disadvantageously affected film production and US production and distribution came to dominate the domestic market in the UK. In 1922 Famous Players-Lasky began to run down its UK operation and made staff redundant, including Alma. Hitchcock, however, survived by continuing to work for other film companies who took leases on the building. In 1924 Michael Balcon, director of both Gaumont-British and Gainsborough Studios, took over the site and gave Hitchcock the chance to direct his first feature film, *The Pleasure Garden* (1925).

Balcon encouraged Hitchcock to study in Germany, where he was to be influenced by Expressionism in the 1920s. Hitchcock returned to work at Gainsborough and directed, among other films, *The Lodger* and *The Mountain Eagle*, and his last two films for the studios, *Downhill* (1927), and *Easy Virtue* (1927). He made one last film, *The Lady Vanishes*, to fulfill a contract with Gainsborough Pictures, at the Islington studios.

The studios closed in 1948, fell into dereliction and were demolished in 2002. Hitchcock moved to British International Pictures, where he made *The Ring* (1927), the first film he scripted. His last silent film was *The Manxman* (1929). Apart from the odd flourish, none of these is particularly striking, and *Blackmail* (1929) was his first sound film.

In 1931 the Hitchcock family went on a world cruise that gave him the idea for *Rich and Strange*. Later films for British International included *The Man Who Knew Too Much* (1934), *The 39 Steps* (1935), *Secret Agent* (1936), *Sabotage* (1936), *Young and Innocent* (1937) and *The Lady Vanishes* (1938).

In 1937 Hitchcock met David O Selznick in America and in March 1939 the family returned to America, which was to be their permanent home. Hitchcock's work has also profoundly influenced a generation of younger film makers.

Hitchcock became an American citizen in 1955 and was awarded an honorary knighthood in 1980. Five months later he died, on 29th April, at home in Los Angeles. His ashes were scattered in the Pacific Ocean.

Hartley, David (1732–1813)

Signatory to the Treaty of Paris, MP, abolitionist and inventor

Tibbet's Corner, near Widcroft Road, Kingston Road, Putney Heath SW15 3EL (obelisk)

David Hartley was not an American but he had a highly significant effect on US history. Member of Parliament for Kingston upon Hull, he was appointed by George III as minister plenipotentiary to negotiate with the American revolutionaries. In this capacity, together with his friend **Benjamin Franklin**, whom he had met when he came to London from his native Suffolk, and others, he put his name to the Treaty of Paris, bringing to an end to the War of Independence with the British, in the Hotel d'York, Rue Jacob on 3rd September 1783.

The treaty set the boundaries between the British Empire and the USA and established matters like fishing rights, restoration of property and prisoners of war. Article 1 of the treaty acknowledged the USA as sovereign and independent.

It was as a scientist that he first came in contact with Franklin, himself a scientist and inventor of note. They became friends and corresponded.

Hartley was an MP, representing his seat from 1774 to 1780 and 1782 to 1784. During this latter period he had a house in Golden Square, Soho in Westminster. Although he had spoken in the House in favour of American independence, he was a close friend of Lord North, prime minister at the time of the revolutionary secession.

Curiously, this obelisk was erected, by the City of London Corporation, near the site of Hartley's former home in 1776, the year of the Declaration of Independence, but it is not his role in that conflict that is

Memorial obelisk to David Hartley (David Anstiss)

129

commemorated, rather the fireproofing which he used in his house, consisting of iron and copper between double doors. The royal family witnessed his experiments, which were deemed successful, and King George III gave 'of a sum not exceeding £2,500' to Hartley to defray his costs to 'ascertain the practicability and utility of his invention for securing buildings from fire'. The stone for the obelisk was laid in 1760 to mark the centenary of the Great Fire of London.

1776 proved to be a triply significant year for Hartley because that year he moved a resolution in the Commons stating that 'the slave trade is contrary to the laws of God and the rights of men'.

CITY OF WESTMINSTER

Adams, John (1735–1826)
Minister to London and 2nd president of the United States
9 Grosvenor Square, Mayfair W1K 5AE ℗

This corner house is where John Adams, one of the Founding Fathers, lived from May 1785 until March 1788, as his country's first minister to the UK.

Adams, who, unlike some of the other Founding Fathers was opposed to slavery, had come to London from representing his country in France and The Netherlands (a post he continued to hold while in London). He had served on the committee, which included **Benjamin Franklin**, that drew up the Treaty of Paris, bringing peace between Britain and the USA.

Adams was eager to go to London but still regretted leaving Paris and the family house in Auteuil, with its large garden, and the company of Thomas Jefferson, with whom, along with Franklin, he had worked in Paris to negotiate the Treaties of Amity and Commerce. London living, too, was expensive, the more so as Congress had opposed Adams having the job and cut his salary by a fifth from £2,500 to £2,000. Visiting London, Jefferson remarked on how very plainly the Adamses lived. Abigail, Adams' formidable wife, had no wish to live in England and begged her husband to refuse 'the parade and nonsense' of public life.

In this house Adams' daughter, also Abigail or 'Nabby', married Colonel William Stephens-Smith, first secretary of the legation, who had been an officer on the staff of George Washington in the Revolutionary Army.

Coming soon after the end of the War of Independence, Adams' London posting marked a thawing of the icy relations between Britain and the USA, for since the Treaty of Paris, Britain had wanted a minister to 'reside constantly' in London, even though it saw no reason to honour treaty obligations toward its weak former adversary.

There remained, all the same, animosity toward the USA, of which the Adamses felt the brunt, and while the royal family were affable, the couple complained of a general lack of civility and politeness. For the most part they were ignored, mixing largely with other expatriates. The press attacked Adams as a nobody, 'pretty fat and flourishing', 'a Pharisee of liberty', and an 'imposter'. Loyalists, now in exile in London, stoked up matters.

Some people stared at the Adamses, as the embodiment of the old enemy and even, on occasion, abused them. Adams took this for guilt and shame, as opposed to anger on his detractors' part, and wrote: 'They feel that they have behaved ill, and that I am sensible of it'. The hostility of courtiers caused John and Abigail to seek out the company of Richard Price, minister of Newington Green Unitarian Church, Stoke Newington, a moral philosopher, radical and republican who was sympathetic to the American cause.

John Adams' home in Grosvenor Square (Terry Philpot)

However, the Adamses enjoyed what London had to offer: they attended a concert in **Westminster Abbey** and went to the theatre, but found the court increasingly tedious and strained. They saw Sarah Siddons, out of retirement, as Lady Macbeth and Desdemona. At Windsor Adams called on Sir William Hershel, the astronomer.

At first, the Adamses stayed in the Bath Hotel, Piccadilly (gone). Grosvenor Square's five acres, the site of the new residence, was the size of the garden at Auteuil. For Adams, London was all 'tumult and hurry'.

George III and Adams shared a love of farming and books. Adams had seen the King's library* during a tour of Buckingham Palace on an earlier visit, and John and Abigail were devoted readers of Samuel Richardson, Laurence Sterne, Tobias Smollett and Samuel Johnson.

George III was 47; Adams 45. Adams said later of the king that he was the greatest talker he had ever known. Adams presented his ambassadorial credentials to the king and said that he hoped to help restore the 'good old nature and good old humor between people who … have the same language, a similar religion, and kindred blood'. The king replied that he was the last person to agree to the breakup between Great Britain and the American colonies, but now that it was done he 'would be the first to meet the friendship of the United States as an independent power'.

John Adams' tenure had two goals: to deal with violations of the Treaty of Paris (which included British troops continuing to hold forts along the Great Lakes) and to create a trade agreement between the two countries. On the first issue there was stalemate when the British insisted that American farmers owed debts, incurred before the war, to British creditors; and there was no trade agreement. However, with Thomas Jefferson, Adams made deals with Prussia and Morocco and secured additional loans from The Netherlands.

Thomas Jefferson visited Adams from Paris in 1786 and the two took off on a tour of the countryside and visited historic sites.

In January 1787 Adams asked to be relieved of his post so he might return home but this was not granted for almost a year. At his last meeting with the king, George told him that when the USA met its treaty obligations Britain would honour its own. The *Westminster Evening Post* opined that he had 'settled all his concerns with great honour; and whatever his political tenets may have been, he was much respected and esteemed in this country'.

Adams left London on 30th March 1788 (the post would remain vacant for four years) to serve George Washington for two terms as vice-president before succeeding him in 1797.

In 1976, marking the USA's bi-centenary, Queen Elizabeth II praised Adams for restoring 'the old good nature and the old good humour between our peoples'.

Adams' son **John Quincy Adams**, who became the 6th President, was later to be minister, as was his grandson Charles Francis Adams.

---

* George III's library can now be seen at the British Library.

Adams, Henry (1838–1918)
Writer and historian
98 Portland Place (formerly 5 Upper Portland Place),
Marylebone W I B I LT **P** *

Henry Brooks Adams was born in Boston, great-grandson of **John Adams** and grandson of **John Quincy Adams**. In 1860 he returned from a two year tour of Italy, France and Germany, where he had studied civil law and the languages and written for the *Boston Courier*, to become private secretary of his father, Charles Francis Adams, a newly elected congressman. Adams had taken the post reluctantly. 'I had little to do', he wrote, 'and knew not how to do it rightly'.

However, the next year, when his father was appointed minister to London by Abraham Lincoln, father and son left for their new London home, which from 1863 to 1866 served as the American legation.

The American Civil War had begun and Henry's thoughts were to seek a commission but he was physically unsuited to the military and his brother, also Charles, urged him to stay in London and advance the Union cause as a writer. He wrote in *The Times, The New York Times*, the *North American Review* and elsewhere. Henry Adams' chief task was to ensure that the UK stayed neutral in the conflict and both Adamses spent time monitoring what the Confederates were up to in the UK, and also attempting to frustrate the building of Confederate ships by UK shipyards. When he was not working for his father Adams also read extensively, as he had from childhood, having been born into a family that boasted the largest private library in the country.

Henry Adams in 1885

In London Adams met Francis Palgrave, Richard Monkton Milnes, John Stuart Mill (whose works he read during his stay) and Sir Charles Lyell. Lyell urged Adams to read Henry Spencer and Auguste Comte. He was exposed to new ideas, especially those of Darwin, and all of this helped shape his thinking on politics, economics and science. Always an intellectual, London convinced the young Adams that his gifts lay as a writer and journalist in shaping his fellows' thoughts.

But London had also shaped him in less positive ways. American society now seemed to him 'a long, straggling caravan, stretching loosely toward the prairies, its few score of leaders far in advance and its millions of immigrants, Negroes and Indians far in the rear'. His writing was marked by cynicism. Washington, he decided, was the best base for the life of a young writer.

Father and son left London in 1868. In 1872 Adams married Marian Clover Hooper and honeymooned mainly at Wenlock Abbey in Shropshire. She was a socialite and talented photographer who committed suicide in 1885 at the age of 42. The couple came to London in 1879 and they took furnished rooms in Half Moon Street, off Piccadilly, near the home of their friend **Henry James** in Bolton Street.

In the USA Adams continued with his journalism and writing and also held academic posts at Harvard from 1870 to 1877, as well as becoming editor of the *North American Review*, which he turned into the organ of the Independents, a Republican grouping opposed to government corruption, while maintaining his scholarly interests. In 1880 he anonymously published *Democracy*, a popular novel set in Washington.

In later life Adams travelled extensively, at first to assuage the depression occasioned by his wife's death, to Japan, the South Seas, Cuba, Mexico, Sicily and Russia, and lived in Paris in the summer. He also retained his political friendships, especially with **Theodore Roosevelt**.

He produced many well-regarded books, including multi-volume histories (a nine-volume history of the USA being one of them) and biographies. One, though, that has remained in print and was named by the Modern Library as the leading non-fiction English language book of the 20th century, is his autobiography, *The Education of Henry Adams*. It was published privately at first, and only publicly after his death. It gained the Pulitzer Prize in 1919.

The book was a critique of western civilisation, and an attempt to come to terms with the 20th century where Adams never felt entirely at home. He felt that man could no longer control the power he had created and was threatened by technology unless a new breed of leader was trained by scientific methods, as traditional education had failed. Maybe such disenchantment and foreboding may partly account for how a man of intelligence, culture and learning also exhibited a virulent anti-semitism.

He died in 1918 at his home in Washington DC.

---

* *The house was severely damaged by war-time bombing but the façade is a close copy of the original. The plaque commemorates both Henry and Charles Adams and the fact that the house was at one time the American legation (which it calls embassy).*

American Bar
Stafford Hotel, 16–18 St James's Place, St James's SW1A 1NJ

It is a certain kind of American – or a certain kind of anyone else – who would be able to savour the delights of a 107-room hotel that marked its centenary in 2010: a wealthy one. The American Bar does, at least, give a less expensive glimpse of the unostentatious luxury in this quiet location, but, more than that, it is for those who wish to have some sense of the great days of the American cocktail bars of London, New York and Paris of the 1920s and 1930s. Many hotels named their bars 'American' to attract overseas clientele and served what were then exotic Manhattans and other cocktails. Most of those bars have long been renamed: the one in The Stafford and the American bar at The Savoy are the two prominent such bars.

Despite refurbishments over the years (the last in 2018) this is just what this is: the genuine article, not a modern-day fabrication.

There's no denying the clubby atmosphere and intimacy with which the adman describes it: an interior of mahogany wood-panelling, a marble bar, emerald green upholstery, vintage glassware and brass fittings, with walls displaying memorabilia and artefacts, together with (often signed) photographs of British and American patrons.

The origin of what's on display is interesting. It began when an American guest gave the then bar manager a small wooden carving of an American eagle. Soon afterwards a wooden model of an Eskimo was given by a Canadian guest, to be followed by an Australian donating a model of a kangaroo. A colourful collection of club ties, sporting mementoes and baseball caps hang from the ceiling.

This must be the only hotel to boast a museum, where can be found, among other things, items left behind by American and Canadian officers during the Second World War. It was then that the hotel became a club for those officers stationed overseas. This led to the formation of the Better 'Ole Club whose membership comprises guests recognised for services above and beyond the call of duty to the hotel.

There have been only three bar managers in the bar's history and the present manager has served 22 years, his predecessor having clocked up 42 years.

American International Church
79a Tottenham Court Road, Fitzrovia W I T 4TB

Today, the American International Church stands in busy Tottenham Court Road but its origins as such rest with members of the United States military who met, during the Second World War, for worship at the Anglican Grosvenor Chapel in South Audley Street, not far from the then US Embassy in Grosvenor Square. The services were led by US Navy chaplains. After the war, while military chaplains still officiated, the congregation grew from the ranks of embassy, State Department and Defense Department families.

In 1969 the church became independent of support from the military when the first settled minister, Rev. William Schotanus, was installed. The congregation made use of several church buildings after leaving the Grosvenor Chapel and came to its present home, the then Whitefield Memorial Church on Tottenham Court Road, in 1972.

The present building was erected in 1955 on the site of a church destroyed by one of the last V2 rockets to hit London on Palm Sunday, 25th March 1945. The old and new churches took their name from George Whitefield, the famous mid-18th century preacher, a contemporary of John and Charles Wesley, and a leader of Calvinist Methodism. Born in England, he served as an Anglican parish minister in Savannah, Georgia, where he was a landowner and, an advocate of slavery, owned 50 slaves. He visited America seven times, making 13 Atlantic crossings. **Benjamin Franklin** was well rewarded through his business relationship with Whitefield as his publisher. Whitefield died in 1770 and is buried in Newburyport, Massachusetts.

The Whitefield congregation, by then part of the United Reformed Church, disbanded in the late 1970s. With that, the American Church joined the United Reformed Church in its present home.

To meet local need, the Soup Kitchen was launched in 1986 and now serves an average of 80 hot meals a day, five days a week. Volunteers also operate a clothes bank, a night shelter and other external ministries that serve the local community.

In the 21st century the congregation has become more varied and international, hence the decision in 2012 to change the name to the American International Church.

Each year, the church participates in the American Thanksgiving Day Service, in partnership with the US Embassy, when more than 2,000 Americans gather at **St Paul's Cathedral**. The sermons are given, in alternate years, by the churches' clergy and those of the International Community Church in Surrey. The service includes African-American spirituals and American hymns.

Arnold, Benedict (1722–1801)

Hero of the American Revolution and traitor to its cause

62 Gloucester Place, Marylebone W1U 8HW 🅿 *
St Mary's Church, Battersea Church Road, Battersea, Wandsworth SW11 3NA

Arnold, whose name is now synonymous with that of traitor, was a hero of the Revolutionary War, so much so that George Washington placed him in charge of West Point.

In 1775 Arnold had taken part in the surrender of the British at Fort Ticonderoga. Later that year he was badly wounded and carried from the battlefield when the British defeated the revolutionaries, whom he led, in their attempt to take Quebec to rouse Canadians to the cause of American (and thus their own) independence, having marched from Maine. The battle enabled the British to retain control of Canada. The next year at the Battle of Lake Champlain Arnold prevented the enemy's invasion of New York.

Benedict Arnold in 1776, three years before his defection to the British

But Arnold felt himself undervalued and unappreciated for all he had done and resigned in 1777 from the continental army when five officers were promoted above him. However, he rejoined to help defeat General **John Burgoyne** at Saratoga. Arnold's feelings were not without justification because General Horatio Oates praised his own efforts at the expense of those of his subordinate in his reports.

In 1778 Arnold became military governor of Philadelphia after another wound in the same leg as at Quebec. There Arnold's second marriage to Margaret (Peggy) Shippen, who had loyalist sympathies, his own extravagance (which led to debt), and resentment that he was not being promoted prompted him to begin to feel that switching sides would be in his own interest.

His lifestyle and the people he mixed with raised suspicions and the censure of the city's supreme executive council, which referred the matter to Congress. Arnold sought a court martial to clear his name and was exonerated on all but two minor charges, though Washington offered a public rebuke.

In 1779 Arnold plotted to hand West Point to the British in exchange for money and the post of brigadier-general. When the British major John Andre, an associate in the plot, was apprehended holding papers that incriminated Arnold, he fled to Canada (Andre was hanged as a spy). Ironically, Arnold's treason boosted the cause he had turned against: American morale had been flagging as they felt that independence was slow in coming. Arnold's treachery revived their spirits. He received half the sum he had negotiated (£20,000), gained a commission in the British army and fought some engagements against his former compatriots, which included sacking and burning towns and the massacre of the men in the New London garrison. Arnold's lame excuse was that he had never supported independence, but sought only that his compatriots' grievances be addressed. He also stated that he could not continue to support the Americans after they allied with France, the enemy of Protestantism.

Friendless among loyalists and rebels alike, when the British surrendered the Arnold family left for London in December 1781. Arnold urged George III and the secretary of state for the Amerian Colonies, Lord George Germain, to renew the struggle against the Americans, which gained support from the Tories, but opposition from the anti-war Whigs, who were in the parliamentary majority. Unable to obtain a permanent British commission or any other useful post, Arnold lived for a while on the £6,315 army lump sum and a pension of £360 a year.

He tried his hand at various unsuccessful ventures, among them land speculation in Canada. When the French Revolutionary Wars broke out, Arnold sailed to Guadeloupe, then in a war zone, where he was captured by the French and threatened with execution, but escaped. He then failed with a venture in privateering. Returning to London in 1791 he lived at Gloucester

Place from 1796 until his death. In 1792 he fought a duel with the Earl of Lauderdale who had referred to Arnold's 'apostasy'.

Arnold was vain, arrogant and tactless, but also a courageous and gifted soldier and, in his last years, plagued by both money problems and ill health. He died in June 1801. He is alleged to have said on his death-bed (though this may be apocryphal) 'Let me die in this old uniform in which I fought my battles. May God forgive me for ever having put on another.' It was said that there were seven mourning carriages and four state coaches, but no military honours at his funeral at St Mary's Church.

He is buried in the crypt with his wife and daughter**. The granite headstone refers to him as: 'Sometime General in the Army of George Washington … The Two Nations Whom He Served In Turn in the Years of their Enmity Have United in Enduring Friendship.' ***

---

*   *The plaque describes Arnold as 'an American patriot'.*

**   *According to contemporary practice Arnold and his wife and daughter were placed in lead-lined coffins in the crypt in 1801. Such 'burials' ended in 1854 and in 1875 the vicar had all the coffins buried under concrete in a hole dug in the crypt. The importance of Benedict Arnold's grave (and that of his wife and daughter) was not realised at the time, but a rough and ready contemporaneous list of the identifiable coffins, including that of the Arnolds, was preserved. The fact of his burial at St Mary's was not established until the 1920s and an individual grave for any of the three cannot be identified.*

*** *The headstone was paid for by Bill Stanley of Norwich, Connecticut, a former state senator and president of the Norwich Historical Society. In 1976 a Mr Lindner of White Plains, NJ, said to be president of the Benedict Arnold Association, paid for the handsome commemorative stained-glass window in the church.*

Astor, William Waldorf, 1st Viscount Astor (1848–1919)

Property owner and newspaper proprietor

2 Temple Place, Victoria Embankment WC2P 3BD*
18 Carlton House Terrace, St James's SW1Y 5AH

For a man who built the Waldorf Astoria Hotel in New York and owned Hever Castle in Kent, Cliveden House in Buckinghamshire and a six-storey Regency home in St James's, a business headquarters like Temple Place, set back by a lawn and gates from the now busy Victoria Embankment, is no surprise.

The Upper Gallery at Two Temple Place (Peter Dazeley)

It is a palatial neo-Gothic mansion, which Astor originally designed for use as his estate's office, work beginning in 1892 with an unlimited budget. It was known for many years as Astor House. Suitably for a man then thought to be the world's richest, the house contained the largest strong room in Europe as well as two other enormous fortified safes. The interior, with wood panelling and intricate carving, is opulent, and testifies to his deepest passions and interests: history, literature and the arts. His passion for art and sculpture had developed when posted to Rome in 1882 as US minister to Italy. In 1885, when his posting came to an end, he published *Valentino: an Historical Romance of the Sixteenth Century* and later wrote two novels. Temple Place was built to include a bedroom, so Astor would have stayed here occasionally, it is believed more so possibly after the death of his wife, Mamie, in 1894.

Astor was born in New York and early in life he served as a Republican in the New York state senate. Before that he had worked as a lawyer and in the family estates. The Waldorf Hotel later became extended as the Waldorf Astoria Hotel and he went on to build the Waldorf Hotel in Aldwych, a short walk from his office.

His father, John Jacob Astor III, had amassed a fortune through fur trading and shipping and then invested heavily in Manhattan Island. When he died in 1890, he left his son a legacy said to be $100 million. That year Astor took his family to London: his wife Mary (Mamie) Dahlgren; their two surviving sons **Waldorf Astor**, later second Viscount Astor, and John Jacob Astor, later Baron Astor of Hever; and a daughter, Pauline. He bought Cliveden in 1893, adding the entire balustrade of Rome's Villa Borghese. In 1899 Astor became a British citizen. This may not be wholly surprising as the *Oxford Dictionary of National Biography* tells us that 'he despised his native country and said so in print'. As a result he was ridiculed and satirised in the New York press.

He bought the *Pall Mall Gazette*, a Liberal evening daily newspaper, in 1892 and turned it into a Conservative one. The following year he launched the monthly *Pall Mall Magazine*. To acquire the services of *The Observer*'s editor, JL Garvin, as editor of the *Pall Mall Gazette*, in 1911 he bought that newspaper. But the *Pall Mall Magazine* was sold in 1912 and the *Gazette* suffered the same fate in 1915. Astor retained the *The Observer*, which was subsequently passed down to his son Waldorf and a later generation.

Astor bought Hever Castle in Kent, which he reconstructed and housed there his collection of pictures and artefacts. He gave to charities and was a substantial donor to the Conservative Party. He became a baron in 1916 and a viscount a year later. His peerage put paid to the career of his eldest son, Waldorf, who became Unionist MP for Plymouth in 1910 and had to step down when he succeeded to his father's titles in 1919. However, this gave leeway to his daughter-in-law **Nancy Astor**, who won her husband's seat in the by-election.

Despite Astor's wealth, a friend wrote in *The Times* of 'the lonely life' he led amid 'surroundings partly noble and magnificent, partly fantastic and baroque'.

The *Oxford Dictionary of National Biography* characterised him as 'a shy, austere and, by all accounts, unlovable man'. He died in another grand house in Brighton in 1919.

---

* The house is open to the public from January to April each year to coincide with its events. (www.twotempleplace.org)

Astor, Nancy (1879–1964)
First woman to take her seat in the House of Commons

Astor, Waldorf, 2nd Viscount Astor (1879–1952)
Politician, race horse owner–breeder and newspaper proprietor

4 St James's Square, St James's SW1Y 4JU ℗ (now the In & Out Club)

Born Nancy Langhorne in Virginia to a family that had made a vast fortune in railway construction, the future Viscountess Astor was divorced after a disastrous marriage to Robert Gould Shaw in 1903, and the next year came to England. She was attracted to the social life and hunting and two years later married **Waldorf Astor**, the New York-born, Eton-educated, wealthy newspaper proprietor and son of **William Waldorf Astor**, later 1st Viscount Astor. As a wedding gift his father gave them the mansion of Cliveden, near Taplow, in Buckinghamshire.

With Astor's enthusiastic help, Waldorf became, as a Unionist, one of the two Members of Parliament for Plymouth, where he supported the 'People's Budget' and the National Insurance Act 1911. 'I married beneath me; all women do', she said of the man who was father to her five children.

Waldorf served in the First World War, though was prevented by a heart problem from taking part in combat. He became parliamentary private secretary to the prime minister David Lloyd George in the coalition and later held ministerial positions.

He made unsuccessful attempts to disclaim the peerage which came to him upon his father's death in 1919, and had to resign his parliamentary seat. He backed his wife as candidate in the by-election, but there were widespread complaints about her candidacy as a woman, and her reputation was such that the Tory party chairman, Sir George Younger, an opponent, said: 'The worst of it is, the woman is sure to get in.'

He was right – she did, with 51 per cent of the vote and a 5,000 majority. Astor's victory was a step forward for women in politics but she had told the electors: 'I am not standing before you as a sex candidate. I do not believe in sexes or classes.' Though Countess Constance Markievicz, the Irish nationalist, had won a Commons seat in 1918, she refused to take it, thus Astor became the first woman ever to sit in the House of Commons. She continued to do so for the same seat until 1945.

Astor was a robust and enthusiastic campaigner for many causes, particularly those affecting women and children, and she supported issues like widows' pensions and raising the school leaving age to 15 in 1944. Financially and as an MP, she supported the pioneering nursery schools of **Margaret McMillan**. Progressive in some ways, she was regressive in others: for example, she opposed information on contraception to married women on the very male Victorian grounds that it degraded women. A teetotaller, she helped pass legislation in 1923 that banned the sale of alcohol to those under 18 years of age.

She felt talk of her clothing in the press trivialised her and so she adopted a simple costume of a white blouse and black skirt, jacket and tricorn hat, with a white gardenia in her buttonhole.

Waldorf's post-House of Commons life consisted of extensive charitable work and becoming a very successful race horse breeder–owner, as well as running the newspapers which his father had bequeathed him.

In 1912 the couple bought 4 St James's Square. The oldest building to survive in the square, it was built in 1726–8. Here, as elsewhere, the Astors entertained lavishly, she liking to invite people with whom she disagreed.

In London Astor was one of the group of London hostesses – the others were **Lady Emerald Cunard** and Lady Sybil Colefax – and she liked to pose at the top of the staircase, sparkling with jewels, to welcome her guests. The magnificent reception rooms and huge ballrooms were the scene of dinners (sometimes for 50 people), balls (with up to 600 guests) and receptions (with a thousand in attendance). The house was requisitioned during the war and used by the Free French forces and suffered bomb damage. The Astors sold it in 1948 to the Ministry of Works at a low price on the condition that it be refurbished for use by the Arts Council.

While in the Commons until 1945, Astor reached her peak in the 1920s, as later other, more articulate and intelligent women held ground. Her inability to offer a well-

Nancy and Waldorf Astor's home in St James's Square
(Terry Philpot)

considered and substantial speech wearied members. This led to her reputation for heckling and interruptions. She said that her fellow MPs 'would rather have had a rattlesnake than me' in the Commons. Her loyalty to her party was never certain – despite her attacks on the Labour party. In 1929 Astor's majority was just 200 and only the National governments that came to dominate the 1930s kept her parliamentary career going as long as it did.

Cliveden gave its name to the so-called 'Cliveden set', a social group that tended to be sympathetic to Germany. In fact, Waldorf was anti-semitic, though he protested to Hitler over Germany's treatment of the Jews, and Nancy, anti-Catholic and anti-Jewish, was opposed to the Nazis, largely on the grounds of women's rights. The 'set' tarnished her reputation, which she restored when she was one of the Tories who unseated Neville Chamberlain and through her patriotism in the Second World War.

Unlikely to retain her seat in 1945, Waldorf informed the local association that Astor would not stand, something she agreed with but resented him for saying. She died at her daughter's home, Grimstone Castle in Lincolnshire, in 1964 and was buried next to her husband at Cliveden, who had died there 12 years previously. A memorial service was held in **Westminster Abbey**.

When Britain's first woman prime minister, Margaret Thatcher, unveiled the plaque on 4 St James's Square in 1987, she said that she herself had been inspired by Astor going into 'that totally male-dominated place'.

Burgoyne, John (1723–1792)

General, politician and playwright
10 Hertford Street, Mayfair W1J 7RL 🅿 *

If Lord North will always be remembered as the prime minister who 'lost' the American colonies, then Burgoyne is the man whose surrender to the rebels at Saratoga on 17th October 1777 created the turning point for the Americans in the War of Independence.

He was most likely born in Westminster, and attended Westminster School, where **Thomas Gage**, later to be an army colleague in America, was also a pupil.

When in 1751 Burgoyne eloped with Lady Charlotte Stanley, the daughter of Lord Derby, her enraged father deprived her of her allowance and Burgoyne had to sell his commission for £2,600 to keep them solvent. After spending time on the continent, they were later reconciled with Derby, when they presented him with a granddaughter, their only child. Burgoyne purchased a captaincy in 1756 in the 11th Dragoons, and bought the Hertford Street house in 1769, moving in two years later, after alterations by Robert Adam.

Burgoyne was a professional soldier (he had distinguished himself in the Seven Years War) and also an MP, being elected to Parliament to represent Midhurst in Sussex in 1761. He served many years in the Commons.

He was a bellicose supporter of North's stand on the colonies and declared in Parliament that 'the soldier draws his sword with alacrity'. After he had pronounced his impatience with talk of tea, taxation and representation 'till one's head grows dizzy with distinctions', he was given the military assignment he requested. In February 1775 Burgoyne was appointed, with Sir William Howe and Henry Clinton, to join Gage, the military commander in America, and suppress the rebels in Boston.

Sir Joshua Reynolds' portrait of Sir John Burgoyne

They were all made major-generals, with Burgoyne the junior and at Bunker Hill, providing only military cover from Copp's Hill. He returned home when he saw no prospect of a senior command and he sent Lord George Germain, the new imaginative and resolute but ultimately unsuccessful, secretary of state for the American Colonies, *Reflections upon the War in America*. Here he suggested using armies from Canada and New York City to separate New England from the other colonies.

Back to the battlefield, Burgoyne left it again to return to England when the British invasion of New York, following the battle against **Benedict Arnold**'s rebels in Quebec, proved abortive.

Returning again to North America, he had command of a force to push south from Canada to end the rebellion by splitting away New England. However, Burgoyne's slow advance gave the rebels the opportunity to concentrate their forces. The plan had been that the British Army in New York City would come to assist him but they moved south to capture Philadelphia. Burgoyne was overcome by superior American forces at Saratoga and surrendered on 17th October 1777. The British lost 184 men, the Americans 30, and there were 264 British wounded, against 100 Americans, with 183 British taken prisoner.

Following Saratoga, France recognised the United States and entered the war the following February. Three years after Saratoga Lord Cornwallis surrendered at Yorktown, effectively ending the war and guaranteeing American independence.

It was agreed that the British would be allowed to return to their homeland on condition that they did not serve again in North America. However, on the urging of George Washington, the Continental Congress reneged on the agreement and those parts of the army in Massachusetts and Virginia were imprisoned.

On his return in May the following year Burgoyne defended his much-criticised conduct but was denied a court martial and an audience with the king. He told Parliament that Germaine had been responsible for what had happened.

Nicknamed Gentleman Johnny, which says something about his approach to life, Burgoyne did not now give himself over to frivolity. In Parliament he opposed the war and later backed the French Revolution. In 1782 he was appointed commander-in-chief of the army in Ireland, resigning two years later.

In 1774 Burgoyne had written a play, *The Maid of the Oaks*, which, extended to five acts by the great actor-manager David Garrick, became a popular feature of the Drury Lane repertory. He now returned to writing with a political satire and success with a comedy, *The Heiress*. It opened at the Theatre Royal, Drury Lane, in 1786, ran for 30 performances, and attained half a century of popularity on the continent and in England.

Burgoyne's wife died in 1776 and he then fathered four children with a married actress, Susan Caulfield. He died at Hertford Street probably of gout and is buried in the North Walk cloisters in **Westminster Abbey**.

---

* *A second plaque on the building shows that the playwright Richard Brinsley Sheridan moved into the house three years after Burgoyne's death.*

Channon, Sir Henry ('Chips') (1897–1958)

Diarist and Conservative MP

5 Belgrave Square, Belgravia SW1X 8PH

Born in Chicago and a naturalised British citizen, Channon was independently wealthy through his family's shipping business when he married Lady Honor Guinness, daughter of the 2nd Earl of Iveagh of the brewing dynasty. He had first come to London after a period as an honorary attaché at the US embassy in Paris and then spent 18 months at Oxford, after which he shared a house in Westminster with Viscount Gage and the future Prince Paul of Serbia. By then he had already come to dislike his homeland.

The Belgrave Square house was purchased in 1935, the year of the birth of the Channons' only son, Paul, and two years later a country home was bought at Kelvedon in Essex. The London house, Channon claimed, was 'not too grand and dirt cheap compared with all the other houses we have seen'.

He went on, '… it has a distinguished air and we will make it gay and comfortable'. They did – £6,000 alone was spent on one room.

Stephane Boudin, whom Channon called 'the greatest decorator in the world', designed a dining room that was 'a symphony in blue and silver, cascades of aquamarine'. On his 50th birthday, 30 guests entered here from an ochre and silver gallery. The artist and designer Rex Whistler made a chimneypiece for the music room.

Another celebrated diarist, Harold Nicolson, described the décor of the vast reception rooms as 'what-ho and oh-no-no and all that. Very fine indeed'.*

The house was the embodiment of Channon's obsession with rank, privilege and wealth (work was one obsession he never had to entertain). It became one of the great centres of inter-war London society, and a scene of his relentless social climbing as he re-invented himself as an upper class European. This was epitomised when he inherited his Southend-on-Sea parliamentary seat from his mother-in-law (which had been his father-in-law's seat and would, in turn, be represented by his son Paul) and was then awarded a knighthood. His friendship with **Wallis Simpson**, however, saw him cold-shouldered by the court after 1936.

Sir Henry 'Chips' Channon, a drawing by Augustus John

Despite Channon's frenetic entertaining and being entertained and parliamentary duties he still wrote two novels, neither favourable to his native country, and a biography of the Ludwig dynasty of Wittelsbach. However, his lasting literary achievement was his posthumously published diaries from 1934 to 1953 – snobbish, self-mocking, informative, endlessly interesting, a portrait of a certain society as seen through the eyes of an unusual, witty, worldly, observant, talented man, a great gossip, who whatever his defects was known for his generosity and kindness. The diaries take in, importantly, the Abdication, appeasement and the outbreak and course of the Second World War.

But he did attract criticism: Lady Gladwyn called him 'that American pipsqueak (alas naturalised British)' and a 'twerp', while another great diarist, James Lees-Milne, thought him 'a flibbertigibbet', and Duff Cooper, Conservative politician, minister and later ambassador to Paris, considered Channon 'a toad'.

About himself he had no illusions:

> I have … an unusual character – able but trivial; I have flair, intuition, great good taste but only second rate ambition: I am far too susceptible to flattery; I hate and am uninterested in all the things most men like such as sport, business, statistics, debates, speeches, war and the weather; I am riveted by lust, furniture, glamour and society and jewels.

Channon was a diligent MP when it came to his constituents, but had little interest in political ideas. He supported appeasement and was pro-German in the way of many of his class at that time, although in his case (and typically) he believed Hitler would restore the German royal family. He never rose above the lowest political ranks with three years as parliamentary private secretary or a ministerial bag-carrier to RA Butler, then under-secretary of state at the Foreign Office.

In 1939 he met Peter Coats, a gay man known as 'Petticoats' and later editor of *House and Garden*, at a dinner given by Lady Emerald Cunard. Bisexual himself, Channon began a life-long relationship that saw separation from his wife and divorce in 1945, although that did not dry up his Guinness funds. He had an affair after the war with the playwright Terence Rattigan.

His sexual voracity continued, as did his entertaining. Channon stayed on as an MP until his death but never gained any further political preferment. He became bloated, suffered heart attacks and his spirits flagged as even his socialising palled. He died, after several strokes, at the London Hospital, Whitechapel.

---

* The grand dining room was severely damaged by war-time bombing. Most of the ornate interiors were taken out when the house came into more prosaic use by the Institute of Directors and then the British Plastics Federation. It is now again privately owned.

Churchill, Jennie (1854–1921)

Society hostess and writer

48 Charles Street, Mayfair W IJ 5EN
2 Connaught Place, Hyde Park W2 2ET *
35a Great Cumberland Place, Marble Arch (now the Rose Court Hotel) W I H 7DS
8 Westbourne Street, Hyde Park W2 2TZ

More formally known as Jeanette Jerome, who became Lady Randolph Churchill, Jennie Churchill is best known for being the mother of Sir Winston Churchill. She was, though, a formidable woman unafraid to use her wiles and influence to advance her son's career as writer, journalist and politician.

She was born in Brooklyn, the eldest of the three daughters of Leonard Jerome, American sportsman and speculator, and his wife, Clarissa Hall. She was invariably known as Jennie after the singer Jenny Lind.

When, in 1874, she married Lord Randolph Churchill (whom she had met the previous year at the Isle of Wight regatta) at the British embassy in Paris, she joined one of the great ducal families, the Marlboroughs. The young couple's wealth was boosted by £50,000 from Leonard Jerome, producing £2,000 a year plus £1,200 from the duke (or over £200,000 at today's rates). There would be two children, Winston and John, always known as Jack, who was born in Dublin, where Randolph was serving his father, the Viceroy.

Charles Street was the Churchills' first home, on a lease from Leonard Jerome, and in 1883 they moved to Connaught Place, where they made it what Jennie claimed to be the first London house with electric light. They were here for nearly a decade before moving to 50 Grosvenor Square, Mayfair (gone: now apartments).

When his mother died, Winston wrote that 'on the whole it was a life of sunshine'. The sunshine in which she basked warmed numerous lovers, said to be 200 during and after her marriage to Lord Randolph, but, as her biographer Anne Sebba says, only she kept count. But Churchill's life was lived at a cost to her sons for she played hardly any part in their younger lives. Cared for largely by a nanny, Winston was then sent off to school at an early age and until he left Harrow never enjoyed his education except at his prep school in Brighton. The *Oxford Dictionary of National Biography* accurately describes Churchill's relationship with Winston as 'affectionate but distant'. However, his love for her was matched by an admiration for his father, who died in 1895 when his son was 21.

Churchill never allowed the social whirl of her London and country life to distract from her husband's career, to which she gave consistent and substantial support – he rose to become Chancellor of the Exchequer – with electioneering, entertaining and active membership of the Primrose League, an organisation founded in 1883 to propagate Conservatism.

However, the marriage was not a strong one – Randolph contracted syphilis, from which he died, and to which he admitted but with which she

The 45 year old Lady Jennie Churchill

was not infected – which led her into her numerous liaisons. Only gradually did she learn discretion, the lack of which had given rise to notoriety.

With her husband's death, Churchill came into her own, not least on behalf of her eldest son: she importuned publishers to take his manuscripts, sought favourable reviews for his books and successfully encouraged the prime minister, Lord Salisbury, to secure him a place on the military expedition to the Sudan led by Sir Herbert (later Lord) Kitchener. Her own first venture into publishing was less successful: *The Anglo-Saxon*, which she founded in 1899, closed after ten issues.

When the Boer War broke out that same year, Churchill went on the maiden voyage to South Africa of the *Main*, a hospital ship provided by a committee of American women, which she chaired. When she came back she was living in Great Cumberland Place up to her marriage in 1900 to a Scots Guards officer, George Cornwallis-West, who was Winston's age. They lived at 2 Norfolk Street (now Dunraven Street, Mayfair), and rented the moated Salisbury Hall near St Albans – and lavishly entertained guests who included Edward VII.

Churchill could hardly rival her son in his literary gifts, but her 1908 memoirs were modestly successful on both sides of the Atlantic and the following year Mrs Patrick Campbell was both director of, and leading lady in Churchill's play, *His Borrowed Plumes*. Alas, George Cornwallis-West's relationship with Campbell led to the couple's eventual divorce and his marriage to 'Mrs Pat'.

During the First World War, Churchill worked with the American Women's War Hospital in Paignton in Devon and nursed in a hospital in London's Lancaster Gate. At the same time, she did some journalism, writing articles for *Pearson's Weekly* that in 1916 appeared as *Small Talks on Big Subjects*.

As the war drew to an end, 64-year-old Churchill entered into her third marriage, with 41-year-old Montagu Porch, a colonial official serving in Nigeria. 'He has a future and I have a past, so we should be all right', she said. She never lived with him in Nigeria but, says a biographer, the marriage was 'placidly successful'. Her second and third marriages she summed up with the words: 'My second marriage was romantic but not successful; my third marriage was successful but not romantic'.

After coming back to England, having quit the colonial service, Porch then returned to Africa in 1921 to seek his fortune. That summer, Churchill died of a haemorrhage at her Westbourne Street home, following a fall when staying with friends in Somerset when she broke an ankle, causing her leg to be amputated and gangrene to set in. She was buried in Bladon near Woodstock, Oxfordshire, next to her first husband and where 43½ years later her son would join them.

Winston's friend, the civil servant and literary patron, Edward Marsh found in her 'an incredible and most delightful compound of flagrant worldliness and eternal childhood', whose love of fashion and luxury combined with 'warm-heartedness, humour, loyalty, sincerity, or steadfast and pugnacious courage'.

Cree (unknown–1734)

Yamacraw leader

St John's Garden, Horseferry Road, Westminster SW1P 4DA

Mahomet Weyonomon was not the first indigenous American known to have been buried in London. In 1734, Cree, whose other names are not known and who is sometimes wrongly identified as Creek, was buried at night by torchlight in what was then the churchyard of St John the Evangelist, Smith Square, ten minutes walk away. The cemetery had been consecrated only three years previously. Added to in 1823, it was closed as a burial ground in October 1853 and was opened as a public garden in 1885.

Cree had travelled with Tomochichi, the leader of several pro-British bands of Yamasee and Lower Creek, who were favourable toward the British. They adopted the collective name of Yamacraw and resettled near the mouth of the Savannah River.

The group had been encouraged to come to England by General James Oglethorpe, founder of the Colony of Georgia. The general said that he 'hop[ed] what they might witness and experience there, would result in lasting benefits to both their nations and the English', according to the Victorian writer Samuel G Drake.

As well as Cree, Tomochici landed at St Helens on the Isle of Wight on 16th June 1734, with Senauki, whom Drake describes as his consort; Toonahowi, his nephew; Hillispilli, a war chief; John Musgrove, an interpreter; and five others: Apokutchi, Stimaletchi, Santachi, Hinguithi and Umphichi.

Tomochichi's cousin Hinguithi died and was said by Drake to have been buried 'according to the custom of the "Cherokee Creeks"'.

Cunard, Lady Emerald (1872–1948)

Social hostess

7 Grosvenor Square, Mayfair W1K 4AG (gone: now apartments, numbered 7)
Dorchester Hotel, 53 Park Lane, Mayfair W1K 1QA

Lady Maud Cunard's 'sudden whim', as she called it, to call herself Emerald, in 1926 at the age of 54, was characteristic of the life she lived – often impulsive, unfettered by convention and unrestrained by the need to earn a living. The new name, too, symbolised her own glittering position in the society she inhabited, entertained and shaped. Her many friends adjusted to the new name with the exceptions of the conductor Sir Thomas Beecham and the Irish novelist George Moore. The latter believed that it signified that she had married a Mr Emerald – and refused to refer to her other than by the name she had always had, as did Beecham. But Emerald is the name by which she is invariably known today.

Cunard was born Maud Alice Burke in San Francisco in 1872, the daughter of a half-French mother and an Irish-American father, who claimed descent from Robert Emmett, the early Irish nationalist leader whom the British had executed in 1803. The Burkes were a wealthy family from the West Coast but a social register below the 'old money' of the East Coast, although young Maud was brought up in New York.

She met Moore when she was 21 and he was 42. He was deeply in love with her and their affair allegedly produced her only child, Nancy Cunard, the writer, heiress and political activist, born in 1896. Certainly, Nancy did nothing to dissuade anyone about her paternity and Moore himself colluded in a rumour that seems to have been unlikely. Indeed, he was believed to be impotent, and, as someone wrote, he was 'one who told but didn't kiss'.

Hearing Wagner at 12, Cunard became devoted to music. She had been engaged to the grandson of the last king of Poland but when he jilted her she married Sir Bache Cunard, the third baronet, in 1895, and grandson of the Canadian-born Samuel, founder of the shipping line. Sir Bache was 21 years older than the new Lady Maud and they lived at Nevill Holt, the Cunard family seat in Leicestershire, which was more baronial than palatial. Emerald's talents lay in entertaining, which she did lavishly, and the arts rather than mothering, which she did, when she did it at all, reluctantly; indeed, she viewed motherhood with distaste.

Hers may appear a sybaritic life but Cunard and her husband, a keen huntsman, had little in common, and with her taste for music, her role as hostess enabled her to indulge what one writer called 'a taste for the arts, or for artists anyhow, especially musicians', of whom she often became patron. She was also well read in literature, both French and English.

In 1911 the Cunards agreed to separate and Maud moved to London with Nancy. Allan Jefferson, the biographer of Thomas Beecham, wrote of her in the capital: 'Soon she had captured all London society, and her … salon became the most important Mecca for musicians, painters, sculptors, poets and writers as well as for politicians, soldiers, aristocrats – indeed anybody so long as they were interesting.' She fell deeply in love with Beecham and she was seen as his companion. She became a tireless fundraiser for him at a time when his finances were stretched.

Cunard invited many politicians to her dinner table, where indiscreet revelations were common, as were her waspish comments. Among her guests were **Wallis Simpson** and the Prince of Wales and Joachim von Ribbentrop, Nazi Germany's ambassador. The disapproval of Queen Mary, the king's mother, led her to hope for preferment at court, as Mistress of the Bedchamber, when the Prince of Wales succeeded to the throne. When her hopes were dashed by the king's abdication, she wept and asked: 'How could *he* do this to me?', which might seem to take solipsism too far.

The war brought an end to lavish society entertaining and when Beecham moved to the United States, Cunard took off in his wake, living in luxury in a New York hotel. Her return to London was prompted by learning from a third party that Beecham was to marry the pianist Betty Hamby.

Cunard set up home in the Dorchester Hotel, where her life was a miserable and lonely one, far removed from her earlier London life. She was 75 when she died in the hotel and her ashes were scattered in Grosvenor Square.

Eisenhower, Dwight D (1890–1969)

Supreme Allied Commander Europe and 34th president of the United States

Norfolk House, 13 St James's Square, St James's SW1 4JR 🅿 *
20 Grosvenor Square, Mayfair W1K 6LE 🅿
Telegraph Cottage, Warren Road, Kingston-upon-Thames KT2 7HU (gone) **

When planning Operation Torch, the Allied landings in North Africa in the autumn of 1942, and, later, Operation Overlord, the D-Day landings in 1944***, Eisenhower lived in Kingston-upon-Thames from 1942 to 1944 which was then a small town in Surrey. It was a private refuge for him from a world at war and his daunting responsibilities in London. No 20 Grosvenor Square was the US embassy from 1938 to 1960 and in war-time was known as Eisenhower Platz.

When he first came to London in 1942 Eisenhower stayed at Claridge's but after a week left for the Dorchester Hotel, which he thought less ostentatious. His first job was to create the Allied Force Headquarters, which he did at Norfolk House, to oversee the Allied landings in North Africa.

He was also at Norfolk House in 1944 for his first months in his new role as Supreme Commander,

Dwight Eisenhower in February 1945 as the war nears its end

a building where he had planned Operation Torch two years before*. In April that year the headquarters of the Supreme Headquarters Allied Expeditionary Force moved to Bushy Park, on the edge of London, and later to France. Eisenhower also commanded the European Theatre of Operations, which directed US operations in part of Europe from 1942, at Grosvenor Square.

Eisenhower was enormously popular with the British public, who would often greet him when he was out in London. They recognised him as a likeable man, simple in his tastes, fun-loving, unshowy and dignified, 'refreshingly naïve', according to one biographer, Stephen E Ambrose. But he refused formal dinners and requests to open events: 'Hell, I've got work to do!' he exclaimed.

London, though, offered no respite and was noisy. Thus, he left the Dorchester and took Telegraph Cottage, a five bedroom house (according to his grandson David Eisenhower; Ambrose says seven), set in ten acres with a golf course nearby. It had only one armed guard. Eisenhower grew fond of his temporary home, even naming his Scottie pup Telek, his contraction for the cottage's name. His grandson's biography calls the house 'a sanctuary, and serious books were banned, along with traces of work'. The latter cannot have been wholly true as he had fellow soldiers as guests, including General Omar Bradley, and the weekend stays that sometimes became half a week demanded work be done.

Eisenhower pottered in the garden, went for walks and famously read Western novels. He also took up painting, probably at the suggestion of Marshal of the Royal Air Force Arthur Tedder, who had previously occupied Telegraph Cottage. Eisenhower, though, never had any illusions about his gift with the brush. When Richard Cohen, the *Washington Post* columnist, was a young reporter with UPI, he toured an exhibition of the work by the then former president, who said of a painting of his Gettysburg home: 'They would have burned this [expletive] a long time ago if I weren't the president of the United States'.

When he was president of New York's Columbia University in 1949 Eisenhower painted a picture of the cottage from an earlier watercolour as a present for his valet. (It failed to reach its price when presented at auction in 2014.) The cottage was destroyed by fire in 1987.

On his first visit to Britain in May 1942 Eisenhower met Irish-born divorcée Kay Summersby, who had acted as his driver. When he returned to live in London, Summersby again acted as his chauffeur and then his secretary, working at the cottage, until November 1945. During her time with Eisenhower she was engaged to an American officer, who died in late 1943. Summersby and Eisenhower were very close and an affair was rumoured, and in 1975 a ghost-written autobiography (she was too ill to write it herself) said that there had been an unconsummated romantic relationship. Most biographers are doubtful; some claim the romance to have been fabricated by the ghost writer, though all acknowledge a very close relationship. Summersby ended the war as a decorated captain, having served in the British Mechanised Transport Corps.

Nine years after leaving Telegraph Cottage and London Eisenhower took up a longer term tenancy – the White House – as president of the United States.

---

*   *Norfolk House and Grosvenor Square both have plaques (Norfolk House has two) which state that Eisenhower planned both Operation Torch and Operation Overlord in the buildings. Most books consulted by the author rarely mention Norfolk House but all mention Grosvenor Square. The details of the use of the two buildings are, as far as can be ascertained in detail, as stated above.*

**   *A plaque commemorating Eisenhower's time in Kingston-upon-Thames has been erected in Warren Road 750 yards from where the house once stood.*

***   *The oft-repeated claim the Eisenhower Centre, Bloomsbury, was Eisenhower's war-time headquarters is untrue. It was a deep underground bomb shelter and is now used for storage. Eisenhower's only connection is that it was named after him.*

Fairbanks Jnr, Douglas (1909–2000)

Actor, businessman, socialite

99 Park Lane, Mayfair W1K 7TH*
8 The Boltons, Brompton, Kensington & Chelsea SW10 9TB

Fairbanks was already internationally known when, with his second wife, Mary Lee Hartford, whom he had married in 1938, he moved to the four-bedroom duplex apartment overlooking Hyde Park. Not only was he the only son of Hollywood legend, Douglas Fairbanks Snr and his equally renowned stepmother Mary Pickford (his parents divorced when he was nine), but in his early 30s he had made a string of popular films, including *Dawn Patrol* (1930), *Little Caesar* (1931), *The Prisoner of Zenda* (1937) and *Gunga Din* (1939). *The Corsican Brothers* (1941) and *Sinbad the Sailor* (1947) reflected something of his father's spirit, although he never attained his father's fame.

From 1920 to 1951 Fairbanks appeared in 59 films, many of which are today forgotten, but often opposite leading ladies of the day, like Greta Garbo and Katherine Hepburn. He was also a socialite, entertaining and

Douglas Fairbanks Jnr in his later London years (Allan Warren)

befriending royalty and actors, and, as a hedge against the fate that awaits many actors who go out of fashion, became a successful businessman and philanthropist. He appeared, too, on US and UK television until the 1980s and on stage: in the UK for the first time in Manchester in 1934 and in London until the 1970s. Noted for his good looks, charm, manners and dress sense, Fairbanks was a governor of the Royal Shakespeare Company and president of a boys' club in south London.

Fairbanks had initially come to London on a delayed honeymoon with his first wife, Joan Crawford. He was an Anglophile, much taken with London. When he met Mary he had been having an affair with Marlene Dietrich, who used to smuggle him into her room in Claridge's.

With US entry into the Second World War, he was commissioned a reserve officer in the US Navy and saw action, receiving American, Italian, French and British (DSC) war-time decorations. Fairbanks was awarded an honorary knighthood in 1949 for his contribution to Anglo-British relations.

Until they moved from their Hyde Park home, it was a place where the Fairbankses, who had three daughters, entertained people like Noel Coward, Laurence Olivier, Gertrude Lawrence (with whom Fairbanks had had an affair), Cary Grant, David Niven and Lord Louis Mountbatten.

A 14-foot-long plunge pool and health spa was installed on the ground floor. It was claimed to be one of the first to be built in a private home in London. Today, the Fairbankses' backlit onyx cocktail bar is one of the several features of the time which have been retained.

After the war, the Fairbankses moved to the large house in The Boltons, where in the 1950s he entertained the Queen and the Duke of Edinburgh. He was said to be one of the men in compromising photographs in the notorious divorce case between the Duke and Dutchess of Argyll, although this is now believed to be untrue, but his name also featured in the 1963 Profumo scandal. The Fairbankses moved to Palm Beach, Florida, in 1973 and there he cared for Mary at her death in 1988. In 1991 Fairbanks married Vera Shelton. He died, aged 90, in New York.

---

* *A plaque on the building commemorates Moses Montefiore, the Anglo-Jewish philanthropist*

Franklin, Benjamin (1706–1790)

Pennsylvania agent to Britain, scientist, inventor, writer and statesman

36 (formerly 7 and later 27), Craven Street, Strand, Charing Cross WC2 5NF ℗ *

Franklin was one of those who put his signature to the Declaration of Independence, but between 1757 and 1785 he lived for only three years in his native land. Nine of those years were spent in Paris and on the Continent, raising funds and military assistance for the emerging United States and (in

1783) signing the treaty which ended the conflict with Britain. From 1757 to 1775, with that interruption, he lived in London, as agent for Pennsylvania and other colonies.

Born in Boston of an English father and an American mother, and with little formal education, Franklin's interests in the arts and scientific inquiry had begun in what was then a far-flung colony of the British empire.

Benjamin Franklin's home in Craven Street (Terry Philpot)

Having been apprenticed as a printer at 12 to his older brother James, he took over his brother's newspaper, the *New England Courant*. Franklin first came to London in 1724 and worked as a printer but left in the summer of 1726 to return to Philadelphia.

The following 22 years were crowded and eventful ones, as a printer, almanac maker, scientist and newspaper owner. Franklin retired from his printing and publishing business in 1748, when he was elected a common councilman in Philadelphia, and more fully gave himself to electrical experimentation, in 1752 inventing the lightning rod and performing kite and key experiments. He was also appointed president of Philadelphia Academy (later the University of Pennsylvania), a justice of the peace, elected to the Pennsylvania assembly, and in 1753 became joint deputy postmaster-general for North America. His literary reputation burgeoned, as did his reputation as a propagandist for the American cause.

Franklin was made agent to London for the Pennsylvania assembly when it vowed to petition the British government for exemption of proprietors' land from taxes, which the British sought to impose.

Taking with him two slaves, Peter and King, he began his stay from 1757 to 1762 by lodging with his illegitimate son William at what was then 7 Craven Street. His common law wife, Deborah (who may have been William's mother and was mother to Franklin's other children, Francis and Sarah) decided to stay in America, fearing the voyage. (She died in 1774, having suffered a stroke, of which Franklin appears to have been unaware.) He lodged with Margaret Stevenson and her daughter Polly, who became a second family to him.

Franklin did not accept the view of the government that, as legislator for the colonies, George II's instructions were law. The British and their government were ignorant, he believed, and began a campaign to enlighten them.

An urban (and urbane) man, he was part of that London society which valued intellectual interests. None of his official responsibilities prevented

155

Franklin's continuing experimentation that sprang from his endless curiosity and led to a literal inventiveness. He attended associations of scientists, philanthropists and explorers (at one he met Capt James Cook, James Boswell, and Dr Samuel Johnson), and visited the Royal Society and the (now Royal) Society of Arts. (Franklin coined the name 'president' for his new nation from the title of the head of the Royal Society.) His scientific work was acknowledged by British universities, as it was by those in the colonies, and he was made an honorary doctor of laws by St Andrews, while Oxford awarded him a doctorate of civil law. Representing his country and making a new nation did not prevent his continued studies like oceanography and meteorology or his inventions, including those of the Franklin stove, bifocal spectacles, the lightning rod, the long arm (for taking down books), a series of chairs with a seat that unfolded to become a ladder and a rocking chair with an automatic fan. He created the world's first electric battery and applied the terms 'positive' and 'negative' for electrical charge. He explained the Gulf Stream and why water evaporates from puddles.

In 1764, three years after his return to Philadelphia, Franklin was elected speaker of the Pennsylvania House of Representatives. He lost his assembly seat by 18 votes but the majority appointed him to join Richard Jackson as the assembly's agent to England. Now Franklin's job was to petition the new king, George III, to seek royal control of the colony against its proprietors, the powerful Penn family. Only gradually did the claims of America itself make themselves clear to him, with independence a last resort.

Once in London Franklin was bogged down in attempts to reject the Stamp Act, which he did by writing essays and letters to London newspapers, but the legislation became law on 22nd March, with effect from 1st November 1765. When in May that year the right of Britain to tax Virginians was opposed by Virginia's House of Burgesses, this gave encouragement to other colonies to do likewise, and mobs threatened the stamp distributors.

Benjamin Franklin in 1767 during his time in London

In 1766, testifying on the Act before a parliamentary committee of the whole House of Commons, Franklin asserted at the suggestion that soldiers be sent to the colonies that 'they will not find a rebellion; they may indeed make one'. By October 1770 three more colonies – Georgia, New Jersey, and Massachusetts – had appointed him their agent.

His essays and pamphlets powerfully advocated the American case, including a treasonous pamphlet published clandestinely and others attacking the king and predicting American independence.

Amidst all this, Franklin found time to visit Germany, France (twice), Scotland (when he stayed with the philosopher David Hume in Edinburgh) and Ireland.

In 1775 when he was sailing for home the War of Independence was signalled by the battles of Lexington and Concord. The day after he arrived in Philadelphia the Pennsylvania assembly unanimously chose him as a delegate to the second Continental Congress.

A personal consequence of the war was Franklin's life-long estrangement from his son, William, the last royal governor of New Jersey, and a Loyalist.**

In 1783 Franklin, **John Adams**, John Jay, David Hartley and Henry Laurens signed the Treaty of Paris, bringing peace between the Britain and the new United States of America. (Franklin was the only person to sign the Declaration of Independence, the Treaty of Paris and the Constitution of the United States, the founding documents of his country.)

Great rejoicing greeted Franklin's arrival back in Philadelphia on 14th September 1785. He was elected to the supreme executive council of Pennsylvania in October and was chosen as its president (effectively governor), serving for three years.

With Thomas Jefferson, Franklin is one of the greatest and most creative of Americans who ever lived; his last public letter was to urge the abolition of slavery.

He died of pleurisy on 17th April 1790 and was buried, beside his wife Deborah and their son Francis, in Philadelphia's Christ Church burial ground.

---

* *Franklin's house is now a museum. For information about tours go to www.benjaminfranklinhouse.org.*

** *William married in **St George's**, Hanover Square, and is buried in an unmarked grave in Old St Pancras Church, Pancras Road, King's Cross, Camden, which may even no longer be there given the extensive clearance in the 1860s for the new Midland railway.*

Gage, Thomas (1719/20–1787)*

Commander-in-chief of the British forces in North America and colonial governor

41 (formerly 22, 29 and 54) Portland Place, Marylebone W1B 1QH Ⓟ

Thomas Gage moved to his town house with Margaret, his American wife, and their children as the property's first residents after he was discharged as commander-in-chief of the British forces facing the rebellious American colonists. He died here seven years later.

Gage was probably born at Highmeadow in the Wye Valley in Gloucestershire, on his mother's family's estate, the second son of the lst Viscount Gage*. He entered the army at about 20 years of age. He engaged in many notable military actions of the period, including the War of Austrian Succession and at the Battle of Culloden during the Jacobite Rebellion and served in Ireland in 1751, that year being promoted to lieutenant colonel in the 44th Foot Regiment.

Three years later Gage was in North America and saw action in the French and Indian War from 1754 to 1763. After successful action in Quebec, in 1760 he was made military governor of Montreal, next year being promoted to major-general.

At the end of that conflict he became commander-in-chief of North America overseeing all manner of issues – from trade to relations with the indigenous people – with more than 50 garrisons and stations under his ultimate command.

However, with the demands growing for independence, Gage misjudged his times and his uncritical and unsympathetic dispatches to London hardened the attitude of prime minister Lord North's government. The Boston Tea Party took place in 1773 when Gage was on leave in England. He told George III that the Americans 'will be Lyons, whilst we are Lambs but if we take the resolute part they will undoubtedly prove very meek'. He came back to America as military governor of Massachusetts, with a charge to enforce draconian new laws, while being promised both large military reinforcements and strong political support at home.

In 1775, in fairly quick succession, occurred the unsuccessful skirmishes at Lexington and Concord in April (with none of the rebel leaders, whom Gage had orders to apprehend, captured) and the disastrous Battle of Bunker Hill. Gage's reports home on the situation – he had failed to point out that the rebellion was not confined to Boston or even New England – led to his being replaced in his post by General Sir William Howe, and he returned to England.

Gage's marriage was now not a happy one as Margaret was sympathetic to her compatriots, and there is evidence that she may have revealed the secret plan of the march to Concord to his American enemies.

In London he was criticised, even ridiculed for his inability to stem the rebellion, though the idea that he could have 'saved' the colonies does not hold water.

Gage kept his salary as Massachusetts governor, a post he was allowed to retain. In 1781 he briefly commanded forces to stem a French invasion. When he was promoted to

Thomas Gage in 1768 by the American painter John Singleton Copley full general, he was given command of the 17th Light Dragoons and later of the 11th Dragoons.

After his death in London, he was buried at Firle, Sussex, the family seat.

---

*   *Gage's actual birth date is unknown and the plaque on his London home gives his birth date as 1719/20, as does the Oxford Dictionary of National Biography. Deborah Gage, curator of Firle Place, Sussex, confirms that this double dating is the best way to express the uncertainty.*

**   *Gage's place of birth is not known but is most likely Highmeadow. Much of his childhood was spent there and to there he returned when on leave from America. His father inherited Firle in 1744 when the Gage family began living between Highmeadow and Firle.*

Harriman, Pamela Churchill (1920–1997)

Diplomat and courtesan

10 Downing Street, Westminster SW1A 2AA
49 Grosvenor Square, Mayfair W1K 2AH

When Harriman was 20 she did not have to be asked twice if she would like to live at 10 Downing Street, courtesy of the fact that her father-in-law Winston Churchill was installed there as prime minister, his son Randolph was away at war, and she had care of the baby Winston.

This was an opportunity not to be missed but one that she probably took in her stride, as she did during her last years when she lived, as Pamela Harriman, in the splendour of the American embassy in Paris as her adopted country's ambassador, having become a citizen in 1971.

For Harriman was born into the British aristocracy, the eldest of the four children of

The then Pamela Digby at her wedding to Randolph Churchill

the 11th Baron Digby and his wife, also Pamela, herself the daughter of a peer. Harriman's aunt was the daughter-in-law of the former prime minister Lord Rosebery and her cousin was the Duchess of Norfolk.

The qualities that would serve Harriman well throughout her life were evident from an early age: vitality, self-discipline, adventurousness and boisterousness. Her infancy was spent in Australia where her father was governor-general and after that she grew up on the family's Dorset estate. Educated mostly at home, there was much emphasis on sport.

Her collateral ancestor Jane Digby had scandalised Georgian society with her many love affairs and her great-great niece had no compunction about following in her wake. Though tutored in the arts of the courtesan by the

Anglo-American heiress, Olive, Lady Baillie, after coming out as a debutante, Harriman had no real lover until she accepted the proposal of Randolph Churchill that they marry on the evening that they met in September 1939. They did so at Caxton Hall, Westminster, three weeks later, despite being warned of the rashness of the arrangement. Her only child was born a year later.

Harriman had a close and happy relationship with her parents-in-law, less so with her husband, whose infidelities, argumentativeness, drinking and debts run up by gambling took their toll. Men she found more agreeable in London included Americans like the future US ambassador to Moscow, Jock Whitney, the president of CBS Bill Paley, and **Ed Murrow**.

She embarked on an affair with the married and much older Averell Harriman (he was 49 and she was 21), the Union Pacific Railway heir, whom **Franklin Roosevelt** had put in charge of Lend-Lease. It is said that the prime minister approved of the relationship as an aid to US–UK relations. When he was sent to Moscow as ambassador, the affair ended.

Pamela and Randolph divorced in 1946 (she was now living in the Grosvenor Square apartment), though she continued to use his name and for a while she worked as a gossip columnist on *Evening Standard*. In 1947 she moved to France, where her lovers included Prince Aly Khan, the owner of Fiat Gianni Agnelli, the shipping magnate Stavros Niarchos and the banker Baron Elie de Rothschild.

She cultivated her men – they were treated as the sole object of her attention: she dressed according to their tastes; she oversaw the decoration of their homes; she adopted their politics; and shared their interests. When she hoped to marry Agnelli she even converted to Catholicism. Shame was not in her vocabulary, resilience was her strength.

In America Harriman married the theatrical producer Leland Hayward as his fifth wife, a marriage that survived until he died in 1971, but by that September she had reacquainted herself with and married the widowed Averell Harriman, now former governor of New York State. Her conservatism gave way to his Democratic beliefs and she acted as hostess and party fundraiser at their Georgetown, Washington DC, home. When her husband died in 1986 Harriman inherited $115 million and a Van Gogh.

Her support for Bill Clinton in the presidential race of 1992 earned her the Paris posting. Here her time was marked as much by energy and hard work as glamour and power. She was 'more than making up in style what she may have lacked in detailed diplomatic knowledge', said her *Times* obituary.

Her Harriman stepchildren instigated a lawsuit alleging that she had squandered $21 million left to them in trust, which cast a shadow over her final years as diplomat.

Harriman was still in office when she died in 1997 at the American Hospital, Neuilly-sur-Seine, having suffered a cerebral haemorrhage while swimming at the Hôtel Ritz, Paris. Washington Cathedral was host to her funeral and she was buried at the Harriman estate in New York State.

Hendrix, Jimi (1942–1970)
Rock musician and songwriter

23 Brook Street, Mayfair WIK 4AH 🅿

Samarkand Hotel, 22 Lansdowne Crescent, Notting Hill, Kensington and Chelsea WII 2NS

Hendrix was born in Seattle of African, Mexican and Cherokee descent. He saw military service as a clerk at Fort Campbell, Kentucky, but was discharged in July 1962 after he broke his ankle in a parachute jump. That June his father had given him his first guitar and, being left handed, Hendrix played it upside-down.

He took to touring, mainly in the South, as a backing musician for Little Richard, Ike and Tina Turner, the Isley brothers, Jackie Wilson and Sam Cooke. He had moved to New York in July 1964, when he formed Jimmy James and the Blue Flames. In residence at Café Wah in Greenwich Village, Hendrix got to know Chas Chandler, bass player with the Animals, and, realising Hendrix's potential, Chandler suggested he return with him to London.

Chandler became his manager and helped Hendrix get a temporary visitor's permit when, in September 1964, they were initially refused entry to the UK.

Jimi Hendrix's home in London (left) next to that of George Frederick Handel (David Holt)

A new band, the Jimi Hendrix Experience, came into being and toured France in October. Here Hendrix established his performative trade marks – smashing the guitar and playing it behind his back, between his legs or with his teeth. He first smashed his guitar accidentally in Germany in October, the other features he had begun in the USA.

In October 1966, the group released *Hey Joe*, their first single, and *Purple Haze*, their second, came along the next February and became Hendrix's signature tune. Both reached the British Top Ten. (*All Along the Watchtower* was his only Top 20 single in his native country.)

Granted a work permit, the Experience could now tour the UK and did so in early 1967. In May the first LP, *Are you Experienced?*, appeared. The act became ever more risqué and sexually provocative, and Hendrix would sometimes set his guitar alight. They were an overnight sensation. Drugs, UFOs and sex were food for the lyrics, accompanied by an astonishing facility with the guitar.

Sometime in the 1960s Hendrix lived for a short time at *34 Montague Square*, Marylebone, which Ringo Starr had bought in 1965 and in which his fellow Beatles John Lennon (for five months in 1968) and Paul McCartney were also to live.

Tours of America, Sweden, France, Italy and the UK followed, with television appearances, and *Electric Ladyland*, the group's third LP, came out in October 1968. Some shops refused to display it, with its sleeve of naked women.

In 1968 Hendrix moved into the Brook Street flat, with his long-time British girlfriend, Kathy Etchingham. The plaque to George Frederick Handel, who had lived at No 25, was said to be an inspiration to Hendrix.

The Experience disbanded after a US tour in 1969 and the Gypsy Sons and Rainbows came into being but didn't last long – when they played at Woodstock, there was a provocative rendering of *The Star-Spangled Banner*. This band was replaced by all-black group, the Band of Gypsies. They disbanded in 1970 to be replaced by The Cry of Love, which performed in Los Angeles and then at the Isle of Wight pop festival in August, along with shows in Europe.

Travelling and little sleep took its toll and Hendrix collapsed on stage in Denmark. While he continued the tour, his last performance was at the Love and Peace festival in Germany on 6th September 1970.

The last time he played in public was later that month when Eric Burden, playing with his new band, brought him on stage at Ronnie Scott's Club, Soho, for the last two songs.

Two days later, on 18th September, he was found to be dead on arrival at St Mary Abbots Hospital, Kensington, after an ambulance was called to the Samarkand Hotel. His death was said to be due to barbiturate intoxication and inhalation of vomit. Hendrix was buried in Seattle.

Later that year, he had a posthumous hit in the UK with *Voodoo Chile*, and there were several subsequent album releases of unreleased, live concert and bootleg material.

162

Ives, Charles (1874–1954)

Composer

18 Half Moon Street, Mayfair W1J 7BE (gone) ℗

Ives was born in Danbury, Connecticut, to a father, George, who was a professional musician, and his wife Elizabeth. George had been the youngest bandsman in the Union army in the Civil War in a band said to be the army's best. He was adept at the cornet, was a band and choir director, and led theatrical orchestrates, as well as taught. Indeed, Danbury was said to be the 'most musical town' in the state.

Ives took drum lessons when he was five and other musical instruction followed. His father was the great influence of his life and he was devastated at his sudden death when Ives was at Yale. George had had him sing in one key while he accompanied in another; he had Ives build instruments to play quarter-tones; and he played his cornet over a pond so that his son could gauge the effect of space. Once George had two bands marching around a park blaring different tunes, to see what it sounded like when they approached and passed.

Ives specialised in the organ and at 14 was the youngest salaried church organist in the state. Two years later the town band played his first composition and in 1893 or 1894 his *Song for the Harvest Season* was composed with parts for voice, trumpet, violin and organ, which were in different keys. He combined his musical talent with sporting skill. Some of the compositions of his teenage years, like *Variations on America* for organ, live on.

Charles Ives, even at 15 an accomplished musician

Ives was a musical innovator and a modernist, who had a profound effect on musical developments in the 20th century, with his use of polytonality, polyrhythm, tone clusters, aleatory elements and quarter tones. He took hymn tunes and traditional songs; he also incorporated melodies of the town band at holiday parade and the fiddlers at Saturday night dances; and used patriotic songs and sentimental parlour ballads. His *114 Songs* (1919–24) for voice and piano comprises ballads, satire, hymns, protest songs and romantic songs. Singing at camp meetings, and playing in band marches, church bells, the power of vernacular music – all were to shape his abilities, compositions and understanding. His work lies deep in American culture and experience, especially that of his native New England. He was known as 'an American original' and one of the first American composers to achieve international recognition.

When Ives graduated he became an insurance clerk in New York and founded Ives & Myrick in 1907, which became a very successful insurance business. He was head of the firm from 1916 to 1930 and most of his work was written before 1915, much of it unpublished until his death. However, he gave up both business and composing due to chronic diabetes and a hand tremor.

Ives was a frequent visitor to London. In August 1924 he stayed at the St James Palace Hotel (gone) and in September at Garland's Hotel, Suffolk Street (gone). In May 1932 he was staying at the Victoria Hotel, off Trafalgar Square (gone), while from April to May and then in June the following year he was in Half Moon Street, and from May to June 1933 was again back in the capital, during which time he recorded at the Columbia Graphophone Co at its Abbey Road studios*. He returned from September to October 1934, when he heard Sir Henry Wood conduct Sibelius. His last visit appears to have been in June and July 1938.

In 1947 Ives received the Pulitzer Prize for his *Third Symphony (The Camp Meeting*; composed 1904–11). His *Second Symphony* (1897–1902) was first performed in its entirety 50 years after its composition.

Ives died in May 1954 but it was another ten years before his status increased and his reputation was such that he began to be considered the greatest American composer.

In his biography, Jan Swafford writes:

> Whenever we reach beyond the trivial and ominous present, whenever we attempt to go beyond ourselves, Ives is there cheering us on, pointing upward and beyond. His vision stretched further than even his great gifts could express, beyond anything plausible, possibly beyond anything we deserve … to the degree that our culture can rediscover a little belief in ourselves and our potential, and in the potential of art and music, we should remember and honour Charles Ives.

---

* Abbey Road studios would become world famous decades later when the Beatles recorded there.

Kent, Tyler (1911–1988)
Spy
47 Gloucester Place, Marylebone W1U 8JE

When on 20th May 1940, Maxwell Knight, (who ran MI5 agents in subversive organisations), Special Branch officers and the second secretary of the American embassy came to arrest Tyler Kent in his second floor flat, they found 1,926 telegrams and other documents in an unlocked suitcase that the embassy cypher clerk had copied or taken from his place of work, when he thought them 'interesting'. Among them was a telegram from Winston Churchill to **Franklin Roosevelt** begging the USA to help in the war effort. This document alone had explosive content – Churchill, then First Lord of the Admiralty, was not to become prime minister until six days after the arrest, while Roosevelt was nearing the end of his second term and battling isolationism at home. Another document was a secret assurance that the United States would support France if it was invaded by the Germany Army.

Kent was born in 1911 in Manchuria, where his father was US consul, into a family that included Davy Crockett and General George Patton. Educated in the USA, at the Sorbonne and at the University of Madrid, he had joined the State Department in 1934. His job in London, to which he came in October 1939, was to code and decipher telegram traffic between the UK and the USA. He spoke French, Greek, German, Russian, Italian and Spanish.

He had been posted to the Moscow embassy in 1934 where, it later emerged, he had passed documents to Nazi intelligence. It was Moscow, according to the writer Malcolm Muggeridge, who, as an MI5 officer attended Kent's trial at the Old Bailey, that 'had given him a manically hostile attitude toward the Soviet Union, and an extra hatred of Roosevelt and his policies, besides fortifying his anti-Semitism'. Kent was, said Muggeridge, 'one of those intensely gentlemanly Americans who wear well-cut, tailor-made suits, with waistcoat and watch-chain, drink wine instead of high-balls, and become furiously indignant'.

Kent had been under surveillance from the off in London, as MI5 first observed his association with Ludwig Matthias, a Gestapo agent. Kent's anti-communism found a ready-made perfect match with that of his fellow defendant, Anna Wolkoff, Russian born but a naturalised British citizen since 1937, and the daughter of Admiral Nikolai Wolkoff, last naval attaché in London to the tsarist government. Fleeing to London, they established the Russian Tea Room, in South Kensington, where members of the pro-Nazi Right Club used to meet. Kent and Wolkoff had met in 1940 and it was at the tea room that Wolkoff introduced Kent to the Club's leader Captain Archibald Maule Ramsay, an anti-semitic Scottish Tory MP.

Kent was himself virulently anti-Semitic: 'All wars,' he believed 'are inspired, formented and promoted by the great international bankers and banking combines which are largely controlled by the Jews'.

At his flat he showed Wolkoff and Ramsay the documents, and in April Wolkoff copied some of them. It was later claimed that they were passed to Duco del Monte, the Italian assistant naval attaché, but he later denied this. However, soon afterwards British wireless interception indicated that Admiral Canaris, head of German military intelligence (Abwehr) had copies of the Roosevelt-Churchill correspondence.

An MI5 agent within the Club alerted the agency to Kent's friendship with Wolkoff, whose pro-German sympathies were known. Another MI5 mole told how Wolkoff had said that Kent was able to give her confidential information about sea battles off the coast of Norway and about conversations between US ambassador **Joseph Kennedy** and Foreign Secretary Lord Halifax. The revelations continued until Maxwell Knight told Guy Liddell, deputy director of MI5's counter espionage. Liddell then met Kennedy, who waived Kent's diplomatic immunity, allowing him to be arrested.

The Special Branch also found the Club's so-called Red Book at the flat, detailing supporters, which Ramsay had given to Kent for safe-keeping. Wolkoff, aged 37, and Kent were tried *in camera* in November 1940. They received ten years and seven years penal servitude, respectively, and she was stripped of her citizenship. On being sentenced, Kent became indignant and said he had acted patriotically to keep his country out of a ruinous war.

In sentencing Wolkoff the judge referred to her 'anti-Jewish obsession … a virus which has entered your system and destroyed your mental and moral fibre'. Ramsay was later interned without trial.

In late 1945 Kent was deported to the USA, where, curiously, he was not charged with spying for the Nazis for which he would have faced a life sentence, but he was investigated six times by the FBI from 1952 to 1963.

In 1946, in Mexico, he married Clara Hunter Hyatt, the heiress to a liver pill fortune, who was 13 years his senior. He relieved her of most of her wealth and for a while he was the publisher of a newspaper that supported the Ku Klux Klan and accused President Kennedy of being a communist. Kent claimed that the president's assassination was the work of Soviet agents because he was abandoning his communist beliefs.

Kent died in poverty in a trailer park in Texas in 1988.

Laughton, Charles (1890–1962)
Actor

Lanchester, Elsa (1902–1986)
Actor

28 Dean Street, Soho WID 3LL*
2nd Floor, 15 Percy Street, Fitzrovia WIT IDS **P** **
47 Farley Road, Hither Green, Lewisham SE6 2AA

Laughton was born in Scarborough, while Lanchester was a south Londoner born in Hither Green, Lewisham. They met in 1927 when both played in *Mr Proback* and for a while lived in Soho in a house formerly inhabited by Karl Marx, before moving to Percy Street in 1928 and marrying a year later. In Percy Street they knocked two rooms into one to make the flat larger but also kept a cottage in Surrey. They had moved out in 1931 to live in New York when a play they were appearing in transferred.

When they moved, Lanchester remembered: 'It was high time, because an Indian restaurant had opened underneath and the smell of garlic and curry, which rose up, was getting stronger and stronger.'

The *Oxford Dictionary of National Biography* (ODNB) refers to the life-long marriage as one of convenience rather than a great love match that brought constant happiness. Laughton's homosexuality caused him unhappiness and, says his *ODNB* biographer, a '... lifelong sense of being a misfit, uneasy in his own skin, and forever on the outside of social, sexual, and familial demands on his upbringing and conditioning'. Soon after their marriage Laughton spoke to Lanchester about an incident with a rent boy, and the matter was never discussed again, according to

Charles Laughton and Elsa Lanchester

Laughton's biographer Simon Callow. There were no children, but the couple shared a common left-wing outlook and pushed at the barriers of pre-war Hollywood without jeopardising their careers. In his last four years he found great comfort and companionship with a much younger man named Terry Jenkins.

Laughton's theatrical journey was rapid. He had been invalided out of the army in 1918 and returned to his parents' home to continue his pre-war training in hotel management (his father was a prosperous hotelier) and returned to London to train at Claridge's Hotel. But in 1925, defying his family, he ditched that and signed on at the Royal Academy of Dramatic Art in London, where two years later he won the Gold Medal. In 1926 he had appeared at non-West End London theatres in classic Russian plays, but fame came two years later when, as the neurotic, greedy, sinister villain in *A Man with Red Hair*, by Hugh Walpole at the Little Theatre in London, he created a type with which he was often to be associated. Then came Christie's Poirot and Dickens' Pickwick, and a Chicago gangster in *On the Spot* by Edgar Wallace (1930).

After the move to the USA in 1931, Laughton went to Hollywood for *The Old Dark House* (1932) and as Nero in *The Sign of the Cross* (1932). When they came back to England in 1933 he made his name as a screen actor in the first of a series of screen biographies, Henry VIII in *The Private Life of Henry VIII* (with Lanchester as Anne of Cleves), and then *The Barretts of Wimpole Street* (1934), *Mutiny on the Bounty* (1935), *Rembrandt* (1936), in which Lanchester also appeared, and the abortive *I, Claudius* (1936).

In 1933 Laughton and Lanchester had joined the Old Vic Company and three years later he became the first English actor ever to appear at the Comédie Française in Paris, playing in Molière's *Le Médecin Malgré Lui*.

The couple settled in the United States in 1939 and became citizens in 1950. Laughton's screen career allowed only occasional stage appearances and his films included *Jamaica Inn* (1939), *The Hunchback of Notre Dame* (1939), *Witness for the Prosecution* (1957), *Spartacus* (1960) and *Advise and Consent* (1962). He rarely came back to his native country, but notably did for David Lean's *Hobson's Choice* in 1954. He returned to the London stage for the last time in *The Party* in 1958 and at Stratford-upon-Avon the following year for *King Lear*. His last film was *Advise and Consent* in 1962.

Unlike her husband's, Lanchester's upbringing was unconventional: her parents were freethinkers and left-wing, and her mother, Edith Lanchester, a noted feminist. It was a peripatetic childhood in south London with little formal education.

With a snub nose and red hair, Lanchester was never destined to be a screen or stage beauty, but nevertheless she had a precocious talent for dancing, gaining a scholarship to Isadora Duncan's Bellevue School in Paris when she was eight. This was frustrated by the outbreak of the First World War and she formed her own dance club and began to teach dance at the Margaret Morris School in Chelsea.

In the post-war years Lanchester exercised her talents in varied ways: a small hall in Charlotte Street, London (not far from her eventual marital home) was from 1918 to 1921 the Children's Theatre, making use of local children for musical entertainments, until the London County Council closed it for exploiting child labour. Then she co-founded a bohemian nightclub, with late-night cabaret and *avant-garde* plays that attracted fashionable London. She worked as an artist's model, posing for **Jacob Epstein**, and even, occasionally, acted as a co-respondent in divorce cases, when such 'evidence' was required.

Lanchester first appeared as an actor at the Kingsway Theatre, Holborn, in 1921, and while taking on other stage roles starred in amateur films written by her friends the young Evelyn Waugh and HG Wells.

Lanchester's was a different career to that of her husband, whose fame overshadowed hers, though she was always supportive of him. In Hollywood she often played spinsters, eccentrics and other character parts. *Come to the Stable* in 1949 gained her an Oscar nomination for the best supporting actress, as did her role as Laughton's nurse in *Witness for the Prosecution* in 1958.

Between 1941 and 1951 she appeared in cabaret at the Turnabout Theatre, Los Angeles and played to packed houses on tour. In 1960 Laughton directed her in a successful one-woman show, *Elsa Lanchester Herself*.

Cabaret, she said late in life, was something she did as she lacked ambition for the great stage roles: 'I only wanted to do vaudeville … I like to get a laugh. I'm a vaudevillian, not an actor.'

Laughton died in Hollywood in 1962 and Lanchester continued to act on television and in films until her death in 1986 in Los Angeles..

---

* The plaque on the building commemorates Karl Marx's tenancy.
** The plaque notes only Charles Laughton.

Legation of the Republic of Texas
Pickering Place, 3 St James's Street, St James's SW1A 1EF **P**

It is easy to miss the site – even the plaque – for the Texas Legation was housed between 1842 and 1846* in premises rented from Berry Brothers & Rudd, the wine merchants, in Pickering Place, a narrow Georgian passageway, at the lower end of St James's Street. The wine shop itself has stood here since 1730, though was established elsewhere in 1680.

The plaque was placed here in 1963 by the Anglo-Texas Society and is headed with the seal of the Republic of Texas. It is set on the 18th century timber wainscoting. The republic adopted all the diplomatic niceties of the time, which are also observed by all nations' representatives in London today, with ministers (now ambassadors) being accredited to the Court of St James.

Photograph: Terry Philpot

By a nice coincidence, the author Graham Greene, one of the founders of the society in 1953, had a flat in St James's Street.

The legation was one of three opened by the Republic of Texas before it acceded to the union of the United States. The others were in Paris and Washington DC. Sam Houston, president of the republic, sent Dr Ashbel Smith to London as his government's diplomatic representative.

Why the legations were opened is subject to debate. Some claim that it was intended to seek international support to ward off any invasion by neighbouring Mexico. Others assert that it was an attempt to make the USA aware that the republic could allow French and British soldiers to amass on the southern border of the larger republic.

Britain had supported Texan independence, even offering to guarantee the borders with both the USA and Mexico. However, in 1845 Texas joined the union. The republic had sought statehood since it gained independence from Mexico in 1836 but nationalist opposition from within Texas and the opposition of abolitionists in the USA had delayed its joining.

Despite British support, the republic left London owing £160 in rent, a debt not settled until 1986 when the Anglo-Texan Society paid the wine shop.

---

* *Some sources give the dates as 1836 to 1845 but the plaque attests to those stated here.*

Lowell, James Russell (1819–1891)

Poet, critic and American minister in London

37 Lowndes Square, Belgravia SW1X 9HA

Lowell came from one of the Boston Brahmin families, the cultured, Anglophile upper class, part of the East Coast establishment that included families in New York and Philadelphia.

A graduate of Harvard, he was a notable poet, an influential critic, and a vocal abolitionist, enjoying a reputation which preceded his appointment as US minister in London in 1880. (Cambridge University had awarded him an honorary degree in 1874.)

Lowell taught at Harvard, his *alma mater*, for 20 years, and travelled in Europe. In 1844, he married Maria White, herself a poet and abolitionist, who died of tuberculosis in 1853. Their daughter Mabel was the only one of their four children to survive infancy. In 1857 Lowell married Frances Dunlap, the same year that he became editor of *The Atlantic Monthly*. He was also the author of a series of essays on the English writers Milton, Shakespeare, Dryden, Wordsworth and Keats.

A crayon drawing of James Russell Lowell 20 years before he served in London

Before his diplomatic appointments he had travelled to England, staying at one time in Down Street, Piccadilly, and on the Continent several times.

In 1876 Lowell was delegate to the Republican National Convention in Cincinnati, Ohio, supporting the presidential candidate Rutherford B Hayes, who won the presidency in 1877. Hayes admired Lowell's *The Biglow Papers* and offered its author the ministry in either Austria or Russia, which Lowell turned down. However, being known for his interest in Spanish literature, Lowell was then offered and accepted the role of the minister's post in Madrid, for which he was paid $12,000 a year and which he held from 1877.

His annual salary was increased to $17,500 with $3,500 expenses, when, in January 1880, he became minister in London. Here he worked at the legation's address in Members Mansions, Victoria Street, Victoria (gone)*. Upon arrival, Lowell lived for a short time at 10 Lowndes Square, Belgravia, and in 1881 moved to No 37 where he lived until his term ended.

This appointment brought him back, he felt, to 'the old home'. In London, as he said in a letter, he 'learned to see as I never saw before the advantages of a great capital that establishes the weights and measures, moral and intellectual, of a whole country'. The trouble for Americans was 'we have as many [capital cities] as we have states'.

Lowell has been described as the 'archetypal New England man of letters, remarkable for his cultivation and charm, his deep learning, and his varied literary talents'. Such qualities, as well as his being a scholar (he became president of the Wordsworth Society) and a gentleman, stood him in good stead as a diplomat.

He dined with the Liberal statesmen John Morley, William Gladstone, William Harcourt and Charles Dilke, as well as the aristocratic Salisbury, Rosebery, Jersey and Derby families. He corresponded with the novelist Thomas Hughes.

Lowell became friendly with the expatriate **Henry James**, who found him 'conspicuously American', as well as the critic and editor Leslie Stephen, and was godfather to Stephen's daughter Virginia Woolf. He impressed the monarch: Queen Victoria found him an ambassador who had never 'created so much interest and won so much regard as Mr Lowell'. His reputation was such that after he was recalled by President Grover Cleveland, he was offered a chair at Oxford, which he declined.

He travelled extensively – to Whitby (a favourite), Hertfordshire, Cornwall and Scotland. In Birmingham in October 1884 he met the 83-year-old Cardinal John Henry Newman. 'He was beguilingly courteous', Lowell wrote 'and we excellenced and eminenced each other by turns. A more gracious senescence I never saw … Supreme decay, like that of some ruined abbey in a woodland dell, consolingly forlorn'. Lowell also took a two-month trip to Germany and Italy.

In his work, though, he applied himself to such unpoetic subjects as the import of allegedly diseased cattle and made recommendations that predated the Pure Food and Drug Act.

Frances died in February 1885 while still in England, which led to Lowell leaving public life. Later that year, he returned to the United States. But he would frequently come back to London: in 1886 staying at 40 Clarges Street,

Mayfair (gone) from May to October; and the next year at 2 Radnor Place, Bayswater; and, again in 1888 and 1899, on each visit travelling elsewhere in the country.

On his final return to the USA, Lowell lived in Deerfoot, Massachusetts, and Boston. He continued to write, but this time was not a happy one, with his friends Henry Longfellow, Richard Dana and **Ralph Waldo Emerson** dead. William Gladstone and Alfred, Lord Tennyson, were among those contributing to a *festschrift* on his 70th birthday. He spent his last two years at the family estate of Elmwood in Cambridge, Massachusetts, where he had been born. He died there and is commemorated by a memorial window and stone tablet in **Westminster Abbey**.

---

* *Members Mansions was next to Broad Sanctuary by Westminster Abbey, so approximately where the Department of Business, Innovation and Skills now stands in Victoria Street.*

Melville, Herman (1819–1891)

Novelist, short story writer and poet

15 Craven Street, Strand, Charing Cross WC2N 5PB Ⓟ

Although it would be two years before *Moby Dick* appeared, when Melville came to London on his short stay in 1849 he was already a well-known author, with four novels to his name. The last two – *Mardi* and *Redburn*, published in the year he crossed the Atlantic – were stories of the sea but did not replicate the critical or financial success of the first two books.

Melville was also an experienced sailor: first as crew member of the *St Lawrence* on a round trip from New York to Liverpool 1839; then on a Mississippi steamboat and on a whaler in 1841; sailing to Rio de Janeiro, round Cape Horn and to Peru; a winter cruise through the Galapagos Islands also in 1841; and to the Hawaiian Islands and other places.

Herman Melville's home in London (Terry Philpot)

He had been married for two years and 1849 was the year that Malcolm, the first of his children, was born.

His oldest brother, Gansevoort, had died in London of cerebral anaemia in 1849, where he had been secretary to the US legation for a year. He had shown a manuscript of his brother's *Typee* to **Washington Irving**, staying in London away from his ambassadorial duties in Madrid, and had placed the book with the publisher John Murray for £100 for the British rights.

When Melville came to the city he was eerily aware that his now deceased brother 'was writing here in London, about the same hour as this – alone in his chamber, in profound silence – as I am now'.

He checked into the boarding house in Craven Street, wearing his new green coat. One reason for his visit was to see Richard Bentley, his British publisher, at his offices at 8 New Burlington Street (gone). The 30-year-old author now wanted to bring out *White Jacket*,

Herman Melville, a few years before his visit to London

another sea-going narrative and in 1851 Bentley was to beat US publishers by a month to bring out *Moby Dick*. Melville also visited other publishers – John Murray and Longman, Chapman & Hall, and others – all to no avail due to problems arising from there then being no international copyright.

Melville hoped to make enough money from the proceeds of his new books to take a year-long Grand Tour of Europe, making notes for another profitable book, and then return to London. He got £100 for *Redburn* and £200 for *White Jacket* and though he did travel to Europe, three months later he was on his way home to the USA.

The writer Philip Hoare speculates that the London stay had a great influence on what was to be Melville's master work, now regarded as one of the greatest novels in any language. It would be, said its author, 'a romance of adventure, founded upon certain wild legends in the Southern Sperm Whale Fisheries'.

Hoare writes: 'Late one night he "turned flukes" down Oxford Street as if he were being followed by a great whale and thought he saw "blubber rooms" in the butcheries of Fleet Street. And when he saw Queen Victoria riding past in a carriage, he joked that the young man sitting beside her was the Prince of Whales … London', Hoare concludes, 'which itself had been a whaling port, was stirring up the ghosts of his past'.

Melville saw JWM Turner's work, a series of whaling scenes with their tempestuous and rolling seas, white foam and the all but audible sound of water. He also visited the Dulwich Art Gallery 'remote from London, but full of splendid treasures'. It is likely that he also saw the 'auto-icon' (a skeleton padded out with hay and wearing the subject's clothes) of philosopher Jeremy Bentham at University College London because, in the novel, he writes about it when Ishmael, the novel's narrator, refers to Bentham's skeleton when evoking the spirit of the whale.

In November Melville attended the public execution of George and Maria Manning. The crowd, he said, was 'brutish' but he was not to know that Charles Dickens was also amongst them . He saw the Lord Mayor's Show and visited the National Gallery. At one point he says he returned to his rooms after midnight with 'an indefinite quantity of Champaigne [*sic*], Sherry, Old Port, Hock, Madeira & Claret in me'.

At Greenwich Melville met a black sailor who had fought at the Battle of Trafalgar, and at Tower Hill he saw a one-legged beggar. Did this plant in his mind the one-legged Ahab, captain of the whaling ship?

On 26th April 1857 he came back to London by steamer from Rotterdam, after being in Italy, and that evening settled at theTavistock Hotel (gone). The next day Melville walked in Hyde Park and Kensington Gardens. He found that Longman had published *The Confidence Man* three weeks before, which had been well received by reviewers. He visited Madame Tussauds and the Crystal Palace ('a vast toy' and 'overdone'), and Oxford before departing for Liverpool, where he visited **Nathaniel Hawthorne**, his New England neighbour and then US consul in that city. He took the voyage home on 6th May.

When Melville died in 1891 his compatriots, the novelists Edith Wharton and **Henry James**, did not even know that he was still alive. There had been what a newspaper called 'the total eclipse of what had been a literary luminary'.

Morse, Samuel (1791–1872)

Painter and inventor of Morse code

141 Cleveland Street (formerly 8 Buckingham Place), Fitzrovia W1T 4QG Ⓟ

The reputation of Morse, who was born to Calvinist parents in Massachusetts, as a painter has been overshadowed by his worldwide fame as inventor of the telegraphic code named after him.

At Yale he supported himself by painting and it was to that he took when he graduated with honours, having studied mathematics and science, as well as religious philosophy. One of his notable early works, *The Landing of the Pilgrims*, caught the attention of Washington Allston, a well-known painter of the day, who arranged with Morse's father that he should spend three years in London, where he would meet the president of the Royal Academy, **Benjamin West**.

Allston and Morse arrived in London in 1811 and by the end of that year Morse had been admitted to the Royal Academy. It was here that he painted what is regarded as his masterpiece, *The Dying Hercules*. He also painted *Judgment of Jupiter* while in London. The next year he moved to the Fitzrovia address, sharing with a fellow pupil, Charles Robert Leslie. Their home was, they said, 'in the very centre of all the artists in London'. They were, said Leslie, 'very comfortable in their new lodgings' and held evening parties for other of West's pupils.

Though only a young man – he was 22 at this stage – Morse became friends with the poets William Wordsworth and Samuel Taylor Coleridge, and the painter JWM Turner. His self-portrait, in London's National Gallery, painted at this time, shows him in profile, an impressive-looking, if not handsome, young man. There is no dour Calvinism about his dress: the high collar and cloak are as a young English aristocrat of the day might have dressed.

In 1812, the British and the Americans were at war and Morse wrote impassioned letters of comment home to his parents, especially deploring the Federalists, although his family were Federalists. Morse sympathised with his parents' religious convictions, but favoured Unitarianism, and his paintings often express spiritual themes or allegories. He was also a gifted portrait painter as is shown by his paintings of the former president **John Adams** and the inventor Eli Witney.

Morse returned home in 1815 and continued to work professionally as a painter, often painting the upper classes (his portrait of the former president James Munroe was a commission). In 1826 he was one of the founders of New York's National Academy of Design, being president from 1826 to 1845 and again from 1861 to 1862. Between 1830 and 1832, Morse travelled and studied in Italy, Switzerland and France to improve his painting skills.

Painting never submerged his scientific interests. He had the idea of his code of 'dots' and 'dashes' in 1832 and it was in general use by 1851. Morse was a contributor to the invention of the single-wire telegraph and helped to develop telegraphy commercially. He became interested in and promoted the daguerreotype (an early form of photograph), when he met its inventor Louis Daguerre in Paris in 1839.

He had married his first wife, Lucretia Pickering Walker, in 1819, with whom he had three children, and, after her death, married Sarah Griswold with whom he had four more children.

Though his invention was one early sign of modernity, Morse's views were seen as reactionary not long after his death. He stood unsuccessfully for mayor of New York in 1836 on an anti-immigrant ticket and was loudly anti-Catholic (connected with

Samuel Morse in 1840

175

his anti-immigration views), while he was a staunch defender of slavery as a natural, divinely ordained condition.

Morse was a generous donor to charities and died with a fortune worth $500,000.

Murrow, Edward R (1908–1965)

Radio and television broadcaster

Flat 5, Weymouth House, 84–94, Hallam Street, Marylebone W1W 5HF Ⓟ

Murrow had been with the Columbia Broadcasting System for two years when he became European director, based in London, with no staff. A former lumberjack, tall, slim and darkly attractive, he took to London life as if born to it: he smoked Camel cigarettes, wore Savile Row suits and drove a Sunbeam Talbot. His sophisticated wife Janet, who was descended from *Mayflower* settlers, was an ideal companion.

Their home in Hallam Street, a short walk from the BBC in Portland Place, where he often worked, welcomed fellow broadcasters, rival journalists, visiting Americans and friends who had lost their homes through bombing. The Czech foreign minister Jan Masaryk was a frequent guest.

As war clouds darkened Murrow gained a team of reporters, known as the 'Murrow's boys', although one was a woman, Mary Marvin Breckinridge. Another was William L Shirer, whom Murrow appointed to his post in Berlin and who alerted Americans to the nature of Nazism and accompanied the German Army to Paris. In Warsaw at the time of the Anschluss, Murrow went to Vienna to make his first broadcast. He announced: 'This is Edward Murrow speaking from Vienna … It's now nearly 2:30 in the morning, and Herr Hitler has not yet arrived.' He did, the next day.

With the outbreak of war, Murrow and fellow American correspondents were seen by the British government as able influencers of public opinion back home, where the USA was neutral. In London during the Blitz, Murrow was given permission to broadcast from rooftops during air raids and his words were spoken as bombs fell and searchlights sought out planes. His nightly broadcast, *London After Dark*, described the Blitz to his compatriots. The BBC repeated his CBS broadcasts and he often appeared on BBC programmes.

His broadcasts began 'This is London', and he would later sign off with an even more famous catch phrase, 'Good night, and good luck.' They related the daily life of the city and the struggles of its citizens, concentrating on how the ordinary man and woman were faring. His tone was calm and deliberate, powerful and intimate.

Murrow's contribution was recognised in December 1941, when temporarily back in the USA, at a dinner in New York in his honour 1,100 people gave him a standing ovation. The poet Archibald MacLeish paid tribute:

Edward R Murrow

> You burned the city of London in our houses and we felt the flames that burned it. You laid the dead of London at our doors and we knew the dead were our dead – were all men's dead – were mankind's dead – and ours.

He flew on 25 bombing missions and reported from the US campaign in Tunisia in 1943. He remained in London to co-ordinate reports on D-Day but went to the Continent when Paris was liberated in August 1944. Murrow was the first Allied war correspondent at Buchenwald. In his broadcast he first warned listeners that they might wish to turn off their sets in view of what he was to say and, after vividly describing the horrors he had witnessed, he said:

> I pray you to believe what I have said about Buchenwald. I have reported what I saw and heard, but only part of it. For most of it I have no words…

In the London years, Murrow had a very open affair with Pamela Churchill (later **Pamela Harriman**), daughter-in-law of the prime minister. She wanted them to marry but when his only son, Casey, was born he ended the relationship.

Murrow was also friendly with Winston Churchill, who entertained Murrow at his country home, Chartwell, in Kent, and offered him the directorship of the BBC, which he declined.

In his final broadcast from the UK, Murrow concluded:

> I am persuaded that the most important thing that happened in Britain was that this nation chose to win or lose this war under the established rules of parliamentary procedure … I have been privileged to see an entire people give the reply to tyranny that their history demanded of them.

At the end of the broadcast, BBC engineers in the studio presented him with the microphone he had used during the war, with an inscription which read: 'This microphone, taken from studio B4 of the Broadcasting House, London, is presented to Edward R Murrow who used it there with such distinction for so many broadcasts to CBS New York during the war years 1939 to 1945.'

Murrow returned to New York in 1946 as vice-president and director of public affairs at CBS, but finding he had no taste for administration, returned to radio broadcasting in 1947. He was also appointed to the CBS board of directors. For the next 12 years he made nightly radio news broadcasts until he was appointed by President **John F Kennedy** as director of the United States Information Agency.

A chain smoker, Murrow died of lung cancer at his home in New York State in 1965.

Page, Walter Hines (1855–1918)

Journalist, publisher and American ambassador

6 Grosvenor Square, Mayfair WIK 6LE
(gone: now apartments, numbered No 7) ℗

By the time that North Carolina-born Page was appointed ambassador to London by Woodrow Wilson in 1913, he was well established as a publisher, writer and journalist.

His career in journalism began on the *St Joseph Gazette* and later included widely circulated articles seeking to show the mutual dependence of the South and the North, as well as the founding of the *State Chronicle* in his native state. But he was also centrally involved in agitation which led to the foundation of North Carolina State University. He was one-time editor of *The Atlantic Monthly* and literary adviser to the publishers Houghton, Mifflin and Company, and then entered Doubleday, Page & Co as partner and vice-president.

In 1880 Page married Willa Alice Wilson (no relation to the future president) and they were to have a daughter and three sons. Two years after the marriage Page and Woodrow Wilson met when the latter was a young lawyer in Atlanta, Georgia. Page supported a Wilson presidency in 1911 and when, two years later, Wilson became president, one of Wilson's first acts was to send Page to London, where he lived with his family in a house on this site.

London suited such a proud Southern Anglo-American as Page: he was accepted by both the British ruling classes – his daughter Kathleen married at the Chapel Royal, St James's – and the general public alike. His standing was

Walter Page Hines when ambassador to London

boosted by his role in the abolition of the toll in the Panama Canal, which the British regarded as discrimatory.

A year after Page came to London, the First World War broke out. Whilst the USA was neutral Page came to see Prussian-dominated Germany as a threat to European democracy. In private letters he expressed his disagreement to Wilson, who held the opposite view, while publicly supporting his country's stance. His was not an easy task in this period: the British claimed the right to stop and search American ships, and also had a blacklist of American firms with whom they barred citizens from having financial and commercial dealings.

The sinking of the British ship the *Lusitania* by a German submarine in 1915, when 100 Americans died, caused Page to call for a declaration of war by the USA. That had no effect, but when Wilson successfully sought Congress's agreement for the USA to enter the war in 1917, it was Page's earlier arguments he deployed. However, Page's stand had not been without cost for he was accused of promoting Britain to America, rather than vice versa.

Page resigned when he became ill in 1918 and went back to live in Pinehurst, where he was born and where he died shortly after his return.

Peabody, George (1795–1869)

Merchant banker and philanthropist

80 Eaton Square, Belgravia SW1 9AP ℗

Peabody, who was descended on both sides of his family from early English settlers, rose to great wealth, and his philanthropy has left its mark in London and the south east, and throughout the USA.

He was born into a very modest family of eight children, who knew real poverty after the death of Peabody's father in 1811. His schooling was never regular and came to an end when he was 11. Apprenticed to a local shop-keeper in his native South Danvers (now Peabody), Massachusetts, Peabody learned to keep accounts. He then worked as a hawker on horseback, was a clerk in his brother's store and worked on his grandfather's Vermont farm.

When working for an uncle in the District of Columbia, he so impressed Elisha Riggs, a local dry goods merchant in Georgetown, that in 1814 they set up a wholesale store for dry goods, which Elisha Riggs financed. The company moved the next year to Baltimore as Riggs, Peabody & Co. Goods were imported from the UK and branches opened in New England, with Peabody as senior partner when Riggs retired in 1829.

Two years previously Peabody had made his first business trip to Britain and, after several more trips, made England his permanent home in 1837.

That year Peabody had capital of $300,000 having opened a counting house and survived a national financial panic. He employed staff and imported to his home country. By 1845 he was a merchant banker but continued in the dry goods market, trading in the USA, Ireland and China, while also financing the foreign trade of others and dealing in American securities until dry goods gave way to banking and finance. He later moved into financing the USA's railways with **Junius Spencer Morgan**, father of **JP Morgan**, as a partner, and his finance house became the largest in London.

Peabody's office was designed to entertain American friends visiting London. Each visitor was given a letter of introduction and he gave sumptuous dinners for American diplomats and other well-known visitors. In July 1855 he recorded that in one week he had given dinner to 80 Americans and entertained 35 at the opera.

When the US government refused to fund the American part of the Great Exhibition of 1851, Peabody advanced £3,000. At the first of his regular Fourth of July dinners, the Duke of Wellington was the guest of honour. Peabody's mark in London society became as pronounced as his impact on commercial life.

Peabody survived a couple of financial crises, one in 1857 when he was saved by a loan of £800,000 from the Bank of England. At 65 he was immensely rich but tired and ill with gout and rheumatism. He had left George Peabody & Co in 1864 and JS Morgan became the senior partner in a company which in 1910 became Morgan, Grenfell & Co.

In the USA Peabody's philanthropy tended to support education across the board. In 1832 he gave South Danvers $30,000 to start an educational institute and five years later ten times that sum was given to create what is now the Peabody Institute of John Hopkins University in Baltimore, which would encompass a library, a gallery of art, an academy of music and prizes to encourage private and public school pupils. There was much else, among which were awards of $1200 annually for gold medals for female high-school graduates in Baltimore; $150,000 to Harvard to found what is the Peabody Museum of Archaeology and Ethnology; and the same sum to Yale that

created the Peabody Museum of Natural History. Newly emancipated slaves benefited from the Peabody Fund for Southern Education set up immediately after the Civil War with $2,000,000.

In March 1859 Peabody created the Peabody Donation Fund with $500,000 to provide model dwellings for 'artisans and labouring poor of London'. The first flats, opened in 1864 in

Statue of George Peabody in the City of London (Mike Hudson)

Commercial Street, Spitalfields, housed 66 low-income families, in a development with shops and laundries.*

Peabody was the first American to be made a freeman of the City of London, but he turned down a baronetcy because he refused to revoke his American citizenship in favour of British citizenship, so attached did he remain to the land of his birth. In 1867 he was awarded the Congressional Gold Medal. Public subscription in England paid for his imposing seated statue, unveiled four months before his death, by the Royal Exchange in the City of London.

Peabody was 6 feet 1 inch tall and broad-shouldered, and the Morgan biographer Ron Chernow characterises him as 'homely', with 'a rumpled face … knobby chin, bulbous nose, side whiskers, and heavy-lidded eyes'. He was jovial company with friends but more formal with his family, many of whom were feckless. While generous publicly, personally he was austere. He is believed to have given away $8,600,000.

Peabody lived in Regent Street for some years. Unmarried, there were persistent 'rumours' (as his biographer, Franklin Parker calls them) of a mistress in Brighton who bore him, it was said, a daughter (whom he treated very generously) or two sons, according to which account one reads. But he had no acknowledged heirs. Peabody had returned from New York via Ireland early in October 1869 and his health determined that he would spend the winter in the south of France. However, ill health caused him to stay with his friend the Vermont-born and naturalised Briton fur merchant Sir Curtis Lampson, and to be nursed at his home in Eaton Square. It was there that he died on 4th November 1869.

Peabody's funeral took place in **Westminster Abbey**, where he was temporarily buried before finally being interred in the tomb that he had built for his parents and other family members in Harmony Rest Cemetery near Salem, Massachusetts.

---

* *In April 2019, Peabody owned and managed more than 55,000 homes across London and the south east, with over 111,000 residents. It also had 8,000 care and support service users.*

Radziwill, Lee (1933–2019)

Socialite and sister of Jacqueline Kennedy

4 Buckingham Place, Victoria SW1E 6HR

Radziwill, born Caroline Lee Bouvier, was in an unhappy, childless marriage to Michael Canfield, a publisher with Harper & Row, a job which never captured his enthusiasm, when they left for London in 1955. They stayed at *14 Chesham Place, Belgravia*, then at *120 Mount Street, Mayfair*, and later moved back to Belgravia to a more spacious home at *45 Chester Square*.

Canfield got a job as special assistant to the ambassador Winthrop Aldrich and had a leave of absence from the publishers.

Jacqueline Kennedy visited her sister in London without her husband, then Senator John F Kennedy, and they spent time in Paris. Radziwill's life was a social whirl – dinners, parties, receptions, country weekends; Ascot, Monte Carlo, Italy; and mixing with royalty, aristocracy and film stars. An obscure American became a fixture in the social scene.

She was homesick when, at a shooting weekend with Jackie at the estate of Lord Lambton in Northumberland, she met Stanislaw ('Stas', pronounced 'Stash') Radziwill and his second wife, Grace. They lived in London, where he had become a British subject and where he had regained some of the family fortune lost in Poland during and after the war. (He had forfeited use of his title, which he insisted, controversially, in London, on using.) Lee and Stas fell in love but the two couples continued to mix socially.

Returning home suddenly at the death of her father 'Black Jack' Bouvier, the Canfields decided to make a go of it in the USA, but in 1958 Stas indicated to Radziwill that he wanted them to marry. She left Canfield, and while she was mildly regretful, he was devastated. Before her second marriage she rented a house in Walton Street, Chelsea.

In 1958, pregnant by Stas, she divorced Canfield the next year and she and Stas were married in a civil ceremony in the USA in March 1959. Her annulment was refused, but with Kennedy's intervention with Pope John XXIII (who seems to have been unhappy at the prospect) the case was reopened and by a tangled, long drawn-out route succeeded, with interventions to the cardinals in Rome, in November 1962. The couple married secretly in Westminster Cathedral in July 1963 by which time she was having an affair with Aristotle Onassis. This was later to sour her relationship with her sister as it was Radziwill who introduced Jackie to Onassis. Jackie and the Greek tycoon were married in 1968, five years after Kennedy's assassination.

Soon after their civil marriage, the Radziwills set up home in Buckingham Place, near Buckingham Palace, part of a terrace described by the architectural historian Nicholas Pevsner as one of 'small, soigné little neo-Georgian and neo-Queen Anne houses'. They lived here, rather than Mayfair or Belgravia, due to Stas's finances.

Between 1957 and 1961 Stas's business had an annual turnover of £1 million. But the Inland Revenue did not believe that there was

The Radziwill home in Buckingham Place
(Terry Philpot)

£500,000 going in and £500,000 going out with allegedly no income at all going into his business. His accountant took ten years to inform Stas that he lived on credit and his capital was in property and shares, not liquid or ready cash. This did not stop the couple acquiring Turville Grange, Oxfordshire, as a large country home.

The couple often met in the middle of the day – at home for lunch from his office in Arlington Street, St James's, or at a restaurant – and were frequenters of the National Theatre and the Royal Ballet. The ballet dancer Rudolf Nureyev stayed with them at Buckingham Place for four months and other visitors included the photographer Cecil Beaton and the composer Leonard Bernstein. The children were educated at the Lycée Français in Kensington.

Radziwill spent much of her time organising dinners, attending auctions and galleries and visiting Italy, France and the USA. She sometimes took her pug Thomas to tea at the Ritz. She rode at Windsor with her husband and went on shooting weekends. The home, with many Radziwill family treasures, had her imprint in design and furnishings. The Radziwills employed the Italian architect and designer Renzo Mongiardino to decorate the house, with the creation of a dining room lined with cordovan (horse-hide leather) and a lavish ground-floor drawing room that was photographed by Cecil Beaton for *Vogue*. The elegance contrasted with Stas's ribald humour and schoolboy jokes. In London Radziwill became a fashion leader, described as 'the epitome of all that is considered chic' by a *New York Times* reporter.

She never liked the Kennedys, whom she regarded as 'dull' with the exception of Jack, whom she found thoughtful and serious. Jack, for his part, enjoyed a good relationship with Stas. The couple spent Christmas with the Kennedy family at Palm Beach.

In 1961 Radziwill went to Paris with the presidential couple, and when the latter came to London from Vienna they made a private visit to Buckingham Place for her daughter Tina's baptism at Westminster Cathedral*, when Kennedy was godfather. But, according to Radziwill's confidante, the writer Truman Capote, she was jealous of her sister for her prominence and success as First Lady and the public idolatry, and became depressed. The biographers Kashner and Shoenberger reveal the differences in the two sisters, when referring to the irony of Radziwill's never attaining the prominence of Jackie as wife of the president: 'One needed to shine on the public stage; one resisted fame and clung to the shreds of her privacy'. In 1962 the sisters went to India on a semi-official visit.

Radziwill was at Buckingham Place when she heard the news of Kennedy's assassination (her husband was at his club). Soon after that event Robert Kennedy, still attorney-general, came to London and she gave two luncheon parties for him.

By the mid-1960s the Radziwills came to see that they had little in common, they lived separate lives and both had affairs (she with, among others, the Labour Cabinet minister Roy Jenkins), though they holidayed together. Radziwill turned, unsuccessfully, to acting. Her career as an actress petered out and for a short while she was an interior designer.

The Radziwills divorced in 1974. She returned to the United States and was a public relations executive and also hosted a talk show. Her third marriage to Herbert Ross ended in divorce.

---

* *Radziwill's book,* Happy Times, *mistakenly says the ceremony took place in* **Westminster Abbey.**

Roosevelt, Theodore (1858–1919)
26th president of the United States

St George's Church, Hanover Square, Mayfair W1S 1FX
Brown's Hotel, 33 Albemarle Street, Mayfair W1S 4BP

Roosevelt was a widower with a baby daughter, Alice, when he began a romantic courtship with Edith Kermit Carow, probably in October 1885. He and Edith had lived next door to one another as children and she was a childhood sweetheart whom he had avoided meeting after his wife Alice's death of Bright's disease two days after her daughter's birth in 1884. (Roosevelt's mother died 11 hours earlier of typhoid fever in the same house.) Edith had attended her future husband's first wedding and he called her 'Her Ladyship'. In November 1885 they became secretly engaged due to the possibility of scandal, he being widowed for only 20 months.

Roosevelt had polled third when he ran for mayor of New York in 1886 and, a few days later, he sailed for England on the *Etruria*, with his then unmarried sister Edith or 'Bamie', who had looked after his daughter. They

spent their first night writing notices of the engagement and the forthcoming wedding. When Roosevelt's brother Elliott, who had seen him off, then attended a society wedding it buzzed with the news of the engagement.

The Roosevelts checked in as 'Mr and Miss Merrifield' but on the boat they were recognised by Cecil Spring-Rice, a young English diplomat who was returning from a holiday in Canada. He was soon to be private secretary to Lord Rosebery, until recently foreign secretary and a future prime minister. The future president was only four months older than the

Theodore Roosevelt in a typically jovial mood

Englishman and they became friendly, so much so that Roosevelt had Spring-Rice for his best man, although, as the latter said, that was because Roosevelt knew no one in London.

There were to be 18 days in London and the Home Counties before the wedding at St George's, and the Roosevelts stayed at Brown's Hotel so that he could establish the residency necessary to marry. Roosevelt said: 'It is as if I were living in one of Thackeray's novels'.

His new-found friend gave him an entrée into London society and, as he remembered, he was 'treated like a prince ... put down at the Athenaeum and the other swell clubs ... had countless invitations to go down to the country to hunt and shoot'. He turned down, regretfully, lunch with the Duke of Westminster and weekends with Lords North and Caernarvon because he 'was anxious to meet intellectual men like [George] Goeshen [Cabinet minister and soon to be chancellor of the exchequer], John Morley [statesman and biographer], [James] Bryce [statesman, scholar and writer], [George] Shaw-Lefevre [Cabinet minister]... I dined and lunched with them all'. This full diary did not find space for the American ambassador, who was not pleased.

Roosevelt wrote to his younger sister Corinne: 'I have been having great fun in London, and have seen the very nicest people, social, political, and literary. We have just come back from lunch at the Jeunes', which was most enjoyable. Edith sat beside [Joseph] Chamberlain, who impresses me very much with his keen, shrewd intellect and quiet force. I sat between [Sir George] Trevelyan, who was charming, and Lady Leamington.' He dined, too, with Parnellites, the Irish nationalist followers of Charles Stewart Parnell.

He also told Corinne: 'You have no idea how sweet Edith is. I don't think even I had known how wonderfully good and unselfish she was; she is naturally reserved and finds it especially hard to express her feelings on paper.'

Edith and her mother and sister were staying at Bucklands Hotel, Brook Street (now the Bath Club), and they called on Roosevelt at Brown's, sitting in his room, finding 'how cosy and comfortable one could be, with a small economical handful of coal in the grate and a heavy fog outside'.

On 2nd December, the day of the wedding, visibility was so poor that link bearers had to be hired to guide Roosevelt's carriage to the church. On the marriage certificate, he had given his profession as 'Ranchman'.

The American wrote of his friend Spring-Rice: 'Characteristically, he had me married in bright orange gloves, which I accepted with a calm, wholly unwarranted'. Edith, who called him 'Dear Springy' (he was also known as 'Sprice'), remembered that on the way to the wedding the two men had an intense conversation about the population of an island in the South Pacific. Spring-Rice wore a frock coat, unusual for him as he was known for being casually and untidily dressed.

The church was almost empty, quiet, unlike his first wedding, 'as the wedding of a defeated mayoralty candidate should be', said Roosevelt in humorous self-mockery.

Edith and Teddy (a name which Roosevelt disliked) took a three-month European honeymoon (it was his fourth trip to Europe), and Edith returned pregnant with Theodore, the first of their five children.

They returned to London on 23rd February, where they spent their last three weeks before sailing from Liverpool. Before that they visited members of both Houses of Parliament, and had lunches and dinners with intellectuals, and supper with Lord Salisbury, the prime minister. Finally, there was a weekend at Wroxton Abbey, with powdered-wigged servants.

'I have had a roaring good time', Roosevelt told reporters. He had met 'all the great political leaders' and had made 'as complete a study as I can of English politics'.

On return to the USA, in March 1887, the New York newspapers ran headlines about Roosevelt and his 'charming young wife'. They lived at Sagamore Hill, New York State, a rambling, handsome mansion, which he and Alice had planned. Over the years, Edith became indispensable to her many-sided husband.

When Roosevelt became president in 1901, succeeding the assassinated William McKinley, 'Springy' became a presidential back channel to London through Edith. Spring-Rice was to rise in the diplomatic service and was appointed ambassador to the USA in 1912, a post he held until 1918. In that capacity he did much to persuade the United States to enter the First World War, a course which his friend, whose presidency had ceased in 1909, also favoured.

The Roosevelts enjoyed 33 years of marriage until his death in 1919.

Roosevelt, Franklin Delano (1882–1945)
32nd president of the United States

Roosevelt, Eleanor (1884–1962)
Politician, diplomat and activist

Brown's Hotel, 33 Albemarle Street, Mayfair W1S 4BP

Eleanor Roosevelt and Franklin Roosevelt (FDR) were distant cousins and married in 1905 in New York in the twin houses of Eleanor's great-aunt Elizabeth Ludlow and her daughter, cousin Susie Parish, with Eleanor's 'Uncle Ted' – President **Theodore Roosevelt** – present. As FDR was a first year law student there was a one-week honeymoon in Springwood, Franklin's family home and his own birthplace at Hyde Park, New York State. In the summer between his first and second year they took their European honeymoon, as his parents, James and Sara, had done 25 years before.

The couple sailed to Liverpool and then London, where, as Eleanor wrote, 'we were horrified to find that in some way we had been identified with Uncle Ted and were given the royal suite at Brown's Hotel (the older Roosevelt had stayed there before his own wedding in London in 1886), with a sitting room so large that I could not find anything that I put down. We had to explain that our pocketbook [wallet] was not equal to so much grandeur, but that made no difference. We lived in it for those first few days in London'.

It was a city both came to love, she said, 'and I learned to like it better than I had ever before, because we poked into strange

Franklin and Eleanor Roosevelt on their way to Washington DC in 1935

corners while he looked for books and prints, with clothes thrown in' – 'thousands of dollars worth' FDR wrote teasingly to his mother, whom he also told they were paying $1,000 a night for the hotel, when it was, in fact, £36 (equivalent to about £2,800 today). They dined at the embassy and at the Carlton.

Wherever the Roosevelts went in Europe there were family and friends to meet. Their journey took them on to Paris, Milan and Venice, the Dolomites, Augsburg and Ulm, through the Alps to St Moritz and out of Switzerland by way of Strasbourg and Nancy, and back to Paris and England. From England, before returning home they travelled to the north of Scotland, and the Firth of Forth, during which time they dined with Sidney and Beatrice Webb, the socialist theorists and economists, who had helped found the London School of Economics and would later found the *New Statesman*.

Selfridge, Sir (Harry) Gordon (1858–1947)

Department store owner

Selfridge's, 400 Oxford Street W1A 1AB
Lansdowne House (now the Lansdowne Club), 9 Fitzmaurice Place,
Mayfair W1J 5J 🅟
2 Ross Court, Putney Hill, Putney Heath, Putney, Wandsworth SW15 3NY

The man born in Ripon, Wisconsin, who left school at 14, has left London with one of its most famous landmarks – the department store that bears his name at the western end of Oxford Street.

Selfridge was brought up by his mother Lois, a teacher, in Jackson, Michigan. After school he became a bank clerk having been rejected by the Navy for being too small, but in 1879 he became a clerk at the department

Gordon Selfridge in 1910, four years after he came to London

store and mail-order firm of Leiter & Co (later Marshall, Field & Co), rising to become manager of the retail department by 1886. It was here that he invented the perennial catch-phrase, 'Only ... shopping days until Christmas'. Four years later he married Rosalie Buckingham, an heiress, who bore him three daughters and a son.

Selfridge had traveled extensively for his employer and when the company, of which he had been made a junior partner in 1890, refused to take on his idea of opening a department store in London like that in Chicago, he left with $300,000 and bought another Chicago firm, Schlesinger and Mayer, from which he made $50,000 profit on a quick sale.

But Chicago did not suit him and he came to London in 1906 (his family followed later) and settled in a large house in Arlington Street, St James's, where he thought again about an American-style department store based on the latest ideas in retailing.

His new store was built by Waring-White to the design of the Chicago architect Daniel Burnham. It opened in 1909, with 1,200 employees, and was announced by £36,000 worth of advertising (for this he engaged leading artists and designers). Selfridge used high salaries to recruit the best buyers from Britain and America. There were exciting new window displays (designed by a Chicago window-dresser) and 130 retail departments, a range of customer services – including a library, rest rooms and a free information bureau – and better working conditions for staff, including staff training. Selfridge observed all this as he made his daily rounds sporting a top hat.

After the First World War, his interests expanded with the purchase of other stores, all of which retained their own distinctiveness. But money problems in the 1920s caused him to create the Gordon Selfridge Trust and Selfridge Provincial Stores Ltd with a registered capital of £5 million, and he received £2 million in exchange for his interest in the company.

However, it was not bad business choices or the economy that brought Selfridge down financially, but his love life and the importunate spending that went with it. His wife died in 1918 during the influenza pandemic, and, always fond of the theatre, he began a series of relationships with well-known actresses. For one, Gaby Deslys, he bought a house. Over eight years French casino resorts profited to the extent of his entire fortune.

In the 1930s the board gave him an option: pay your debts or retire, and he stepped down in 1939 with the honorary title of president, which he gave up in 1941, and a modest salary (for him) of £6,000. In 1937 he became a British citizen.

Selfridge's London mansion, Lansdowne House, leased for £5,000 a year from the 5th Marquess of Lansdowne from 1921 to 1929, and Highcliffe Castle, his country home in Dorset, which he began leasing in 1916, reflected his generous side, with his vast entertaining attracting many important people of the day. Despite the sorry state that his choices had brought him to, he was gregarious and optimistic.

In 1947 Selfridge died all but penniless at Ross Court, Putney Heath, where he lived with his daughter Rosalie.

Smithson, James (c1765–1829)

Founding donor of the Smithsonian Institution, mineralogist and chemist

9 Bentinck Street, Marylebone
W1U 2EH ℗

James Smithson in 1816

Given the circumstances of Smithson's birth, he might have been an obscure outcast. Instead his name is perpetuated in the world-famous institution he funded, in a country in which he never set foot.

He was born James Lewis Macie, the illegitimate son of Elizabeth Hungerford Keate Macie and Hugh Smithson, 1st Duke of Northumberland. He grew up in Paris and later took his father's family name in 1801.

Smithson graduated from Oxford in 1786 and quickly established a reputation as a chemist and mineralogist. He experimented, took meticulous notes, and while wealthy he was determined on recognition as a scientist. This was achieved when, only a year after leaving Oxford, he was admitted to the Royal Society of London in April 1787. The Society published many of his papers, which included those on the chemical content of a woman's teardrop, the crystalline form of ice and a superior way of making coffee. It also brought him into contact with other scientists. After his death a zinc ore was named Smithsonite.

He died in 1829 in Genoa, Italy and was buried in the Protestant cemetery. Only three years before he had written his will, leaving his considerable estate (which most likely came from his mother's family) to his nephew,

Henry James Hungerford. The will stated that should Hungerford die without an heir, then the money should go 'to the United States of America, to found at Washington, under the name of the Smithsonian Institution, an establishment for the increase and diffusion of knowledge among men'.

This is exactly what happened, but delay was caused by Congressional advocates of states' right arguing that the constitution did not allow for the creation of such an institution.

When the Federalists prevailed a Philadelphia lawyer, Richard Rush, secured the bequest for the USA in a two-year suit in the Court of Chancery in London. In 1838 the estate (then worth $508,318.46) came to the USA but provoked a decade-long debate in Congress as to the nature of the proposed institution. It was not until 1846 that Congress brought in a law to create the Smithsonian.* It is now a collection of 19 museums, which encompass air, space and science; African-American art culture; American history; a zoo; and art galleries.

Smithson may never have visited the land which owes him so much nor do we know why he chose the USA for his beneficence, but, in many ways, he had the optimistic American frame of mind. As Heather Ewing writes:

> Smithson was part of a small elite who … [i]n the French Revolution … found not a threat to Britain's security, but triumphant confirmation that even the most hierarchical of societies could be transformed. And in America's unprecedented system of government, founded upon the rights of man, where each person was to be valued for his contribution rather than his pedigree, they saw the future – the most promising foundation for the pursuit of knowledge and the advancement of society.

---

* A fire in 1865 in the Smithsonian Castle destroyed many of Smithson's letters, diaries and other papers originally acquired by the Institution. This included the handwritten draft of the last will and testament.

Statues of Presidents of the United States

There are seven statues of American presidents in London, running from the first (George Washington) to the 40th (Ronald Reagan), and with Washington and Eisenhower being both military commanders. However, one president has two statues: Roosevelt, who stands on his own in Grosvenor Square, also shares a bench in New Bond Street with Winston Churchill.

George Washington (1732–1799; served 1789–1797)
Trafalgar Square, Westminster WC2N 5DX

The bronze statue of the first president stands outside the National Gallery in Trafalgar Square, looking across on his plinth, to Nelson, while his cloak rests on a bundle of 13 fasces, the symbol of the original 13 states. It is claimed that Washington, who was of English descent, said he would never set foot on London soil again and so under the statue, which was given to Britain by the Commonwealth of Virginia in 1924, is said to be some American earth. There is, however, no evidence that Washington ever came to England. The statue is a replica of that by Jean Antoine Houdon, which stands in the State Capitol, Richmond, Virginia. It is considered one of the most accurate representations of its subject.

George Washington overlooking Trafalgar Square

Abraham Lincoln (1809–1865; served 1861–1865)
Parliament Square, Westminster SW1P 3PD

Lincoln, the 16th president, is generally regarded as the greatest president, who led and preserved the Union during the Civil War and ended slavery, but was assassinated in 1865. Rightly, then, his statue, which captures his sombre, thoughtful self, stands with other international statesmen (and now one woman, Millicent Fawcett) and looks across to the statue of Winston Churchill and the Houses of Parliament beyond.

Like the statue of Washington, this, too, is a copy, this one of the original by Augustus Saint Gaudens, which is in Lincoln Park, Chicago. The first statue of an American president to be erected in London, it was unveiled in 1920 by Prince Arthur of Connaught to commemorate a century of peace between the two countries.*

The unveiling was preceded by a meeting at Central Hall, Westminster, where the American ambassador formally presented the statue to the prime minister David Lloyd George. (A statue was to be unveiled in 1914 but there was a discussion as to whether the statue chosen should be that by George Gray Barnard which had recently been unveiled in Cincinnati, but which was considered artistically inferior to this one. That statue now stands in Manchester.)

Abraham Lincoln looks across Parliament Square (James)

* In fact the USA ratified The Treaty of Ghent in 1815.

191

Franklin Roosevelt (1882–1945; served 1933–1945)
Grosvenor Square, Mayfair W1K 2HP

What is interesting about this statue, unveiled in 1948 by **Eleanor Roosevelt**, the president's widow, is that it shows Roosevelt, standing, feet apart and with a stick that looks as if he does not really need it. Roosevelt's paralysis, caused by polio, which he contracted in 1921, was carefully hidden from the public. Rarely were there photographs of him using the wheelchair that he needed.

The 32nd president led his country through the Depression with the New Deal, and the Second World War, and died in April 1945 when the German surrender was three weeks away. The Japanese would surrender in September. Roosevelt is the only president to be elected for four terms and at his death Congress changed the constitution to limit presidential terms to two, or a maximum of eight years. The statue was created by William Reid Dick and paid for with money raised in a week by 160,000 Britons paying 5 shillings (25p) each.

Franklin Roosevelt and Winston Churchill
New Bond Street, Mayfair W1S 3SU

Allies, by the American-British sculptor Lawrence Holofcener, is an entirely different type of statue from the usual ones of statesmen, and certainly the London presidential statues. Given by the Bond Street Association to Westminster Council and the people of London, it shows the two men, friends and war-time allies, smiling, talking amiably and leaning toward one another on a bench (Churchill, of course, holds a cigar). It was unveiled in 1995 by Princess Margaret to mark 50 years of peace, which the two men had done so much to achieve.

Dwight D Eisenhower (1890–1969; served 1953–1961)
Grosvenor Square, Mayfair W1K 2HP

The statue of Eisenhower, the 53rd president, stands, appropriately, near that of Roosevelt, for Roosevelt was the Commander-in-Chief and Ike, as he was popularly known, was his Supreme Allied Commander Europe during the Second World War, charged with the planning and supervision of the D-Day invasions and North African landings. Several presidents in the past have been related to one another, closely or less so, but in modern times (excluding Bush, father and son, and unless one counts the rather distant kinship of Franklin and Theodore Roosevelt) Eisenhower is the only one who has that distinction: his grandson David married Julie, the daughter of his vice-president and a presidential successor Richard Nixon.

John F Kennedy (1917–1963; served 1960–1963)
Marylebone Road, Marylebone WIB IPF

Only four presidents have been assassinated and two are commemorated by London's presidential statues – Lincoln and Kennedy (the others to fall to the murderer's bullet were James A Garfield and William McKinley). This bronze bust, which is set on a pedestal of polished black granite, is a brisk walk from **Winfield House**, the American ambassador's residence in Regent's Park, and was unveiled by Robert Kennedy, the 35th president's brother, who himself was to be assassinated in 1968. Kennedy studied at the London School of Economics and for a time lived at the then ambassador's residence in Kensington, when his father, **Joseph Kennedy** was ambassador. This bust, which is erected two years after Kennedy's death, was paid for with £50,000 raised by readers of *The Daily Telegraph*, sending in £1 each. Another bust by the same sculptor, Jacques Lipchitz, stands in the Military Park, Newark, New Jersey.

Ronald Reagan (1911–2004; served 1981–1989)
Grosvenor Square, Mayfair WIK 2HP

Ill health prevented Margaret Thatcher from unveiling this statue to the 40th president. She and Reagan were friends, ideological allies: they were both wedded to market solutions and less involvement by the state in most walks of life, and both played a part in the downfall of Communism and the end of the Cold War. Thatcher famously said that, on meeting the Russian leader Mikhail Gorbachev, she could 'do business' with him, while Reagan met him for ground-breaking weapons limitation talks. The statue shows Reagan in a typical pose – smiling and well dressed in a suit. At ten feet this is the tallest of the presidential statues and it was paid for by the Ronald Reagan Foundation and unveiled in 2011, the centenary of the president's birth.

Ronald Reagan's statue in Grosvenor Square
(Ham)

St George's Church

Hanover Square, Mayfair W1S 1FX

The main connection for Americans with this magnificent church, opened in 1725, is the fact that the future president **Theodore Roosevelt** married there.

The wedding is alleged to have set a fashion for church weddings by Americans and *The New York Times* would regularly report on Anglo-American weddings at the church in the late 19th century and into the early 20th century.

However, its first American connection was the wedding of William Franklin, the illegitimate son of **Benjamin Franklin**, to Elizabeth Downes, daughter of a Barbados sugar planter, in September 1762. The next year they moved to New Jersey, where Franklin was the last governor. He was estranged from his father as he was a Loyalist during the American War of Independence, when he was imprisoned. He later returned to live in Britain and saw his father once more when the latter was passing through London after his negotiation of the Treaty of Paris.

The church has also seen the weddings of Lulu Pfizer, New York-born granddaughter of the German-American pharmaceutical manufacturer Charles, to Major-General Charles Holland in 1905, when three bridesmaids were English and three American; Elizabeth Berlin, daughter of the composer Irving; as well as the daughter of oil and railroad magnate Henry Clay Pierce, once one of America's four richest men.

The church organ, made by Richards, Fowkes & Co, installed in 2012, is the first American organ to be commissioned for a London church.

St George's Church, Hanover Square (Angelo Hornack)

Van Buren, Martin
(1782–1862)

Minister to Britain and 8th president of the United States

7 Stratford Place, Marylebone W I C I AY ℗
2 Chandos Street, Marylebone W I G 9DG

Irving, Washington
(1783–1859)

Writer, essayist, historian and diplomat

8 Argyll Street, Soho W I F 7TF ℗

Martin Van Buren, the presidential years long behind him

On 16th August 1831 Van Buren sailed on the packet the *President*, to take up his post as minister (or ambassador) to England, accompanied by his son John, who would be an attaché at the legation. They were met by Washington Irving, acting as *chargé d'affaires* in the interregnum between Van Buren's arrival and the departure of Louis McLean, his predecessor.

Two years before Irving had been appointed secretary to the legation by Van Buren, who was then secretary of state. In this capacity, working with McLean, in 1830 he had successfully negotiated a trade agreement between the USA and the West Indies. In 1830, too, Irving was awarded a medal by the Royal Society of Literature, followed by an honorary doctorate of civil law from Oxford in 1831.

Irving had previously resigned but took to the new minister and agreed to serve under him. He said: 'The more I see of Mr Van Buren, the more I am confirmed in a strong personal regard for him. He is one of the gentlest and most amiable men I have ever met with; with an affectionate disposition that attaches itself to those around him and wins their kindness in return.'

Irving had moved to Argyll Street in about 1830 and lived there until 1832, having arrived in London in 1829 to serve in the legation in Chandos Street. By the time he arrived he was already established as a writer – *Rip Van Winkle* had been published in 1819 and *The Legend of Sleepy Hollow* in 1820 – and it was in this house that he finished *The Alhambra*, published in 1832, under the pseudonym of Geoffrey Crayon.

Irving lived with Van Buren when he leased the house in fashionable Stratford Place at £500, according to Irving 'spending out of his own pocket, $2,600 [*sic*] for servants and £310 on carriages', although he had imported his own carriage.

When King William IV met Van Buren the monarch spoke of President Andrew Jackson's election, in 1828, as creating alarm among 'all classes of his subjects'. But, he added, 'I have kept myself free from those alarms for I

Washington Irving about 25 years after his stay in London

have made it a rule through life never to condemn an untried man; and in respect of other matters, I regarded Mr Jackson as placed in that position. I said to those who addressed to me their apprehensions: "I will judge Mr Jackson by his acts". I have done so, and I am satisfied that we shall have no reason to complain of injustice at his hands.'

Born in New York, Irving was of Scots-English parentage and knew England for his older brothers had paid for him to make a European tour in 1804–06. In 1815 he came to London to attempt to salvage their London business, damaged by the war of 1812 but, when that failed, he took to writing, which became *The Sketch Book of Geoffrey Crayon* (in which both of his best known works are included). He was a member of the American Antiquarian Society, with a great passion for history, and in his story *London Antiques* Geoffrey Crayon visits the ancient Charterhouse (once a monastery, in Irving's day a school, and now a residential home), where he sees a line of grey-haired men clad in long black cloaks, and a number of school boys playing sports.

Irving then lived in France and Spain, where he researched his biography of Christopher Columbus and his book on Granada.

Thus, Irving was Van Buren's ideal guide as they set out on a holiday, in an open carriage, to Oxford, Blenheim Palace, Stratford-upon-Avon, Warwick and Kenilworth Castles, Newstead Abbey and Hardwick Castle. They spent a fortnight over Christmas at Barlbrough Hall, Derbyshire, where they ate boar's head 'crowned with holly', imbibed wassail in old taverns and watched mummers and Morris dancers.

In London Van Buren enjoyed the sophisticated and enjoyable society that was the legacy of the late King George IV. He savoured receiving political gossip from the USA and Jackson wrote, too, to bring him up to date with news, saying that he missed his minister as a member of his 'harmonious' cabinet. Jackson, whose health was poor, even proposed that his minister should share the ticket with him and that he, Jackson, would retire after a year and Van Buren succeed him. He longed, he said, for retirement and 'the peaceful shades of the Hermitage', his family home.

But Van Buren had his enemies at home – John C Calhoun, the vice-president; Henry Clay, Van Buren's successor as secretary of state; and Senator Daniel Webster planned his downfall. Though Van Buren was already in London, Jackson only now sent his name to the Senate for approval, as it was a recess appointment, and he heard news that his opposition were planning its rejection.

Opposition came from Van Buren's negotiations as secretary of state over the North east boundary with Canada, and his views on fugitive slaves (he came increasingly to oppose slavery).

In the Senate debate on his confirmation, Van Buren was charged with putting his party and self before the country he was supposed to serve. Clay said that when it came to the Republic all was wrong; when it came to Britain all was right. He was 'prostrating the American Eagle before the British Lion'. Two days later confirmation was refused when Van Buren found only four defenders versus a dozen who spoke against him. Calhoun said: 'It will kill him, sir, kill him dead. He will never kick, sir, never kick.' Van Buren responded: 'There is such a thing in politics as killing a man too dead.' Jackson gave public support to Van Buren, dismissing what had been said against him, and referred to his private and public worth and dignity. Van Buren had learned of the vote just before attending a party given by Charles Talleyrand, the French ambassador. Meetings of protests were held in towns and villages in upstate New York.

Van Buren was lying in bed ill when a letter from US Representative Churchill Cambreleng told him: 'Come back as quick as you can – we have not triumphal arches as in ancient Rome, but we'll give you as warm a reception as any Conqueror had'. He would be nominated for vice-presidency, he was told. Van Buren rose from his bed and cheered Irving by showing him the letter at the breakfast table. At Buckingham Palace later that day the king told him that he was satisfied that the rejection was caused by partisan considerations and that his respect for him was unimpaired.

In April 1832 Van Buren travelled to Paris and then to Germany and thence to The Netherlands, his ancestral country where William I received him. In June he and his son sailed for home, landing in New York on 5th July to find that he had been nominated at the National Democratic Convention on 31st May, with Jackson's support, as vice-president.

In 1836 Van Buren was elected president. Among his policies was maintaining peaceful relations with Britain. In 1844 Van Buren was the leading candidate for the Democratic Party's nomination for president, but his continued opposition to the annexation of Texas aroused the opposition of Southern Democrats and the party nominated James K Polk. Van Buren grew increasingly opposed to slavery after he left office, and he agreed to stand on a third party platform in the 1848 presidential election, but he finished a distant third.

Irving returned to the diplomatic service as US minister to Spain from 1842 to 1846 and then spent the rest of his life at Sunnyside, his home near Tarrytown in New York State. He continued to write with enduring success, including a five-volume life of George Washington, whom he had met at the age of six, soon after the president's inauguration. A supporter of the Union in the American Civil War, he died at his estate in New York State.

West, Benjamin (1738–1820)

History painter

14 Newman Street, Fitzrovia W1T 1PB (gone)

Whatever the hyperbole contained in John Galt's two-volume *The Life, Studies, and Works of Benjamin West, Esq, President of the Royal Academy of London*, published in 1816 and 1820, at a young age West had a deep belief in his own abilities that would ensure great fame.

He was the tenth and youngest child of a Quaker family in Springfield (now Swarthmore), Pennsylvania, and advanced through his mother's encouragement, as his early artistic training and education were quite basic (even as an old man he was awkward at speaking and writing).

Before he was ten West was instructed by the English artist William Williams and others. As a teenager he produced *Storm at Sea* and *Landscape with Cow*, two oil panel overmantels, for the Pennsylvania Hospital, Philadelphia, along with two small portraits. Around this time he took a commission to produce the genre for which he would be later renowned, in this case *Death of Socrates*. The Rev William Smith, who was visiting Philadelphia, was so impressed that he offered West a classical education that would suit an artist, and West moved to Philadelphia to study at the new College of Philadelphia (now the University of Pennsylvania).

He studied and painted in Italy for three years, where, in 1762 in Venice, he met Richard Dalton, librarian to George III, who commissioned from him

Self-portrait by Benjamin West
(Baltimore Museum of Fine Art)

a royal painting of *Cymon and Iphigenia*. In 1763 West went to England in the hope of further royal patronage. Although he envisaged a short stay before a return to his homeland, he stayed for the rest of his life, encouraged as he was by his reception and the potential to become a noted history painter. His looks and personality helped – he was handsome, well-built, good natured, well-bred and capable, kindly and generous, if, at times, self-aggrandising.

West was engaged to Elizabeth Shewell, and within a year she came to London and they were married at St Martin-in-the-Fields, Trafalgar

Square, in 1764. A year after his arrival West was exhibiting at the Society of Artists.

A versatile artist, West was a history painter in the neo-classical style, beginning with his 1764 *The Choice of Hercules*, in a London populated by portrait painters. His American origins did not bar him from appointment to the royal household: he was history painter to the king in 1772 and Surveyor of the King's Pictures in 1791. After the death of Sir Joshua Reynolds, West was elected as second president of the Royal Academy in 1792.

His *The Death of General Wolfe* in 1770 introduced a new degree of realism to history painting and would become one of the most commercially successful prints ever produced. For many years it became a model for history painters, although history painting never gained great traction with artists, and West was the only artist to whom George III gave such commissions.

West painted six history paintings to hang with *The Departure of Regulus* at Buckingham House (later Palace). After that he worked on decorative schemes for the restoration of Windsor Castle from 1779 to 1801 that would help make it the main royal residence. Nevertheless, his ambitious series of 18 large canvases on biblical themes for the Royal Chapel at Windsor was halted due to the king's illness in 1801. They were never installed and were returned to the family. (Seven of the group can be seen in the War Memorial Chapel at Bob Jones University, Greenville, South Carolina.)

His work in the Royal Chapel and a commission from the writer and art collector William Beckford for scenes from the Book of Revelation for Fonthill Abbey, Wiltshire, made the artist the country's best-known painter of religious subjects.

In the last ten years of his life, West painted and exhibited three huge biblical compositions: *Christ Healing the Sick* in 1811; *Christ Rejected* in 1814; and three years later *Death on the Pale Horse*.

West produced more than 700 known works that ranged from history and biblical paintings on a grand scale, to oil sketches. He is today best known for his *Death of Nelson*, which he completed six months after the admiral's death. West dramatised the event by placing Nelson on the deck when, in fact, he died in the cockpit. It is said that 30,000 members of the public came to see it when he exhibited it in his studio. The sad irony was that Nelson, who admired West's *Death of General Wolfe*, had said when they met that he would like to be the subject of West's next work.

West refused a knighthood in about 1792, mistakenly believing that he would be granted a hereditary peerage. He was repeatedly re-elected president of the Royal Academy. He died at his home and, as president, lay in state at the Royal Academy before being buried in **St Paul's Cathedral**.

Westminster Abbey

Memorials

Dean's Yard, Westminster SW I P 3PA

The memorial to **Franklin Delano Roosevelt**, 32nd president, is the only commemoration to a foreign head of state in the Abbey. However, it is far from being the only memorial of interest to Americans.

There is the tomb of William Pitt the Elder, prime minister from 1766 to 1768. He informally led the Cabinet from 1756 to 1761 (with a brief interlude in 1757) during part of the duration of the French and Indian Wars (1754–1763), which led to France's defeat.

He was no longer in office and was a member of the House of Lords, as the lst Earl of Chatham, when the American War of Independence broke out, and adamantly supported the sovereignty of Parliament but with generosity and conciliation toward the colony. That was 1774 and while he still sided with the colonists, by 1775 he sought reconciliation, proposing a Provisional Act, which would meet colonial needs while preserving the sovereignty of Parliament. He conceded that there be no taxation without consent; an independent judiciary; trial by jury; and recognition of the American Continental Congress. The Lords rejected the idea in February 1775. But Pitt, 'glorious and immortal', the 'guardian of America', became a hero to the colonists. In Bristol County, Massachusetts, a toast was raised to 'Magna Carta, the British Constitution – PITT and Liberty forever!'

In 1921, after a later conflict, General John J Pershing conferred the Congressional Medal of Honor on the Unknown Warrior, the year after the grave was created, and a month before the present black Belgium marble stone was unveiled. The medal now hangs in a frame on a pillar near the grave. In 2013 the Congressional Medal of Honor Society presented its official flag and this is framed below the medal.

TS Eliot and **Henry James**, both Americans who became British citizens, are among the writers commemorated in Poets' Corner. The Rev Martin Luther King is one of the modern martyrs whose statues stand above the Great West Door. British General **John Burgoyne**, who surrendered at the Battle of Saratoga in 1777, is buried in the North Walk of the Cloisters.

The funeral service of the philanthropist **George Peabody** was held in the Abbey, where he was also temporarily interred.

In the vestibule of the Chapter House is a memorial to **Walter Hines Page**, the US ambassador during the First World War. It is below the memorial window to **James Russell Lowell**, the poet, who was US minister in London from 1880 to 1885, who also has a stone tablet.

Winant, John (1889–1947)

US ambassador

7 Aldford Street, Mayfair W I K 2AQ ℗

Winant moved fairly swiftly up the political and diplomatic ladder after four years (1913–1917) as a history teacher in his old school, St Paul's in Concord, New Hampshire, during which time he was elected to the New Hampshire House of Representatives. He was the first person to serve three two-year terms as governor of New Hampshire.

Winant, known as 'Gil' for his middle name Gilbert, was born in New York to a prosperous family and educated at St Paul's, and then Princeton, which he left without graduating. With America's entry into the First World War he trained as a pilot and served in France as a captain. In 1919, he married Constance Rivington Russell, and they had two sons and a daughter. He became a New Hampshire senator in 1920, but lost money in the Wall Street Crash of 1929.

Some of Winant's terms as governor were served during the Great Depression, when, while a Republican, he closely followed **Franklin Roosevelt**'s New Deal policies: he introduced an Emergency Credit Act which allowed the state to guarantee debts of local authorities; and pushed through the Fair Labor Standards Act to create a minimum wage. He improved the state's highways. In 1935 he became head of the Social Security Board.

In 1939 Roosevelt appointed Winant to head the International Labour Organisation. But in 1941 Roosevelt sent him to London as ambassador, where, sympathetic to the British cause, he succeeded the isolationist **Joseph Kennedy**. 'I'm very glad to be here. There is no place I'd rather be at this time than in England', he said on arrival. He refused to live at the ambassador's official residence and took a small flat, near the embassy, in Aldford Street. Tall, handsome, charming, if at times socially awkward, given to self-doubt and dark moods, he took to the British and they took to him.

Winant's was a crucial role in London, with the USA still neutral, and he was close to George VI and Winston Churchill, often spending weekends at the Prime Minister's country estate, Chartwell in Kent. He was with Churchill when the news came through of the

John Winant's London home in Aldford Street
(Terry Philpot)

bombing of Pearl Harbour. The two would often tour London's devastated streets the morning after a bombing raid. Winant also had an affair with Sarah, Churchill's 27-year-old married daughter, which lasted through the war but ended when she rejected him. At the end of the war he took a lease on 9 *Rex Place* around the corner from Aldford Street.

President Harry Truman made Winant his country's representative to UNESCO, although he had hoped to be made Secretary-General of the UN. He resigned his post in 1946 to retire to Concord to write his memoirs. In 1947 Winant was the second (and last) American to be made an honorary holder of the Order of Merit, following General **Dwight Eisenhower**.

But Roosevelt was dead, Winant was exhausted, life was far less exciting and momentous than it had been, and he was deeply in debt, with an estranged wife who lived in New York. Depressed, Winant shot himself in his home. Churchill sent four dozen yellow roses to Winant's funeral.

Windsor, Duchess of (Simpson, Bessie Wallis) (1896–1986)

Socialite and royal consort

5 Bryanston Court, Bryanston Square, Marylebone W1H 7HA

Mrs Wallis Simpson and her second husband Ernest came to live at this apartment when they settled in London for his business after their marriage in 1928. He became a naturalised British citizen, part of his self-reinvention as an English gentleman. The flat was large enough for 14 to sit for dinner and the couple had four servants. Many well-known guests came to their table, including Sir Oswald Mosley, when British fascist leader.

One guest was Edward, Prince of Wales. At a fateful meeting in 1931 Wallis and Edward had met at Burrough Court, the Leicestershire home of Viscountess Furness and her husband, when Lady Furness was engaged in an affair with the heir to the throne, as he also was with Lady Freda Dudley-Ward, another woman married to an aristocrat. (Lady Furness was the daughter of the US diplomat Henry Hays Morgan Snr.)

Lady Furness had urged her Baltimore-born friend to 'look after my little man' while she went off to the USA in the early months of 1934, and upon her return in May it was obvious that Simpson had taken her duty all too seriously, even though at the dinner the prince had shown no obvious interest.

When the affair did get underway, Simpson was said by one intimate to be Edward's 'perfect woman', a sexual and intellectual companion. He never gave much thought to anyone else's opinion (certainly, none to the potential constitutional implications of what was happening), and their relationship and passion were open within their circle. Although the British press wrote as if nothing were happening, overseas newspapers reported the relationship.

When Ernest Simpson's business began to falter and his wife had little money after the Wall Street crash – the chauffeur-driven car and holidays abroad gave way to economy – Edward gave her an allowance of £6,000 a year (£303,975 in 2017), not to mention lavishing very valuable jewellery upon a woman said to be 'mean and acquisitive'.

Even before their marriage, Edward and Simpson had been known for their pro-German sympathies. Pro-Nazi German aristocrats, some related to the prince, were entertained at his London home, York House, St James's Palace; Fort Belvedere, his home near Windsor; and also at Bryanston Court.

The Duke and Duchess of Windsor

Among these was Joachim von Ribbentrop, Hitler's special commissioner for disarmament and, from 1936–1938, German ambassador to London. He used to send Simpson 17 carnations (or roses) every day to the apartment.

Simpson began divorce proceedings against her husband on the grounds of his adultery with Mary Raffray, whom he went on to marry. (He moved from the apartment to his club.) Yet he had been a complaisant cuckold, saying in 1935, that he thought Edward wanted to marry his wife and he hoped for a peerage when (not, if) Edward succeeded to the throne. The coronation was due in May 1937 and Edward abdicated in December 1936, four months before the Simpson divorce became final, to allow the couple to marry. She moved from the apartment to another in Cumberland Terrace, Regent's Park after receiving poison pen letters, a brick being thrown through a window and graffiti appearing on neighbouring properties (harassment alleged to have been prompted by the newspaper owner Lord Beaverbrook). She then moved to Fort Belvedere and, finally, to France.

However, the King's determination to marry was trumped by his lack of political perception, even naiveté, for Simpson was now twice divorced with two husbands living. He abdicated on 10th December 1936. The pair married seven months later in France and Wallis Warfield, as she had become by deed poll, became the Duchess of Windsor.

Apart from war-time governorship of the Bahamas, Edward never again held an official position. They spent the rest of their lives living in France but travelled frequently, including meeting Hitler where the duke gave the stiff-armed salute. They were effectively ostracised by members of the royal family and rarely came back to the realm he had forsaken: in 1952 he attended the funeral of his brother George VI, and the next year visited his mother Queen Mary before she died, but he did not return for the coronation of his niece, Elizabeth II later that year. In 1967, the Windsors were invited to attend the unveiling of a plaque to Queen Mary. His last visit to his former kingdom was to attend the funeral of his sister-in-law Princess Marina, Duchess of Kent.

Edward died in their Paris home in 1972 and she died, also in the French capital, in 1986. Many had greeted with disbelief his claim that, as king, Edward could not live without her, but they remain together in death, lying beside each other in the royal burial ground of Frogmore at Windsor.

Bibliography

In writing this book the *Oxford Dictionary of National Biography* has been invaluable, while the *Encyclopaedia Britannica* has often proven useful.

The following publications I have read or consulted:

Ambrose, Stephen E, *Eisenhower: Volume 1: Soldier General and President-elect 1890–1952*. London: George Allen & Unwin, 1984

Anonymous, 'James Russell Lowell', *The Spectator*, 22nd February 1919

Ackroyd, Peter, *T.S. Eliot: A Life*. London: Penguin, 1993

Ackroyd, Peter, *Poe: A Life*. London: Chatto & Windus, 2008

Ackroyd, Peter, *Alfred Hitchcock*. London: Chatto & Windus, 2015

Albright, Madeleine, *Prague Winter*. London: HarperCollins Publishers, 2012

Ashton, Rosemary, *142 Strand: A Radical Address in Victorian London*. London: Chatto & Windus, 2006

Bease, Ray and Read, Anthony, *Conspirator: The Untold Story of Churchill, Roosevelt and Tyler Kent, Spy*. London: Macmillan, 1991

Blight, David W, *Frederick Douglass: Prophet of Freedom*. London: Simon & Schuster, 2018

Bourne, Stephen, *Elisabeth Welch, Soft Lights, Sweet Music*. Latham, Maryland: Scarecrow Press, 2005

Brown, Richard, 'Birt Acres', in Herbert, Stephen and McKernan, Luke (editors), *Who's Who of Victorian Cinema: A Worldwide Survey*. London: BFI Publishing, 1996

Bryant, Barbara, *Two Temple Place: A Perfect Gem of Late Victorian Art, Architecture and Design*. London: Two Temple Place, 2013

Callow, Simon, *Charles Laughton: A Difficult Actor*. London: Methuen, 1987

Caute, David, *Joseph Losey: A Revenge on Life*. London: Faber and Faber, 1994

Chandler, David and Collins, James (editors), *D-Day Encyclopaedia*. London: Simon & Schuster, 1994

Chapman, Gary, *London's Hollywood: The Gainsborough Studio in the Silent Years*. Stroud: Edditt Publishing, 2014

Chernow, Ron, *The House of Morgan*. New York: Simon & Schuster, 1990

Clough, Brian, *State Secrets: The Kent-Wolkoff Affair*. Hove: Headway Publishers, 2005

Chisholm, Anne, *Nancy Cunard*. London: Sidgwick & Jackson, 1979

Clymer, Adam, *Edward M. Kennedy*. New York: William Morrow and Company, 1999

Collier, Peter and Horowitz, David, *The Kennedys*. London: Pan Book, 1984

Crompton, Samuel Willard, *Alexander Graham Bell and the Telephone*. New York: Chelsea House Publishing, 2009

Dallek, Robert, *John F. Kennedy: An Unfinished Life 1917–1963*. London: Allen Lane, 2003

Davis, John H, *The Kennedys*. New York: SPI Books, 1984

Dobbs, Michael, 'Albright's Family Tragedy Comes to Light', *Washington Post*, February 4th 1997

Drake, Samuel G. *The Book of the Indians of North America*. Boston: J Drake, 1833

DuBois, Diana, *In Her Sister's Shadow: An Intimate Biography of Lee Radziwill*. New York: Little, Brown and Company, 1995

Edel, Leon, *Henry James: A Life*. London: Collins, 1987

Eisenhower, David, *Eisenhower at War 1943–1945*. London: Collins, 1986

Ewing, Heather, *The Lost World of James Smithson: Science, Revolution, and the Birth of the Smithsonian*. London: Bloomsbury, 2007

Flint, Peter, 'Ava Gardner is dead at 67', *New York Times*, 26 January 1990

Foote, Joseph, 'John Gilbert Winant: The Most Important NH Man You Never Knew', *New Hampshire Magazine*, June 2017

Frederick, Frank S and Magistrale, Anthony, *The Poe Encyclopaedia*. Westport, Connecticut: Greenwood Press, 1997

Freedland, Michael, *Bob Hope: A Biography*. Bath: Chivers Press, 1999.

Freedland, Michael, 'Elisabeth Welch', *The Guardian*, 17th July 2003

Gardner, Ava, *Ava: My Story*. London: Bantam Press, 1990

Goodwin, George, *Benjamin Franklin in London: The British Life of America's Founding Father*. London: Weidenfeld & Nicolson, 2016

Gwynn, Stephen, *The Letters and Friendships of Sir Cecil Spring Rice: A Record. Volume 1*. London: Constable & Co, 1929

Hamilton, Nigel, *JFK: Life and Death of an American President. Volume One: Reckless Youth*. London: Random House, 1992

Hanc, John, 'The Curious London Legacy of Benedict Arnold', *The Smithsonian*, 8th July 2010

Hannah, Leslie, 'J.P. Morgan in London and New York before 1914', *Business History Review*, Spring 2011.

Harbaugh, William, H, *The Life and Times of Theodore Roosevelt*. Oxford: OUP, 1975

Hiney, Tom, *Raymond Chandler: A Biography*. London: Chatto & Windus, 1997

Hoare, Philip, 'White whale in the Big Smoke: How the geography of London inspired Moby Dick', *New Statesman*, 2nd December 2015

Hyde, Montgomery H, *Henry James at Home*. London: Methuen & Co, 1969

James, Robert Rhodes (editor), *Chips: The Diaries of Sir Henry Channon*. London: Weidenfeld, 1993

Jefferson, Alan, *Sir Thomas Beecham: A Centenary Tribute*. London: Macdonald and Jane's, 1979

Jenkins, Roy, *Churchill*. London: Macmillan, 2001

Kashner, Sam and Shoenberger, Nancy, *The Fabulous Bouvier Sisters: The Tragic and Glamorous Lives of Jackie and Lee*. London: HarperCollins, 2018

Kern, Susan, *The Jeffersons of Shadwell*. New Haven and London: Yale University Press, 2010

Koch, Daniel, *Ralph Waldo Emerson in Europe*. London: IB Tauris, 2012

Kohn, Edward P, *A Most Glorious Ride: The Diaries of Theodore Roosevelt 1877–1886*. Albany: State University of New York Press, 2015.

Kukil, Karen V (editor), *The Journal of Sylvia Plath 1950–1962*. London: Faber and Faber, 2000

Lash, Joseph P, *Eleanor and Franklin: The Story of their Relationship based on Eleanor Roosevelt's Private Papers*. London: Andre Deutsch, 1972.

Little Ealing History Group, *An American President in Ealing: The John Quincy Adams Diaries 1815–1817*. Ealing, London: Little Ealing History Group, 2014

Loeffler, Jane C, *The Architecture of Diplomacy: Building America's Embassies*. New York: Princeton University Press, 2011

Lucas, John, *Thomas Beecham: An Obsession with Music*. Woodbridge: Boydell Press, 2008

Lynch, Denis Tilden, *An Epoch and a Man: Martin van Buren and His Times. Volume 11*. Port Washington, New York and London: Kennikat Press, 1971 (first published 1929)

McCullough, David, *John Adams*. New York: Simon & Schuster, 2001

McCullough, David, *1776: America and Britain at War*. London: Allen Lane, 2006

Mellow, James R, *Nathaniel Hawthorne and His Times*. Boston, Mass: Houghton Mifflin and Company, 1980

Miller, Edwin Haviland, *Salem is My Dwelling Place: A Life of Nathaniel Hawthorne*. Iowa City, Iowa: University of Iowa Press, 1991

Merton, Thomas, *The Seven Storey Mountain*. New York: Harcourt, Brace, Janovich, 1948

Moorehead, Caroline, *Martha Gellhorn: A Life*. London: Chatto & Windus, 2003

Moorehead, Caroline (editor), *The Letters of Martha Gellhorn*. London: Chatto & Windus, 2006

Morris, Edmund, *The Rise of Theodore Roosevelt*. New York: Random House, 2010

Morton, Andrew, *17 Carnations: The Windsors, The Nazis and the Cover-up*. London: Michael O'Meara Books, 2015

Morton, Brian, *Edgar Allan Poe*. London: Haus Publishing, 2010

Muggeridge, Malcolm, *Chronicles of Wasted Time. Vol 2: The Infernal Grove*. London: William Collins, 1973

Murray, Nicholas, *Real Bloomsbury*. Bridgend: Seren Books, 2010

Murray, Nicholas, *Bloomsbury and the Poets*. Presteigne: Rack Press Editions, 2014

Nagel, Paul C, *The Adams Women: Abigail and Louisa Adams, Their Sisters and Daughters*. Oxford: OUP, 1987

Norton, CE (editor), *The Letters of James Russell Lowell: Volume II*. London: Osgood, McIlvanie and Co, 1894

Olson, Lynne, *Citizens of London: The Americans who Stood with Britain in its Darkest, Finest Hour*. London: Scribe Publications, 2015

Parker, Franklin, *George Peabody: A Biography*. Nashville, Tennessee: Vanderbilt University Press, 1971

Parker, Hershel, *Herman Melville: A Biography. Volume 2, 1851–1891*. Baltimore, Maryland, 2002

Parker, Hershel, *Melville Biography: An Inside Narrative*. Evaston, Illinois: Northwestern University Press, 2012

Philpot, Terry, *Beside the Seaside: Brighton's Places and Its People*. Brighton: Step Beach Press, 2015

Ritcheson, Charles R, 'Van Buren's Mission to London, 1831–1832'. *International History Review*, February 1886. Vol VIII, No 1

Radziwill, Lee, *Happy Times*. New York: Assouline, 2000

Reynolds, David, *America, Empire of Liberty: A New History*. London: Allen Lane, 2009

Robinson, Corinne Roosevelt, *My Brother Theodore Roosevelt*. New York: Charles Scribner's Sons, 1921

Rollyson, Carl and Paddock, Lisa, *Herman Melville A–Z: The Essential Reference to His Life and Work*. New York: Facts on File, 2001

Roosevelt, E, *The Autobiography of Eleanor Roosevelt*. New York: Harper & Brothers, 1961

Satterlee, Herbert L, *J. Pierpont Morgan: An Intimate Portrait*. New York: The Macmillan Company, 1940

Schlesinger, Arthur M, *Robert Kennedy and His Times*. New York: Houghton Mifflin, 1978

Sebba, Anne, *Jennie Churchill*. London: John Murray, 2007

Severs, Dennis, *18 Folgate Street: The Tale of a House in Spitalfields*. London: Random House, 2001

Sheppard, Edward M, *American Statesman: Martin Van Buren*. Boston and New York: Houghton, Mifflin and Company, 1888

Smith, Jean Edward, *FDR*. New York: Random House, 2007

Smith, Jean Kennedy, *The Nine of Us: Growing Up Kennedy*. London: HarperCollins, 2016

Spalding, Frances, *Whistler*. Oxford: Phaidon, 1979

Spencer, Howard (ed), *London's Blue Plaques*. Tewkesbury, Gloucestershire: September Publishing, 2016

Stamp, Gavin, 'Dennis Severs'. *The Guardian*, 10th January 2000

Stront, Cushing (ed), *Hawthorne in England: Selections from Our Old Home and the English Note-Books*. Ithaca, New York: Cornell University Press, 1965

Sumeray, Derek and Sheppard, John, *London Plaques*. Oxford: Shire Publications, 2011

Summers, Anthony and Robbyn Swan, *Sinatra: The Life*. London: Doubleday, 2005

Tait, Tim, *Hitler's Traitors*. London: Icon Books, 2018

Thrush, Coll, *Indigenous London: Native Travelers at the Heart of Empire*. New Haven: Yale University Press, 2016

Vaughan, Alden T, *Transatlantic Encounters: American Indians in Britain, 1500–1776*. Cambridge: Cambridge University Press, 2006

Whalen, Richard J, *The Founding Father: The Story of Joseph P. Kennedy*. New York: The New American Library, 1964

White, Duncan, 'The fast life of Billy Fiske'. *The Observer*, 3rd February 2002

Williamson, Audrey, *Thomas Paine: His Life, Work and Times*. London: George Allen & Unwin, 1973

Wilson, Andrew, *Mad Girl's Love Song: Sylvia Plath and Life Before Ted*. London: Simon & Schuster, 2013